Deconstructing Eurocentric Tourism and Heritage Narratives in Mexican American Communities

This book attempts to dismantle the unfounded Eurocentric view of US-born and immigrant Mexican peoples, that groups together the identities of Latinx, Chicanx, and other indigenous peoples of the Southwest into Hispanics whose contributions to the cultural, historical, and social development of the Southwest are marginalized or made non-existent.

The narrative and performative legacies that tourism and fantasy heritage produce are promulgated and consumed by both Latinx and non-Latinx peoples and cultures. This book endeavors to expose these productions through analysis of on-the-ground resistance in the service and spirit of intercultural dialogue and change. This book will offer a precise set of recommendations for breaking away from these practices and thus forming new, veritable identities.

With a strongly heritage-oriented discourse, this book on deconstructing Eurocentric representation of Mexican people and their culture will appeal to academics and scholars of heritage tourism, Chicano studies, Southwest studies and Native American studies courses.

Frank G. Pérez is Associate Professor of Communication at the University of Texas, El Paso, where he also teaches Chicano Studies.

Carlos F. Ortega is Lecturer in Chicano Studies at the University of Texas, El Paso. His research interests include educational policy, Chicano film and music, and the erasure of cultural heritage. He is co-editor of *Chicano Studies: Survey and Analysis*.

Routledge Cultural Heritage and Tourism Series

Series Editor: Dallen J. Timothy, Arizona State University, USA

The Routledge Cultural Heritage and Tourism Series offers an interdisciplinary social science forum for original, innovative and cutting-edge research about all aspects of cultural heritage-based tourism. This series encourages new and theoretical perspectives and showcases ground-breaking work that reflects the dynamism and vibrancy of heritage, tourism and cultural studies. It aims to foster discussions about both tangible and intangible heritages, and all of their management, conservation, interpretation, political, conflict, consumption and identity challenges, opportunities and implications. This series interprets heritage broadly and caters to the needs of upper-level students, academic researchers, and policy makers.

Valuing World Heritage Cities
Sustainable Tourism Practices in the Mediterranean

Waterways and the Cultural Landscape
Edited by Francesco Vallerani and Francesco Visentin

Heritage of Death
Landscapes of Emotion, Memory and Practice
Edited by Mattias Frihammar and Helaine Silverman

Industrial Heritage and Regional Identities
Edited by Konstantinos Andriotis, Dimitrios Stylidis and Adi Weidenfeld

Deconstructing Eurocentric tourism and Heritage Narratives in Mexican American Communities
Juan de Oñate as a West Texas Icon
Frank G. Pérez and Carlos F. Ortega

For more information about this series, please visit: https://www.routledge.com/Routledge-Cultural-Heritage-and-Tourism-Series/book-series/RCHT

Deconstructing Eurocentric Tourism and Heritage Narratives in Mexican American Communities

Juan de Oñate as a West Texas Icon

Frank G. Pérez and Carlos F. Ortega

LONDON AND NEW YORK

First published by Routledge

2 Park Square, Milton Park, Abingdon, Oxon, OX14 4RN
605 Third Avenue, New York, NY 10017

Routledge is an imprint of the Taylor & Francis Group, an informa business

First issued in paperback 2020

Copyright © 2020 Frank G. Pérez and Carlos F. Ortega

The rights of Frank G. Pérez and Carlos F. Ortega to be identified as the authors of this work have been asserted by them in accordance with sections 77 and 78 of the Copyright, Designs and Patents Act 1988.

All rights reserved. No part of this book may be reprinted or reproduced or utilised in any form or by any electronic, mechanical, or other means, now known or hereafter invented, including photocopying and recording, or in any information storage or retrieval system, without permission in writing from the publishers.

Notice:
Product or corporate names may be trademarks or registered trademarks, and are used only for identification and explanation without intent to infringe.

British Library Cataloguing in Publication Data
A catalogue record for this book is available from the British Library

Library of Congress Cataloging-in-Publication Data
A catalog record has been requested for this book

ISBN: 978-0-367-13679-6 (hbk)
ISBN: 978-0-367-77681-7 (pbk)

Typeset in Times New Roman
by Taylor & Francis Books

For Areli and Diego, in loving memory of my parents, Manuel Antonio and Francisca Pérez, as well as my late mentor and friend, Everett M. Rogers—F.G.P.

To Rachel and all those who struggle to authentically express themselves culturally—C.F.O.

Contents

	List of illustrations	ix
	Acknowledgements	xi
	Introduction: Juan de Oñate, fantasy heritage, and heritage tourism in the Southwest	1
1	Fantasy heritage in southwest tourism	14
2	San Elizario's First Thanksgiving of the Americas and the Juan de Oñate fantasy heritage	56
3	Mediated debate, historical framing, and public art: The Juan de Oñate controversy in El Paso	88
4	Inclusive tourism and public memory	109
5	On public memory and ethnic conflict in the current era	145
	References	164
	Index	181

Illustrations

Figures

1 A mosaic of three Lower Valley missions under the César Chávez/Juan de Oñate Border Highway welcomes visitors to the area. 16

2 Statue of Colonizer Juan de Oñate at *Parque Municipal Cuatro Siglos* (Four Centuries Municipal Part), Ciudad Juárez, Mexico. 23

3 A sign explaining the history of Presidio Chapel in San Elizario that includes the chapel's original name, San Eliceario. 60

4 The 2016 First Thanksgiving cast outside the San Elizario Chapel. 66

5 Murals at Lincoln Park beneath Interstate 10, possibly El Paso's most visible Chicano artwork. 91

6 A photo of the Juan de Oñate/César Chávez Memorial Highway with US border fencing and the Ciudad Juárez "X" (equis) statue in the background. 93

7 El Paso leaders celebrate the unveiling of the Equestrian statue in April 2007; protestors were forced to remain across the street. 95

8 An Oñate protestor holds an effigy of an amputated foot, a reminder of Oñate's brutality against the Acoma Pueblo peoples. 101

9 A sign that directs visitors to the Oñate historical marker. 110

10 The historical marker that commemorates the approximate location where Oñate's colonizing party may have crossed the Rio Grande. 111

11 A mural in El Paso's *Segundo Barrio*. The legacy of Father Harold Rahm who served at the Sacred Heart Catholic Church from 1952 to 1964 is represented by the man on the bicycle. 127

12 Skyline of El Paso 150

13 *Los Lagartos* fountain at San Jacinto Plaza, a symbol of El Paso's Mexican American cultural reality and a denial of its fantasy heritage. 156

x *Illustrations*

Table

1   A framework for culturally inclusive heritage tourism and related
     projects   132

Boxes

Case study 2.1 How men become "real Alaskans"	74
Case study 3.1 South Africa, the 2010 World Cup, and media representations	96
Case study 3.2 Marketing unpopular tourism destinations	102
Case study 4.1 Creating a tourism mecca in Okinawa	120
Case study 4.2 Maintaining historical accuracy to create local identity: the case of Chemnitz, Germany	124
Case study 5.1 Gastronomy as a tool for culturally sensitive tourists	154
Case study 5.2 Tourism efforts in a second-tier city	157

Acknowledgements

Numerous processes led to the creation of this book and many people were instrumental to our ability to complete the project. UTEP Reference Librarian Juan Sandoval, recently retired, provided us with his private collection of documents about the Juan de Oñate controversy in El Paso. Juan's views counter our own but his commitment to professional ethics and sincere desire to promote scholarship show through in his generosity. We thank him for his support.

Frank G. Pérez thanks his wife, Areli Chacón Silva, and son, Diego Antonio Pérez. During the writing of this book, their love and support kept me motivated to finish. I also thank my parents, Manuel Antonio and Francisca Pérez, whose deaths prevented them from seeing the finished product. Their love and the examples they set taught me to value education and the value of giving back to one's community, and they motivate my advocacy for social justice. Their sacrifices were many and I am the sole beneficiary. My doctoral advisor, mentor, and friend, the late Everett M. Rogers selflessly helped me as both his student and to launch my professional career. Ev's love and support allowed me, a first-generation college student, to learn much about research, writing, and academic life. John G. Oetzel has also been instrumental in my professional development, as a teacher, mentor, and friend. He and Keri Bolton Oetzel made my time at the University of New Mexico a very special period.

I also thank Irasema Coronado, Dennis Bilxer-Márquez, Kathleen Staudt, Krishna and Bindu Kandath and family, Roberto Perezdíaz, Guillermina "Gina" Nuñez-Mchiri, W. Gill Woodall, Patricia Witherspoon, Arvind Singhal, Stacey K. Sowards, Larry A. Erbert, Richard D. Pineda, Roberto Avant-Mier, Kenneth C. C. Yang, Eduardo Barrera, Yolanda Chávez Leyva, David D. Romo, Azuri L. González, Kimberlee Pérez, Daniel Chacón, Eli García, Rosie Antillon, Maria Rubio, Teresa Yañez, Michelle Ronquillo, Norma Gaines, Delia Smith, Tim Davis, Pablo L. Barron, Leonel Monroy, Jr., Mary Monroy, Marco A. Terán, Samantha Dena, and my students. Finally, I thank the De La Rosa, Romero, Alonzo, Pérez, Chacón Silva, Enríquez, Giner, Terán, Villanueva, and Chagoyán families.

xii   *Acknowledgements*

Carlos F. Ortega thanks his wife, Rachel Valenzuela Ortega for her support and patience during the many hours of writing and rewriting. I also offer thanks to the following UTEP colleagues for their support: Dennis Bixler-Marquez, Yolanda Chavez-Leyva and Kathleen Staudt; from the California State University, Northridge: Rodolfo Acuña for showing that the role of history is also to build counter-narratives, Fermin Herrera for opening up the door to Pre-Columbian Mexico, especially Nahuatl Language and Culture, and Rafael Perez-Sandoval who taught me the importance of being erudite. Finally, to my students who asked questions about this project and supported our efforts.

No book is the product of only its authors. We thank everyone who has helped us along the way and apologize to those we may have missed in this section. All errors and omissions are ours.

Introduction

Juan de Oñate, fantasy heritage, and heritage tourism in the Southwest

On the night of January 7, 1998, in the small New Mexico town of Alcalde, just north of Española, two individuals approached a bronze statue of Spanish colonizer Juan de Oñate and sawed off its right foot. The next day the *Santa Fe Reporter* received a letter stating the foot was removed on behalf of the Acoma People.[1] The Acoma reservation sits sixty miles west of Albuquerque and the actual "Sky City" pueblo is located fifteen miles from Interstate 40. The Acoma who reside atop the imposing rock are descended from a tribe whose members have inhabited the mesa for more than 2,000 years. It is one of, if not the only site where people have continuously resided for that space of time in what is now the United States. Removing Oñate's right foot was not an act of vandalism.[2] It was a symbolic protest to remind the public that 400 years ago Oñate amputated the right foot of twenty-five Acoma Pueblo warriors during his colonizing efforts in New Mexico.[3]

Days earlier, the State of New Mexico had begun its year-long *Cuatro Centenario* (the Fourth Centenary) celebration of the region's founding by Juan de Oñate. The celebration and the statue's "amputation" contributed to a long-standing debate surrounding the failed Spanish colonizer, Spanish iconography in the region, public art, and how those items relate to heritage tourism. New Mexico's tourism economy relies on and heavily emphasizes the state's ties to Indian cultures, colonial Spain, and Anglo settlers, while it simultaneously downplays the state's Mexican/American peoples[4]. In truth, the area's indigenous peoples are often exiled to a forgotten past and a contemporary existence limited to pottery making and casinos.[5] *El Cuatro Centario* triggered much civic debate over the virtues of the type of men who settled New Mexico at the expense of the Pueblo peoples and the omission of the area's Mexican-origin populations in state tourism efforts.

Three hundred miles south of Santa Fe, a local businessman inspired El Paso area leaders to launch their region's "First Thanksgiving" festivals that same year. An early supporter of the Oñate fantasy, Sheldon Hall, saw it as a potential monetary generator for the economically depressed region. In 1998, El Paso and Socorro each presented a reenactment of Oñate's entry to what is now West Texas. In 1598, a Spanish colonizing party led by Oñate had reposed by and forded the Río Grande in this area as it made its way north.[6] Only the San Elizario event

2   *Introduction*

survives and is known as the *First Thanksgiving Celebration* (formerly *First Thanksgiving of the Americas*). The Spaniards were seeking treasures in what is now northern New Mexico. Although their dreams failed to materialize, El Paso leaders were thrilled to honor the colonizers, believing a First Thanksgiving event would attract tourist dollars.

While First Thanksgiving supporters focused only on Oñate's arrival, going so far as to honor him with a Catholic mass to soften the Spaniards' image, recent developments have seen some community leaders challenge this framing. In 2014, Al Borrego, President of the San Elizario or *San Eli* (Texas) Historical Society referred to the event as a "marketing campaign" that "cannot be proven" to be first.[7] His comments forced locals to ask whether Oñate was really central to their past. If this thanksgiving was first, why is that important? Can anyone prove it was the first one? For example, in 1959, the Texas Society of Daughters of the American Colonists installed a marker near Canyon, Texas, claiming that the Francisco Coronado expedition held a "first" Thanksgiving in Palo Duro Canyon in 1541.[8] Did the indigenous not celebrate something similar prior to the Europeans' arrival?

First or not, Oñate has been used to appeal to tourists for many years. While local supporters objected to Borrego's comments, he was not the first to question the Spanish fantasy. In 2008, former El Paso Mission Trail Association executive director Ben Sánchez told the *El Paso Times*: "The whole idea is to celebrate [the First Thanksgiving] and draw on it for tourism purposes."[9] Similarly, in a 2008 PBS documentary titled *The Last Conquistador*, City Representative Larry Medina recalled the El Paso City Council's reaction to a proposal to build an Oñate sculpture for the downtown:

> The first thing that came to our mind was tourism and economy because we are the tenth poorest city in America. So, we need all the help we can get when it comes to tourist attractions and raising economy [sic] and the level of living and so on.[10]

Economic necessity was a central incentive in the creation of the First Thanksgiving myth.

The series of the aforementioned inaugural events took place throughout the El Paso metropolitan region on the weekend of April 24–26, 1998. Socorro, Texas, six miles north of San Elizario, held a small celebration in the Lower Valley's Cougar Park. A larger reenactment was staged at the Chamizal National Memorial, a federal park in El Paso. An Oñate descendent, Manuel Gullon y de Oñate, a banker whom the *El Paso Times* categorized as an "authority" on his notorious ancestor, was in attendance. Gullon spent much of the weekend defending his progenitor, claiming "[O]ñate should be judged by all his actions in founding New Mexico, not just the battle of Acoma."[11] A month earlier, El Pasoans learned of sculptor John Houser's proposed statue of Juan de Oñate, now formally called *The Equestrian*.[12] Supporters quickly linked Houser's work to Oñate's status as an *adelantado*, a man approved by the Spanish King to colonize a region, and to the First Thanksgiving to strengthen the tourist angle.

Introduction 3

The First Thanksgiving promotion recounts the Spaniards' celebration of thanks along the banks of the Río Grande, prior to the Pilgrims' well-known occasion. Early in its history, the First Thanksgiving's high point was a reenactment of the Spaniards' celebration of thanks for reaching the Río Grande. It included Oñate's reading of *La Toma*, a colonial decree that claimed the lands of far West Texas and New Mexico for King Phillip II.

At the time of this writing, only San Elizario continues to host a First Thanksgiving event, El Paso abandoned these efforts years ago. San Elizario continues the tradition and even includes a one-day conference that examines this historical period (in a strangely sympathetic manner). A Catholic mass is celebrated by the local bishop and held at San Elizario's Presidio Chapel. However, the mass omits that Oñate's actions would today be considered crimes against humanity. Oñate enslaved the Pueblo peoples of northern New Mexico and ordered an assault on Acoma Pueblo, resulting in the murder of 800 Acoma Indians, including 300 women and children. He was convicted of these and other crimes, resulting in his being permanently barred from New Mexico.[13]

The greater El Paso area is surrounded by Oñate markers that bring the failed colonizer local and regional name recognition. Besides the cultural marker in the township of San Elizario, Texas, another, denoting where the Spaniards allegedly crossed the river sits on the banks of the Río Grande, a quarter-mile south of the current University of Texas at El Paso campus. A central roadway, Loop 375, is officially designated both the Don [sic] Juan de Oñate[14] Trail and the César Chávez Border Highway. This naming links the savage colonizer with a pacifist civil rights leader. Nearby Oñate High School in Las Cruces, New Mexico testifies to locals using the colonizer's myth in shaping local history, even if his time in these cities was limited to a few days.

While debates on Spanish colonialism continued to rage in New Mexico during the late 1990s, the events in El Paso grew into a storm of controversy with the announcement for a planned statue of Juan de Oñate for the downtown. Whether a statue of Oñate should even be placed in the city was a moot point. Citizens rapidly took sides. Was Oñate an explorer who brought civilization to the Southwest? Was he a brutal murderer who, despite his attempts at a "bloodless conquest" as one local newspaper account claimed, defended himself and his party because his soldiers were attacked by the Acoma?[15]

To place these questions in context, we examined newspaper accounts, looked to historical scholarship, tapped into indigenous and Chicano historical memory, as well as theoretical and conceptual frameworks to help us argue our concerns regarding this aspect of Southwest public memory. We wanted to understand why El Paso leaders embraced an individual who only spent a few days in the region. Hammond and Rey's archival research on the Oñate expedition notes the Spanish colonizers reached the Río del Norte, today's Río Grande, on April 20, 1598. One week later, on April 27, the Spaniards traveled up river and on April 30, Oñate claimed possession of

4 *Introduction*

the land by reading *La Toma*, claiming what is today West Texas and New Mexico under the sovereignty of the Spanish Crown. The colonizing party then moved on to northern New Mexico.[16] How did El Paso's embrace of these events shape local identity? To what extent did this process ignore historical actors, such as the indigenous peoples of the area and later the Mexican community? Did local El Pasoans take historical accounts that proclaimed Oñate the city's founder to heart? El Paso was not founded until the 19th Century. Did they take the local tourism industry and media accounts at face value?

The chapters that follow reflect our search for and discussion of the myth and reality centered on local heritage tourism and public memory, which in turn reflects the economic goals of a small local elite. Tourism is often developed and promoted by government and business leaders via chambers of commerce and professional or organizational committees and bureaus.[17] This work reflects our desire to open a dialogue in order to examine the issue, so people might then decide for themselves whether to accept Oñate as a hero, reject him as a failed Indian killer, or simply find him to be a man of his times. The community deserves the information to make an informed choice.

Here, we offer an explanation we believe can help the reader understand why the controversy continues to divide the peoples of the Southwest. Carey McWilliams critiqued the mythmaking of the Spanish Southwest that converts Spanish colonizers into heroes and the importers of culture to the area. He termed this phenomenon *fantasy heritage*, noting its ability to erase past injustices from public memory.[18] A local Anglo businessman reflected this view when he told one of the authors that Oñate-era history is, "our history." Yes, Oñate is part of local history but historical accounts are open to multiple interpretations and many who support fantasy heritage fail to see the complexity of previous eras in the Southwest. Such a stance whitewashes the past and creates a hegemonic view where history is reduced to food, fun, and fiesta. The term hegemony is appropriate here as it offers insight to the idea of control but more importantly, the act of control as conceded to by the colonized. We are thus concerned with the hegemonic effects of fantasy heritage presentations to the public as an accurate presentation of the past.[19] As it stands, we contend that fantasy heritage leads to the hegemony that historian David Romo characterized as existing at a "Disneyfied, McDonalized-level, without really seeing the guts and the gore of history."[20]

If fantasy heritage representations of Oñate and the reduction of indigenous and Chicana/o history to a secondary status diminishes or marginalizes the Other, what does this say about taking tourist-oriented events at face value? If people believe a sanitized and tourist-friendly framing of the past, our contention is they will remain blind to the history of violence that shaped our current world and how that legacy preserves privilege for some at the expense of others.[21] We will explore how and why fantasy heritage appears natural, normal, and/or complete, so as to understand how history became so sterile. Oñate has long been the central figure in the area's tourism plans. He has been favorably depicted in monuments, historical reenactments, coloring books and in elementary-level books assigned to students in El Paso schools. These efforts reflect a despicable attack on schoolchildren who have yet to develop advanced critical thought. The end result is the building of pro-Spanish attitudes that deny most area students the opportunity to thoroughly understand their mestizo culture. Eighty-two percent of the community is of Mexican ancestry or origin.[22]

While we do not argue against the practice of using history to attract visitors to a region, we argue for a form of tourism that recognizes the diversity of peoples and their stories. If other tourism venues across the globe have started to acknowledge past wrongdoing, why does El Paso lag behind?[23] Historian Marsha Weisiger explains: "The public is hungry for an understanding of the past that is less about the sugar-coated, mythic West and more about its sometimes less palatable historical realities. People are seeking a past that explains the present."[24] A more complex treatment of Spanish colonialism would likely meet this goal and possibly increase area tourism. It would also have a positive effect on the local community's understanding of its identity.

Oñate's presence in the community affects local identity, leading to the question: Who are we? Whether expressed by the media, school, business, or political leaders, the region's Mexican-origin community (other Latinos as well) are viewed as Hispanic. But, are we, members of the Chicana/o, Mexican American, and Mexican immigrant community, actually Hispanic? Do we come from Spain? Do we adopt the term "Hispanic" just because social institutions tell us to do so? Some of our students at the university appear to validate this view, at least until we clarify the terms for them. Many believe they are Hispanic because throughout their public or parochial school years, this is what they have heard from teachers and staff members. When they enrolled in school, these same students and their parents were forced to choose Hispanic as an ethnic marker because the only other options are often Asian, Black (non-Hispanic), or White (non-Hispanic). Other than a label adopted by the US Census Bureau to collect demographic data, the Hispanic label reveals the shaping of a generation whose personal choice in selecting an identity has been denied.[25] This whitewashing is remarkable, particularly on the US-Mexico border, where a vast majority of the population is of Mexican origin, whether they identify as Mexican, *mexicano*, Mexican American, *tejano*, or Chicana/o.[26]

We are reminded of Jonathan Kozol's idea that the problem with schools is not that they fail to work, but rather, that they actually do.[27] His point is that schools successfully socialize our youth to fit into a mold that satisfies the goals of the institution and mainstream society. While many Hispanics quip, "What is the big deal?" Simply put, how we see ourselves is crucial to our identity. Adopting a Hispanic identity for Spanish-speaking peoples in the Southwest places their historical memory at risk. Understanding our past affects how we understand and navigate our present. Questioning the colonialism of the region requires a "contested history," as Linda Tuhiwai Smith

6   *Introduction*

writes. Viewed as a challenge to Western history, this approach looks at the other side of the historical coin and poses questions that provide a different view of the story.[28] To that end, case studies that highlight how these central concepts play out across a variety of other intercultural contexts are interspersed throughout the book.

The chapters that follow have their genesis in El Paso and New Mexico's centennial celebrations of Juan de Oñate's 1598 arrival to the region. These events began in the late 1990s and relied heavily on the use of fantasy heritage to make Oñate a marketable tourism commodity. As we examined the controversy surrounding various events, for example, a binational dinner that included events in El Paso and Ciudad Juárez, academic conferences (again strangely sympathetic to the colonial experiment), and the announcement of a Juan de Oñate statue commissioned by the El Paso city council, we noted many problems. The region's embrace of this "heroic" Spanish figure coincided with the erasure of his indigenous victims at Acoma and other areas of colonial conquest. No one can deny indigenous communities have inhabited the Southwest for millennia. Witness the pictographs that exist across the area (e.g., Hueco Tanks State Park in Texas or Petroglyph National Monument in New Mexico), the numerous Southwest pueblos, and the many Indian reservations throughout the region.

Ironically, those who promote the Oñate fantasy prove incapable of seeing or unwilling to see this side of history. One of the authors, for example, was invited by an Oñate sympathizer to "imagine how those brave Spanish men and women must have felt, knowing they faced death to settle the area. The women knew they could be killed or raped by the Indians." The person who made these comments could not grasp that the Indian "attacks" could also be framed as the Indian defense of their homeland. The Spanish were little more than an invading military force that included Catholic clergy who imposed a new spirituality on penalty of death on the indigenous. Still, regional tourism rhetoric suggests it is the Indians who were "ungrateful" for what the Spanish offered, as noted by a member of the New Mexico Hispanic Culture Preservation League.[29] Apparently, whatever is bad for tourism is shunned or inverted by people with this degree of desire for tourist dollars or, in the case of some minorities, social acceptance in White society.

Our research allowed us to develop themes around questions of fantasy heritage and its role in Southwest tourism. We are, admittedly, not supporters of the Oñate statue in El Paso. Yet, our purpose here is to promote a critical dialogue between ethnic and social class sectors of the Southwest community—Asian, Black, Brown, Indian, White, and anyone else who wishes to join in the examination. The voices represented here are not those of victims but of a unified community whose concerns should be heard. There must be dialogue among Chicanas/os, Mexican Americans, Natives, Whites, and others on the question of identity. Discussions designed to identify progressive forms of teaching in the education of our students, particularly at the elementary through secondary levels, should become standard. If we achieve even a portion of this goal then our work will have been worth the effort.

Oñate, rightly, belongs more to New Mexico than to West Texas and our dialogue extends into that state. However, the ramifications of the Spanish fantasy resonate throughout the entire Southwest and West. From San Elizario's *First Thanksgiving* to Santa Fe, New Mexico's *Fiestas* to the *Old Spanish Days* of Santa Barbara, California, much remains to be learned about and from Spanish colonialism. The landscape of the Southwest is a living tapestry reflecting both its current state and the conflict-filled past that shaped it.[30] The chapters that follow address our key concerns related to Juan de Oñate, fantasy heritage, public memory, and tourism in the Southwest.

Organization of the book

Chapter 1 presents a short overview of Juan de Oñate's life. It contextualizes his era and seeks to present him as more than an evil, failed colonizer or a misunderstood but well-intentioned saint. In truth, Oñate was a man, no more, no less. This chapter represents him as such and also corrects many of the fantasy accounts told about him in the Southwest. For example, many in the Southwest believe Oñate was born in Spain, sailed to the New World, held the First Thanksgiving in El Paso, and peaceably settled New Mexico. Many local newspaper and television news accounts paint this image as well. Some researchers who have utilized the historical record ignore Oñate's crimes when interviewed by the local media. The fact is Oñate was born in or near Zacatecas, New Spain, failed in his efforts to colonize New Mexico, stood trial for and was found guilty of the murder of 800 Acoma Indians, and died a mining inspector in Spain.[31]

The first chapter also examines the concept of fantasy heritage that was introduced by Carey McWilliams in 1948 in his book, *North from Mexico*, and its relation to contemporary concepts of heritage tourism and public memory. Fantasy heritage is our central concept and serves to frame our discussion throughout the book. We provide examples of how dominated groups are rendered invisible by the use of stories and myths that give colonizers an air of noble grandeur. These stories and myths also drive a market system of profit in real estate, art, museums, and other cultural areas. As one of our colleagues mentioned in passing statues of Indians and buffalos at Albuquerque's Sunport Airport, "It's a shame that Americans have to push people and animals to the brink of extinction before they can be celebrated." Regrettably, extinction and genocide create a longing for the past, a central element in selling Southwest cultures to tourists and locals alike.[32] As anthropologist David Berliner reminds us, "nostalgic discourses and practices are foundations underlying the fields of heritage and tourism."[33] The nostalgic past is transmitted to public memory in the Southwest via heritage tourism events, public art, and memorials, the elements of study in this book.[34]

In addition to public art and memorials, the Southwest also reflects this nostalgia in everyday forms. In many Southwest communities, for example, the streets of middle- and upper-middle class neighborhoods are named in

8 *Introduction*

Spanish but are primarily inhabited by Whites. The opposite is true of low income and lower-middle class spaces. This strategy of naming reflects some of what our colleague observed at the airport; the poor are socialized to love the US. In contrast, the economically privileged need to know they are living in an exotic space, believing they are at peace with the local culture. One need only walk the Santa Fe Plaza to see that many of the gallery owners are White, often transplanted from other places. These owners sell and benefit from fantasy heritage constructions, often to the detriment of native-born locals.[35] While these same owners often profess a love for the multicultural or Spanish or indigenous aspects of their adopted culture the economic inequalities that permeate the Southwest are glaringly obvious. The Natives sell their jewelry and handicrafts on sidewalks not galleries.

Chapter 2 examines the annual reenactment of "the First Thanksgiving Celebration" in San Elizario, Texas. The three-day event's high point is a thirty-minute reenactment that represents the Spaniards as noble Christians who entered the area to civilize the region's indigenous populations. It culminates with Oñate reading *La Toma*, thereby usurping the indigenous people's lands and initiating the colonization of New Mexico. In time, the colonial experiment made the indigenous subjects of the Spanish Crown, forced their conversion to Catholicism, stripped them of their lands, and enslaved countless people. The climactic part of the play lays bare the goals of colonization via a much softened representation—the reading of a colonial era document. The chapter traces the evolution of the First Thanksgiving from a minor tourism curiosity to the long-struggling El Paso-area tourism program it has become. The late Sheldon Hall's influence and that of a small group of local area business and political elites continues to be felt. The First Thanksgiving reenactment was previously staged by David Mills and Hector Serrano in conjunction with El Paso Community College.[36] In 2014, the University of Texas at El Paso's "Opera UTEP" led the 25th anniversary reenactment. In 2015, educator Joe Estala took over the play's production. The chapter provides a semiotic reading of the play to examine the hegemonic glorification of the Spanish past via fantasy heritage.

Chapter 3 examines a thirty-six-foot tall statue of Oñate, renamed *The Equestrian*, as a form of public art outside the El Paso International Airport. Here, we are concerned with how the push for the statue served to ignore the cultural experiences of the Chicana/o community by using public art to promote a neocolonial view of history in a city that is eighty-two percent Mexican origin. The chapter examines these topics via the analysis of more than twenty years of print media stories and editorials in El Paso area newspapers, building heavily on our previously published work.

Chapter 4 ties the earlier chapters together by examining the framing of El Paso's identity through heritage tourism and public memory. There are many elements to tourism in the city but as anyone who flies into El Paso quickly learns, it all begins and ends with Juan de Oñate. Business leaders within the Chamber of Commerce as well as politicians help to shape area tourism policies, few are Mexican American or socially progressive. For them the solution seems to do anything that brings people to town, regardless its historical accuracy or lack thereof. We also examine the Oñate controversy, the neocolonial nature of contemporary El Paso, and recent trends to reinvent its downtown.

In 2013 and 2014, the Office of State Senator José Rodríguez sponsored day-long meetings regarding heritage tourism in El Paso. It is welcome relief that there are others in the city creating a more representative approach to heritage and public memory. Still, some in the audience at the 2014 tourism summit expressed shock when Senator Rodríguez noted that the Juan de Oñate myth ignores Indians. How could the senator make such an assertion? The entire point of this book is to demonstrate why comments such as those voiced by the senator are important. The only way to achieve a better sense of historical inclusion is for members of the El Paso community, with differing points of view, to sit down and discuss the complex issues that shape El Paso's public memory and tourism. This goal has been part of the senator's heritage tourism efforts. Many more El Paso politicians and business leaders need to understand that a holistic tourist policy is doable and is indeed happening in many other communities. El Paso's failure to keep up with current trends may bring about the demise in popularity of its First Thanksgiving efforts. Such a demise may happen as the city's focus is now on the downtown.

Chapter 5 offers a multiple-step strategy for developing more ethnically-inclusive tourism projects. We would hope to take it to the schools, as well as local business, political, and academic communities. It is a process, not a short-term solution, that addresses the importance of contextualizing the past from a multicultural angle. The chapter ends with suggestions for creating a holistic, but tourist-friendly, public memory that does not focus on fantasies. It also illustrates how dialogue can help communities come to grips with the notion of colonialism and promote a more inclusive representation of its past. This chapter concludes our study and offers a series of ideas regarding the process of heritage tourism.

A Word about Terminology

Writing about both the Mexican and Mexican American populations leads authors to struggle with ways to avoid the redundancy of terms such as "Mexicans and Mexican Americans" throughout the work. Inspired by Michelle A. Holling's[37] use of Mexican(American) to denote both populations, we use the following: Mexican (a Mexican citizen), Mexican American (an American of Mexican descent), and Mexican/American in reference to both groups. The plural form of the last term shall be Mexican/Americans to denote both a multiplicity of Mexicans and Mexican Americans. Throughout this study we also use Chicana/o. It speaks to a generation of individuals who, from the 1960s to the present day, have fought to reclaim a community's dignity through self-determination and activism. It speaks to the realization that the Mexican community in the US is one of social injustice and has been

10 *Introduction*

for many generations. Younger generations have through personal experience offered a new term, one of greater inclusion, Chicanx. They have incorporated the "x" as a signifier of inclusivity, one that moves beyond the traditional and heteronormative female/male dichotomy.[38] We support this effort and see ourselves as Chicana/o/x allies in the struggle for social justice; however, we opted to retain the Chicana/o label. We believe Chicana/o is not outdated but is a reflection of our experience, not only in academics but through engaging the activist tradition.

Notes

1 Thomas H. Guthrie, *Recognizing Heritage: Multiculturalism in New Mexico* (Lincoln, NB: University of Nebraska Press, 2013), 148. The number of individuals became known only in October 2017, when the self-confessed transgressor agreed to be interviewed by the *New York Times* and revealed it was he and a friend who had committed the foot removal. See: Simon Romero, "It Takes a Foot Thief," *New York Times*, October 2, 2017, A1. Abridged story available online: https://www.nytimes.com/2017/10/02/insider/new-mexico-statue-conquistador-foot-thief.html. Retrieved March 8, 2019.

2 Christopher Cordess and Maja Turcan, "Art Vandalism," *British Journal of Criminology*, 33 no. 1 (1993): 95–102. Cordess and Turcan's review of the literature on art vandalism led them to create two categories. Major acts included "acts of slashing, stabbing, and shooting of canvasses, and of arson, or of smashing sculptures or vases … [and] Minor acts tended to be surreptitious and anonymous" (p. 97). However, they report that "Minor acts were described correspondingly lightly and were thought of as merely the result of 'daring' by adolescents or school children or by 'parties of foreign students'" (p. 98). The Acoma incident led to an explanatory letter being sent to a major New Mexico newspaper. Thus, we argue the Alcade amputation was a political act. Cordess and Turcan mailed ninety-two, seven-item questionnaires to galleries and museums in Great Britain. They reported receiving sixty replies that support the information taken from p. 98.

3 David J. Weber, *The Spanish Frontier in North America* (New Haven, CT: Yale University Press, 1992), 85–87.

4 As will be discussed later in the chapter, we use Mexican(s) in reference to a person (s) from Mexico, while Mexican American(s) refers to Americans of Mexican descent. Mexican/American refers to both Mexicans and Mexican American people.

5 Guthrie, *Recognizing Heritage.*

6 Weber, *Spanish Frontier*

7 On January 12, 2014, *El Paso Times* reporter Aileen Flores reported that Al Borrego, President of the San Elizario Historical Society, questioned the First Thanksgiving myth. Borrego earned the ire of leaders in his small community and from some El Paso area business leaders, particularly that of the family of the late Sheldon Hall who introduced the First Thanksgiving tourism ploy. Borrego publicly referred to the First Thanksgiving as a "marketing campaign," adding that he and other San Elizario historians and residents want to abandon the concept because, "[supporters] can't prove it really happened." See: "San Eli's Claim is Labeled a Campaign: Historical Society's Chief Calls It a Creation to Attract Tourists," *El Paso Times*, January 12, 2014, A1, A7.

8 According to the texasalmanac.com, "later research indicated that grapes and pecans were gathered by the celebrants for the feast, and neither grow in Palo Duro Canyon." See: https://texasalmanac.com/topics/history/timeline/first-thanksgiving. Retrieved September 14, 2018.

Introduction 11

9 Darren Metz, "San Eli's First Thanksgiving Pays Homage to Town's People," *El Paso Times*, April 27, 2008, B5.

10 John J. Valadez and Christine Ibarra, *The Last Conquistador*. Medina's comments appear at 8:18–8:34.

11 Ken Flynn, "Spanish Descendent Calls Oñate Builder, Not Killer," *El Paso Times*, April 26, 1998, A6.

12 Darren Hunt, "Making an Impression: Giant Statue Promises National Recognition," *El Paso Times*, March 29, 1998, 12, Sunday Special Supplement.

13 Ibid. While Guthrie (2013) claims that Oñate "was eventually cleared of all charges" (p. 146) related to the Acoma slaughter, Weber (1992) notes Oñate devoted great effort to trying to rebuild his reputation but received only a "partial pardon" (p. 87). According to Weber, although Oñate received a coveted knighthood in the Order of Santiago, he remained barred from New Mexico (p. 87).

14 Writers sympathetic to Oñate use the honorary title, *Don* (of noble origin), signifying him as a member of the Spanish colonial nobility. We refrain from using this title because we see no reason to revere a man convicted for what today would be crimes against humanity.

15 Laura E. Gómez, *Manifest Destinies: The Making of the Mexican American Race* (New York: New York University Press, 2007), 22. Oñate assumed his conquest would be "bloodless" because he foresaw no one to challenge his claim to the region. Although Indian resistance was a regular occurrence, the bloodless theme seems to capture the colonial history of New Mexico as framed via heritage tourism. The concept is used, for example, in the Santa Fe Fiestas to describe Diego de Vargas' expedition in 1692 to reconquer New Mexico after the Pueblo Revolt of 1680. By enlisting the support of three Pueblo governors, de Vargas was able to secure support for his objective without warfare. However, not all pueblos supported the Spanish incursion and through 1701 resisted and battled the Spanish until they decided it was not possible to continue their struggle. Finally, the bloodless conquest also describes the taking of New Mexico without a shot during the US-Mexico War in 1846. Weber (1992) notes a pattern of rebellion among many Indian peoples below the contemporary US-Mexico border during the late 1680s (p. 137).

16 George P. Hammond and Agapito Rey, *Don Juan de Oñate: Colonizer of New Mexico, 1595–1628, Vol. V & VI* (Albuquerque, NM: University of New Mexico Press, 1953).

17 Brij Maharaj, Reshma Sucheran, and Vino Pally, "Durban – A Tourism Mecca? Challenges of the Post-Apartheid Era," *Urban Forum* 17, no. 3 (July 2006): 262–281. An example of this type of tourism development is provided in Maharaj, Sucheran, and Pally's study of Durbin, South Africa's development into a tourism attraction. See p. 264–266.

18 Carey McWilliams, *North from Mexico: The Spanish-speaking People of the United States* (New York: Praeger, 1948/2016).

19 Frank G. Pérez and Carlos F. Ortega, "Mediated Debate, Historical Framing, and Public Art: The Juan de Oñate Controversy in El Paso," *Aztlán: A Journal of Chicano Studies* 33, no. 2 (2008), 121–140. This point is addressed in Chapter 2 and builds on our earlier work.

20 Valadez and Ibarra, *Last Conquistador*. Romo's comments appear at 10:55–11:02.

21 Edward W. Said offers a compelling explanation of this situation in terms of the "Orient" and its relation to the West in his seminal text: *Orientalism* (New York: Vintage Books, 1978). Eduardo Bonilla-Silva provides a contemporary interpretation of how racism has evolved in a US context in his work: *Racism without Racists: Color-blind Racism* 4th Ed (New York: Rowman & Littlefield, 2014). He specifically examines how Whites in the US use rhetorical mechanisms to downplay the nation's history of racism and its effects on contemporary society. See

12 *Introduction*

also: Tim Wise, *White Like Me* (Berkley, CA: Softskull Press, 2011). The book, auto-biographical in nature, illustrates the many benefits Whites enjoy in contemporary society as well as the many additional obstacles encountered by people of color in the US. Given our study's focus on race and hegemony we recommend the reader review Kuan-Hsing Chen and David Morely, *Stuart Hall: Critical Dialogues in Cultural Studies* (New York: Routledge, 1996), 411–441.

22 The actual figure is 81.6% according to the City of El Paso, Office of Economic Development. We rounded the figure for ease of reading. See: https://www.elpasotexas.gov/economic-development/business-services/data-and-statistics/population.

23 Perhaps the most extreme example of tourism grounded in the atrocities of the past comes in the form of former Nazi death camps that are toured for educational purposes. See, for example: Schlomo Romi and Michal Lev, "Experiential Learning of History through Youth Journeys to Poland," *Research in Education* 78 (2007): 88–102. Other examples include Clinton van der Merwe's summary of the heritage tourism literature in his essay, "The Limits of Urban Heritage Tourism in South Africa: The Case of Constitution Hill, Johannesburg," *Public Forum* 24, no. 2 (2013): 573–588.

24 Marsha Weisiger, "No More Heroes: Western History in Public Places," *Western Historical Quarterly* 42, no. 3 (2011): 295.

25 Pablo Vila addresses the competing meanings of the label Chicana/o in El Paso from the perspectives of different interviewees. His respondents view the term and its related identity from several perspectives in both *Crossing Borders, Reinforcing Borders: Social Categories, Metaphors, and Narrative Identities on the U.S.-Mexico Border* (Austin, TX: University of Texas Press, 2000) and in *Border Identifications: Narratives of Religion, Gender, and Class on the U.S.-Mexico Border* (Austin, TX: University of Texas Press, 2006). The index in either book can provide the reader with specific page numbers. However, to fully grasp the discourses addressed by Vila, we suggest one read the corresponding sections in their entirety. Much of what Vila's respondents claim about Chicanas/os is inaccurate, suggesting that a strong anti-Chicana/o hegemony permeates the region.

26 The issue of identity in the Mexican community is complex and contested. Cultural attitudes, general, social, and institutional values shape ethnic identity. The result is at times an individual who is confused about who they are, or who may reject their heritage markers, or may altogether, simply choose an identity and ignore all assumptions about who they are supposed to be. See as an example: Pablo Vila, "The Competing Meanings of the Label 'Chicano' in El Paso," *The U.S.-Mexico Border: Transcending Division, Contesting Identities*, ed. Kathleen Staudt and David Spencer (Colorado: Lynne Rienner Publishers, 1998), 185–211.

27 Jonathan Kozol, *The Night is Dark and I am Far from Home* (New York: Bantam Books, 1977), 1.

28 Linda Tuhiwai Smith, *Decolonizing Methodologies: Research and Indigenous Peoples*, 7th ed. (London: Zed Books Ltd., 1999).

29 Valadez and Ibarra, *Last Conquistador*. The name of the man who makes this comment is not provided. His comments appear at 35:40. One gains more context by viewing the entire scene: 35:14–35:55.

30 Andrea Hammer, "Memory Lines: The Plotting of New York's Military Tract," in *Rhetoric, Remembrance, and Visual Form: Sighting Memory,* ed. Anne Teresa Demo and Bradford Vivian (New York: Routledge, 2012). Hammer uses the analogy of the landscape as a living tapestry in reference to "New York State Surveyor General Simeon De Witt's original 1789 survey of central New York State's Military Tract," 15.

31 Hammond and Rey, *Don Juan de Oñate*; John L. Kessell, *Pueblos, Spaniards, and the Kingdom of New Mexico* (Norman, OK: University of Oklahoma Press, 2008); Marc Simmons, *The Last Conquistador: Juan de Oñate and the Settling of the Far Southwest* (Norman, OK: University of Oklahoma Press, 1993).

Introduction 13

32 Edward H. Spicer, *Cycles of Conquest: The Impact of Spain, Mexico, and the United States on the Indians of the Southwest, 1533–1960* (Tucson, AZ: University of Arizona Press, 1962). Spicer covers the process of conquest as well as the results of that contact and the process of cultural change. One should also consult: Richard Drinnon, *Facing West: The Metaphysics of Indian-Hating and Empire-Building* (New York: New American Library, 1980). Drinnon takes the reader on a much longer journey by addressing the conquest of indigenous lands in the United States, a mere first step in the larger program of conquest and colonialism.

33 David Berliner, "Multiple Nostalgias: The Fabric of Heritage in Luang Prabang," *Journal of the Royal Anthropological Institute* 18, no. 4 (2012), 769–786.

34 Although a number of scholars have examined this topic, with interest growing in recent years, we have drawn on the work of Carole Blair, Greg Dickinson, and Brian L. Ott in the Introduction of Greg Dickinson, Carole Blair, and Brian L. Ott, *Places of Public Memory: The Rhetoric of Museums and Memorials* (Tuscaloosa, AL: University of Alabama Press, 2010), 1–54.

35 Andrew Leo Lovato recounts how the influx of people from outside Santa Fe has forced native Santa Feans to move to housing beyond the city limits because native Santa Feans can no longer afford to live in their own city. He also addresses how the entry of this population has shifted local politics toward a more conservative political orientation. See: *Santa Fe Hispanic Culture: Preserving Identity in a Tourist Town* (Albuquerque, NM: University of New Mexico Press, 2006). Chris Wilson's *The Myth of Santa Fe* (Albuquerque, NM: University of New Mexico Press, 1997) provides a detailed account of how Santa Fe became a tourism mecca and the impact this objective has had on a variety of social areas.

36 John Hall, "First Thanksgiving: 1598 Oñate Arrival Celebrated." *El Paso Times,* May 1, 2011.

37 Michelle A. Holling. "A Dispensational Rhetoric in 'The Mexican Question in the Southwest'," in *Border Rhetorics: Charting Enactments of Citizenship and Identity on the U.S.-Mexico Border,* ed. D. Robert DeChaine, (Tuscaloosa, AL: University of Alabama Press, 2012), 65–85.

38 For additional insights into the use of the "x", please consult Ed Morales, *Latinx: The New Force in American Politics and Culture,* New York: Verso Press, 2018; Alan Peleaz Lopez, "The 'X' in Latinx is a Wound Not a Trend," *EFNIKS,* September 13, 2018. Retrieved at http://efniks.com/the deep-dive-pages/2018/9/11/the-X-in-Latinx-is-a-wound-not-a-trend.; and Rigoberto Marques, "What's in the 'X' of Latinx?" Center for comparative Studies in Race and Ethnicity, Stanford University, July 9, 2018.

1 Fantasy heritage in southwest tourism

Romantic tales of outlaw gunslingers, noble Spanish explorers, and images of gentle Natives lure visitors to the desert Southwest. The region's political and merchant class have long recognized tourism's economic impact here, particularly in relation to marketing the past.[1] In this book, we examine *heritage tourism* as the simplistic framing of history that sanitizes important events to create marketable tourism myths[2] We want to understand how heritage tourism impacts the Mexican/Americans[3] of the Southwest. Often tied to a locale's desire for tourist dollars, heritage tourism has been decades in the making in places such as Santa Fe, New Mexico,[4] and is on the rise in neighboring West Texas. In fact, heritage tourism is an international concern worth billions of dollars annually on a global scale.[5] Regrettably, it has also been characterized as "largely a pastiche with no higher purpose than entertainment."[6]

As a cultural enterprise, heritage tourism is a mixture of past and current events, a union between history and its use, often through exploitation, by contemporary community or regional elites.[7] The marketable representation of the area's past, complete with heroes and villains typically overlooks historical complexities to distill the past into easily digested story lines promoted by elites.[8] "As a branding term, it has broad marketing appeal in its associations with the past, with traditions and perhaps with craftsmanship."[9] Tourism scholars Hazel Tucker and John Akama note that heritage tourism is replete with "hegemonic structures of language and representation [that] have created particular conceptions of 'truth' and 'reality' for both tourism practice and tourism destinations."[10] They add that "concepts such as gender, class, ethnicity, and race, [have] become a ground for 'internal colonialism' in which identities are constrained and oppressed, selectively represented."[11] In short, "all heritage is someone's heritage and therefore logically not someone else's: ... any creation of heritage from the past disinherits someone completely or partially, actively or potentially."[12] Themes of ownership and authenticity are central to our analysis of Juan de Oñate as a Southwest Spanish heritage icon, the central focus of our work.

Tourism as a field of study operates "as a site of contestation in which cultural imagery, politics, economics, and [even] international relations"[13] may come into play among competing social segments. Thus, heritage tourism greatly influences a locale's collective recollection of the past or its framing—*public memory*. Building on communication scholars Carole Blair, Greg Dickinson, and Brian L. Ott, we call the reader's attention to the six key premises linked to this concept: (1) memory is activated by present concerns, issues, or anxieties; (2) memory narrates shared identities, constructing senses of communal belonging; (3) memory is animated by affect; (4) memory is partial, partisan, and thus often contested; (5) memory relies on material and/or symbolic supports; and (6) memory has a history.[14]

The elements of public memory contribute to fantasy heritage and vice versa. They build on one another and extend beyond buildings to include intangibles such as "rituals, tales, performing arts, crafts, and ceremonies ... that act as symbols of identity in the present."[15] Heritage is political, economically driven, and exists in various manifestations, physical and otherwise.

With a focus on heritage tourism and its impact on public memory, in this chapter we seek to explain how the Southwest's tourism industry has turned a superficial and Eurocentric understanding of the past into an economically questionable hegemonic construct. Carey McWilliams addressed *fantasy heritage* [16] in terms of California's "Spanish" identity. He explained that fantasy heritage reinvented the Spanish colonial era into an Eden-like world that never existed. Here, noble Dons cared for their Native charges while introducing new technologies to the area; Spanish friars, driven by their Christian love of humanity, brought religion to the Natives and "civilized" them. Fantasy heritage omits the genocide, enslavement, forced religious conversion, unjust imprisonment, rape, murder, and exploitation that defined the Spanish conquest of the Americas.[17] It refers to efforts that frame the colonial period via a simple, Eurocentric framework that hides the usurption and cultural erasure of Native and Mexican resources and culture.

Many other groups were also erased; regrettably, due to space limitations they fall beyond the scope of this particular project. Fantasy heritage tells the experiences of oppressed groups whose stories are preserved using: (1) a Christ-like hero who is free of any apparent moral deficiencies, particularly as represented by their academic sympathizers, tourism organizers and marketers;[18] (2) a story line involving a noble colonizing force who "settled" a region to improve the life ways of its native inhabitants;[19] (3) the framing of forced religious and/or political indoctrination as voluntarily accepted by the colonized;[20] (4) the acknowledgement of the imposition of a new economic order,[21] also framed as voluntarily adopted; and (5) the failure to address the complexities of the commemorated era or event in the present.[22] These elements create a Eurocentric hegemonic frame that represents colonialism as human progress by ignoring or distorting past key elements or events, for example, the colonized's knowledge, military violence, or slavery.

Historical reenactments must be both interesting and relatively accurate in terms of names, dates, and locations. Citing the extant literature, Melody K. Pope, April K. Sievert, and Sheree L. Sievert emphasize that "authenticity is a crucial and fundamental factor in attracting tourists."[23] Fantasy events sanitize, standardize, and whitewash history. They rely on creative license and perspective to craft a marketable experience.[24] For example, the Polynesian aha'äina (eating gathering) was reinvented as the Hawaiian "luau" for tourists.[25] The original meaning was lost but became synonymous with visits to Hawaii in the minds of many. Santa Barbara's *Old Spanish Days* festival celebrates the Spanish colonization of California, erasing any traces of the state's "Mexicanness." This tendency permeates the entire US Southwest and West where tourists are sold fantasy heritage myths that normalize the regions' racial segregation. We will use fantasy heritage[26] to show how the Spanish colonial experiment and related myths promote a simple and Eurocentric framing of the Southwest region's past.

Tourist or visitor? Individual understandings of fantasy heritage tourism

Increased public interest in urban sightseeing, cultural heritage, and civic festivals leaves many cities and regions facing intense competition for tourists.[27] To broaden their appeal many heritage reenactments adopt a "talk television" production style that favors emotional appeals over rational thought, rewrites political discourse as entertainment, and that replaces democratic community participation with low-grade cultural fare.[28] People's beliefs and experiences shape their interpretations of heritage tourism events. Some unquestioningly

Figure 1 A mosaic of three Lower Valley missions under the César Chávez/Juan de Oñate Border Highway welcomes visitors to the area.
Credit: Leonel Monroy

accept information they are presented at heritage sites, while others engage them with greater skepticism. Many attendees are oblivious to the position of power their disposable income and leisure time provide. As Daniela Fiorini and Paula Socolovsky[29] remind us, tourists often come from more economically developed or prosperous places than those they visit,[30] allowing some tourists to "see themselves as ... explorers in exotic lands. This distancing can lead to greater powers of observation or, conversely, to oversimplifications and naïve ideas."[31] They add that "Because foreign tourists are not aware of the meaning of most of the signs in any culture, they can only participate in these cultures through myths – that is, by means of stories or discourses."[32] For these reasons, we have categorized those who visit heritage sites into tourists and visitors, as explained below.

Visitors and Tourists

The eclectic nature of contemporary tourism may be, at least partially, responsible for the use of several lowest common denominator strategies. However, not all heritage attendees take the information they receive to heart. Some may attend heritage events despite holding views contrary to the promoted fantasy or to learn about history and then augment their experience with supplemental knowledge (e.g., reading books on the topic, interacting with locals). Still others may visit to examine how the past is being presented in the contemporary era. Those who visit heritage tourism sites seeking more than fantastic and "official" histories are termed *visitors* throughout this work. Visitors are individuals who: (1) typically engage tourist venues and heritage performances from a contemplative or, possibly critical, perspective; (2) realize contemporary views of the past are influenced by different standpoints; and (3) comprehend that economic goals influence heritage tourism venues. Visitors are travelers who interact with locals and who seek activities and venues outside the tourism districts. As Josiah Tucker summarized in 1757, visitors see travel as a form of personal growth and sophistication, to become global in contemporary parlance.[33]

In contrast, *tourists* seek great predictability in their travel and interactions with natives. They often: (1) visit only tourist districts, (2) minimize "unscripted" contact with locals, and (3) use only their own cultural scripts when engaging others.[34] Tourists reduce culture "into iconic visuals such as traditional dress, digestible sound bites such as a greeting in the Native tongue, and standardized ethnographic information."[35] They engage other cultures via their own "prior knowledge, expectations, fantasies, and mythologies."[36] Daniel Boorstin suggests that, "Tourist 'attractions' offer an elaborately contrived indirect experience, an artificial product to be consumed in the very places where the real thing is as free as air."[37] When the "real thing" sold is actually artificial, facts become inconsequential.[38] Fantasies are important because, as Jonathan Culler observes, tourists "are as mindless and docile as a flock of sheep but as annoying as a plague of insects when they

18   *Fantasy heritage in southwest tourism*

descend upon a spot they have 'discovered.'"[39] Tourists seek novelty and do not care about facts. A happy story fits their purposes well.

In addition to fantasies, tourists require material comfort. Thus, it is hardly surprising that the tourism industry frames a Westernized lifestyle as a universal norm. This framing is tied to tourists' desires for predictability. A successful heritage event can prove profitable for a locale, particularly when they offer creature comforts and develop a positive reputation for their longstanding hospitality, suggesting a rewarding experience. When executed correctly tourists will spend money across several economic sectors while visiting. For example, New Mexico promotes its annual *Fiesta de Santa Fe* as dating from 1712.[40] The event and its related activities are a successful tourism draw to the city.[41] The Fiesta commemorates the fantasy of the "bloodless" Spanish Reconquest of Santa Fe in 1692 by Diego de Vargas. It also allows the city to sell its gastronomic, artistic, and recreational opportunities to tourists. People spend money on more than a hotel room and reenactment tickets.

Heritage and public memory in the Southwest

Popular representations of the past reflect contemporary mores and influence societal views, for example in mass media.[42] Heritage tourism similarly transforms perceptions of self, place, and other. The geophysical landscape is a living tapestry that reflects both its current use and the past that shaped it.[43] As historian Fan Ying explains:

> Public urban spaces are a repository and vehicle for recording historical events and shaping and passing down collective memory. They are clearly symbolic public landscapes, often becoming a landmark for a city or even a certain district on a visual and psychological level; they play a decisive role in the formation of spaces for public memory.[44]

Monuments are important physical manifestations that celebrate the past. Whether in the shape of pyramids, statues, memorials, or grandiose buildings that served as sites for the gods (e.g., Temple to Athena), monuments affect the landscape and are political. One way in which one can understand them is through public art, as reflections of how the artist "sees" his or her commissioned topic and in how the state wants certain histories remembered. While one group may love a monument, others may be less than pleased with its topic or depiction. What often happens with these projects is the development of a "monument controversy," according to Ronald L. Grimes.[45]

One need only think of the Eiffel Tower, its initial rejection by many Parisians, and its contemporary status as a symbol of France, to grasp Ying's point. In the Southwest a violent past shaped and influences the present. Associations between the past and contemporary representations make heritage sites and public memorials contested spaces. They also influence people's views. Thus, scholars must examine how social discourse affects public memory and how it, in turn, influences societal perceptions. While scholars have examined heritage tourism across a variety of areas, we will focus on public memory's hegemonic influence on the identity of the Southwest and its inhabitants through tourism.

Southwest public memory glorifies the Spanish colonial era and disregards indigenous and Mexican/American plight and contributions, heritage tourism being a prime example. Thus, some Mexican/Americans deny their ethnic roots.[46] This is not surprising because public memory evolves from political discourses and struggles about how to interpret culture.[47] This struggle "takes the form of an ideological system with a special language, beliefs, symbols, and stories, people can use [to] privilege some explanations over others."[48] Grimes provides an example via a monument erected in Santa Fe's Plaza in 1866–68. The plaque on the monument reads in part, "To the heroes who have fallen in various battles against savage Indians." By the 1960s, Pueblo peoples involved in their civil rights cases took a stand demanding the removal of the monument and plaque. As the city council considered the possibility, supporters of the monument and plaque responded in kind by demanding that nothing of the sort would occur. As things became even more heated, the city council announced that the removal of the word "savage" would help the situation. Ultimately, to quell the antagonisms on both sides, the city council decided that another plaque would explain the situation. As Grimes correctly noted, opponents of removal based their arguments on what-is-done-is-done, while supporters of removal argued that symbolically, the monument did not reflect a plain historical fact but rather it symbolically represented a present-day continuation of "the past into the present;" that is, conquest and colonialism.[49]

As may be expected, those with greater access to economic capital, support from (non)academic experts, and access to the mass media typically dominate these discourses. At present, identity politics and cultural diversity create a situation where those interested in heritage tourism and its related sites "cannot agree on what the proper tone or overarching narrative should be."[50]

This issue is further complicated today because many cultural workers lack formal academic training in the humanities or social sciences. An increasing number of individuals with no formal training in history or a related field (and often without funding) head history-oriented projects.[51] Benjamin Filene terms such individuals "Outside history makers" and includes "heritage tourism developers in this category."[52] He notes that such people, "Unmoored by institutional expectations ... respect the past, but unbound by professional affiliation or, often, training ... can break the rules about disciplinary rigor, form, and footnotes."[53] He suggests museums can use outside history makers in a positive way, offering examples from a project in Minnesota.[54] The foremost element in his example is for professionals to guide outside historians as they work together on projects. While his results were positive, and we are sure in many other places they are, our concern stems from places, such as El Paso, where academic experts in relevant areas are generally absent from heritage tourism efforts or dialogue

20 *Fantasy heritage in southwest tourism*

on the topic. A key example stems from the paucity of guest columns by academics that appeared over a twenty-plus year period in El Paso print media on the topic of Juan de Oñate and the First Thanksgiving.[55] Local planners possibly believe that tourists are interested only in heritage events that exclude violence and the general messiness of history. It may be easier to sell stories, souvenirs, and food to people seeing a fantastical account, than to sell such items to people learning about brutalities in the past. Perhaps inadvertently, if you will, but El Paso area merchants appear to seek out only tourists. Visitors are not actively recruited.

The lack of professional training in heritage tourism is complicated when Anglos in the Southwest have worked to erase the area's Mexican/American cultural presence for more than a century. A strong anti-Mexican hegemony permeates the region. There are about twenty-five traditional high schools in the greater El Paso area, none named in honor of a Mexican American.[56] Consider also how in and of itself Oñate High School in Las Cruces may not influence people to view the failed Spanish colonizer in a particular way. Yet, when El Paso installs a four-story statue in honor of Juan de Oñate and San Elizario annually celebrates him as the founder of "The First Thanksgiving," the potential for residents to develop a positive perception of Spanish colonialism grows exponentially. The aggrandizement of the Southwest's Spanish past also reflects the longstanding Anglo tendency to marginalize or ignore the area's Mexican and Indian past.[57] The Spanish colonial era is represented as one where well-meaning Spaniards received the irrational ire of uncivilized and bloodthirsty Indians.

It is easier to tell, or more accurately sell, stories of noble Spaniards "civilizing" the Indians than to admit colonization's brutality against Native peoples.[58] It is easier to praise the "Hispanic" culture that grew from the ashes of Spain's colonial adventure than to talk about the racism endured by Indians and Mexican/Americans since then.[59]

Visitors to contemporary tourism sites seek out interaction with locals outside of scripted tourism activities, craving something "authentic".[60] Thus, some locales attain economic success by using a holistic approach. For example, Xcaret Park near Cancun, Mexico, features a nightly show whose first part tells the story of Spanish colonialism through dance. It includes the Spaniards' arrival, enslavement of the Indians, and forced religious indoctrination; it is one of the park's most popular draws.[61] Tourism venues in South Africa address the injustices of the apartheid system,[62] the National Civil Rights Museum in Memphis, Tennessee, is housed in the Loraine Motel where civil rights leader Dr. Martin Luther King, Jr. was assassinated.[63] Many other examples exist across the globe. Monuments operate as public memory signs. Often in support of heritage tourism efforts. They are rhetorical, affective, shape the landscape, and grounded in an area's history.[64] When combined with other similar elements they operate as part of a system of semiotic signs that form a hegemonic web of association that emotionally ties people and geography into public memory. Next, we explore the life of failed Spanish colonizer Juan de Oñate, a central icon in West Texas' heritage tourism efforts.

Enter Juan de Oñate as a tourism draw

Throughout the Southwest, Juan de Oñate (c. 1550–1626) has been resurrected to promote heritage tourism as an iconic representation of the Spanish colonial era. He is the key focus of this book and a beneficiary of fantasy heritage representation. This chapter presents a short biography of his life and a review of the literature on fantasy heritage and related theoretical constructs. We then address how the Oñate myth operates as a hegemonic construct throughout the Southwest and what this framing means for the inclusion or exclusion of Mexican/Americans from regional public memory. We seek to complicate Oñate as more than a tourism icon, seeing him as a human being, neither completely sinner nor saint. The Spanish colonizer is touted as either a noble and benevolent leader or, as we saw on one protester's sign, *Hitler's brother in genocide*. We will explore the controversies in New Mexico and far West Texas that surround Oñate's legacy.

The Life of Juan de Oñate

This section draws heavily from Marc Simmon's authoritative biography, *The Last Conquistador*, [65] supplemented with other academic references. On June 3, 1626, Juan de Oñate entered a mine he was to inspect in the Guadalcanal region of the Sierra Morena Mountains, north of Seville.[66] Stripped of his role as colonial governor and permanently barred from New Mexico, Oñate arrived in Spain in 1624 intent on reclaiming a high social position. His violence against the Natives of New Mexico led to the death of more than 800 Acoma Pueblos (including 300 women and children) and resulted in his being placed on trial. Convicted in Mexico City of these deaths, cruelty toward his own colonizing party, the Indians, and adultery, Oñate was sentenced to a lifetime ban from New Mexico, banishment from Mexico City for four years, and ordered to pay a fine. Despite the outcome, Oñate still requested the title of marquis from the Council of the Indies. Their denial led Oñate to Spain to negotiate with the King. He earned an unpaid royal appointment as a mine inspector. Juan knew the industry first-hand. His father had made a fortune mining silver in Zacatecas and Oñate's expertise allowed him to generate reports on the status of mining operations throughout Spain. He also made recommendations for further mining development. Oñate assumed the role might allow him to renegotiate for a better post later.

During a series of mine inspections, Oñate became seriously ill en route toward Guadalcanal from Cartagena. He reached his destination but lay near death for weeks; slowly he mustered the strength to begin the inspection. Having survived countless personal tragedies, Oñate must have believed this

22   *Fantasy heritage in southwest tourism*

illness was just another conflict he would in time defeat. However, he collapsed in the Guadalcanal mine and died shortly thereafter, ending a tumultuous life. In death, he became a repository for fact and fiction, myth and reality, and, depending on whom one asks, god-like or guileful. While technically a *criollo*, a person of Spanish parents who was born in the Americas,[67] Oñate exemplified the colonial ideology of the elite social classes of his day. To better understand such an orientation let us consider Oñate's family legacy.

Family origins and the Oñate historical narrative

In the 16th Century, few Basque people traveled to the Americas, yet those who did often found wealth or influence, sometimes both. It is in this context that Oñate's family history begins. Cristóbal Pérez de Narrihando resided in the town of Oñate. When his son, Juan Pérez, married and moved to Vitoria in the Alta Province, he became known as Juan Pérez de Oñate and was father to two children: Cristóbal and Juan II. Cristóbal, born about 1504, came to the Americas around 1524. This was three years after the fall of the Mexica and a time when México-Tenochtitlán was being transformed into a new Spain. A wonder to Spanish eyes, Hernando de Cortés described it "as one of the most beautiful cities on earth."[68] Yet, the Spaniards were compelled to extract its riches, namely precious metals and land.[69] Juan II's arrival coincided with the then-ongoing Spanish colonial efforts. His brother, Cristóbal, soon became an assistant to the accountant of the royal treasury. He left that position shortly after and in 1529, both brothers joined Nuño de Guzmán's expedition into the Pacific Northwest of Mexico—Nueva Galicia. Cristóbal is said to have respectfully interacted with the indigenous people of Mexico. If true, he was likely influenced by friars who sought to "civilize" through nonviolent means. Interestingly, Juan also joined the expedition but unlike his brother tortured and slaughtered native peoples.

The Spaniards' saw their New World efforts as "a moral crusade to spread [their] culture and Catholicism to pagans in all parts of the Americas."[70] Semantics played a role in this effort. If the Americas were a "New World," Europeans from the "Old World" possessed superior knowledge, gained from Europe's experience, and the Spaniards saw fit to educate their juniors, as noted by Chicano historian Rodolfo F. Acuña.[71] This framing conditioned the colonizer into a superior role and the colonized into a subservient one.

By 1534, Cristóbal was appointed governor of Nueva Galicia by the Viceroy of New Spain. He was later replaced by Francisco Vásquez de Coronado but remained as lieutenant governor. Hearing of treasures in the north, Coronado in 1540 organized a large party and departed to search for great fortunes. Cristóbal was in charge during his absence and the Spanish quest for wealth would now begin to change what became the US Southwest. The area's indigenous groups united to resist Spanish encroachment and to restore the former social order.[72] Between 1540 and 1542, Viceroy Antonio Mendoza ordered Cristóbal to suppress the Mixton War. He overcame the Mixton people's opposition. In 1543, Mendoza sent Cristóbal to quell a disturbance in Zacatecas.

Figure 2 Statue of Colonizer Juan de Oñate at *Parque Municipal Cuatro Siglos* (Four Centuries Municipal Part), Ciudad Juárez, Mexico.
Credit: Frank G. Pérez

Cristóbal

The Spanish quest for treasure allowed entrepreneurs to enter into contracts with the King.[73] These *adelantados* were encouraged to colonize places, sharing their wealth and success with the Crown. Cristóbal

24 *Fantasy heritage in southwest tourism*

garnered great wealth via the *encomienda* system in Nueva Galicia as well as in mining. In 1549, Cristóbal married Catalina de Salazar. They had seven children of whom Juan may have been the second or third eldest. Juan was born in 1552 in or near Zacatecas. He received a traditional Spanish upbringing, adjusted to meet New World contexts. He may also have been a twin, according to historian Marc Simmons. Fellow historian Stan Hoig goes so far as to state that Oñate's twin "was Don Alonso, who eventually became procurator general of the mines in New Spain."[74] In his youth, Oñate "shifted between Zacatecas and Mexico City, permitting him to experience both the rough milieu of the frontier silver-mining camp and the urbaneness of the Mexican capital."[75]

He also learned the family business and "was well versed in the arts and the sciences of the period."[76] Oñate was educated about his right to rule over Indians, displaying the Spanish contempt for native peoples.[77] He lived in a social order based on privilege and rank with little regard for ethnic diversity. Stories of elder Spaniards and their battles against Indians likely influenced the young Oñate to go soldiering, a social institution that allowed Spanish elites to support the Church and their King. As Simmons writes: "members of the frontier gentry ... spent literally millions of pesos ... to underwrite the military enterprises that benefitted the King, and to sponsor the construction of churches, missions, and monasteries ..."[78] Conquest was in Oñate's family culture and his desire to conquer may have been driven by a longing to succeed where others had failed.[79] He "was very wealthy ... [had] a solid military reputation as an Indian fighter, a proud Basque heritage, and a sound social and political position in Mexico."[80] His wealth was due to having wealthy maternal and paternal ancestors, as well as a wealthy wife.[81] Oñate believed that success as a conquistador would further enhance his family's already excellent social status and make him a hero.

Juan de Oñate: a life of privilege and failure

Oñate married in the 1580s and his wife, Isabel de Tolosa Cortés Moctezuma, was the granddaughter of Hernan Cortés and the great granddaughter of the late Mexica/Aztec emperor Moctezuma.[82] The mestizaje, so often denied or downplayed in fantasy heritage,[83] was well in effect during this time. Once wed "Oñate worked and exploited the silver mines of Sombrerette, San Martin, and Aviño, all of which had been discovered by Isabel's father."[84] This success brought him favorable treatment by the government, since his work generated great tax revenues.[85] Oñate's colonizing party later brought the mestizaje and short-lived colonial rule to New Mexico after his appointment as an *adelantado* and colonial governor.

In 1583, the King issued a *cedula* calling for a wealthy colonist to undertake the settlement of New Mexico and various men sought to gain permission to meet this mission.[86] Yet, the Viceroy was held back on selecting someone. Observing the negotiations for two years, Juan de Oñate was able to prepare a proposal for a major exploration and on September 21, 1595, Oñate and the Viceroy entered into a formal contract.[87]

> Viceroy Luis de Velasco wrote to his successor, the Count of Monterrey [Gaspar de Zuñiga y Acevedo], explaining ... 'Since Don Juan de Oñate had become a widower and was free to negotiate in regard to this project, I chose him.'[88]

For the next two years, Oñate developed his plan and used the time to enlist investors and find officials to manage his affairs. He also jockeyed to be independent of the Viceroy and responsible to the King, while feeding his party of 500 colonists who awaited their departure. The key element on which Oñate should have concerned himself is that the *cedula* required adherence to Spain's Comprehensive Orders for New Discoveries of 1573,[89] which "prohibited the entry of unlicensed parties into new lands, under 'pain of death and loss of all their property.'"[90] As Oñate, his two nephews, Vicente and Juan de Zaldívar, and the rest of the colonizing party would soon find out, although New Mexico proved to be a treacherous place, the Crown expected the colonists to comply with the law, to include calls for the humane treatment of Indians.

Even before leaving, Oñate faced an unexpected challenge. Count Zuñiga y Acevdo expressed doubts about Oñate's leadership that in retrospect seem valid and he was certainly kept under tight control. As Hoig recounts:

> Oñate would no longer have permission beyond the outset to recruit soliders and colonists. He would not be permitted to appoint officials in New Mexico or set their salaries. He was not permitted to evade the authority of New Spain, reporting instead directly to the Spanish Council of the Indies. He was denied the authority to determine the amount of tributes Indians would pay. His ability to grant *encomiendas* was subject to an accounting and regulation; it was required that his colonists must serve five years to become hidalgos; and his request to have his New Mexico colony supplied by ships twice annually was denied.[91]

The expedition was put on hold and an inspection was ordered, to be carried out by Lope de Ulloa y Lemos, the man delivering the *cedula*. Simmons claims Oñate's enemies had been at work to see him fail but the contract was instated in April 1597.[92] However, Hoig posits that Oñate was an ineffectual leader and we agree with him, based on the scandals that seem to have followed Oñate throughout much of his adult life.

Shortly before the party's departure, a rarely discussed event took place that highlights the improbability of the fantasy heritage of a moral and pious Oñate. Desperate for supplies and colonists, one of Oñate's captains and six soldiers raided the estate of wealthy silver miner and Oñate rival, Juan de Bautista de Lomas. In addition to "oxen, clothing, and equipment," the

26 *Fantasy heritage in southwest tourism*

soldiers captured Indian women.[93] Estate foreman Juan de Aritaga told the soldiers the women were all married, to which one of them replied that Oñate said the soldiers could take the women. They eventually left with at least two Indian women—Clara and María—as well as two Indian boys, one named Melchor. The name of the other is not known. No actions were taken against Oñate. He proceeded to prepare for his journey.[94]

When the colonizing party departed, the colonists headed north from Santa Barbara to the Río Grande and then turned toward New Mexico. They reached the river about twenty-five miles south of what is now El Paso. On April 30, Oñate's scouts found a suitable crossing further upstream, at which point Oñate stopped the caravan near modern day San Elizario. He ordered a ceremony to include *la toma*, literally the taking, a ritual that claimed the land for the King. After "several days" the Spanish headed out;[95] their San Elizario visit was a short one. The colonizing party later crossed the Río Grande twenty-five miles out of San Elizario near what is now West El Paso. While the exact spot cannot be known, a historical marker stands along this part of the river. As the party moved up the riverbank, the Spaniards met an indigenous group identified as *Manso* Indians. Oñate took the name to mean "the peaceful people" because *manso* means meek in Spanish. Like those who trekked this land before him, Oñate entered into agreements with various villages along the way. How well the Spaniards could understand the indigenous and vice versa cannot be known. Perhaps the Spaniards simply assumed the Native peoples understood them.[96]

By May 4, Oñate camped at what Simmons alleges Oñate called "the pass of the river ford,"[97] north of today's downtown El Paso. After following the Indian route that became the *Camino Real de la Tierra de Adentro* (Royal Road of the Interior Land), the party entered *La Jornada del Muerto* (the journey of the dead), ninety miles of desert with little water in central New Mexico. As the Spaniards moved forward, the Pueblo peoples would abandon their villages once they spotted the approaching convoy.[98] Historical records suggest that those Pueblos whom the Spanish did meet on their journey were friendly. New Mexico quickly provided the Spanish colonizers with a series of challenges beyond translations, including a shortage of food well before reaching their northern destination, and a freakishly harsh winter that enveloped the entire globe.[99] Ignoring the Comprehensive Orders for New Discoveries, the Spanish soldiers would visit Pueblo villages to take what food they could from the Indians.[100] This appropriation meant starvation and death for many Indians and bred hostility. The Spaniards' sexual abuse of indigenous women led the Pueblo peoples to fear and despise them.

According to colonizing party member Fray Franciso de Zamora, "When he [Zamora] instructed the Indians to become Christians, they asked why they should become Christians when it was Christians who caused them so much harm."[101] Still, the colonizers continued their mission. After reaching Yúngé village, close to the Chama River, Oñate founded San Gabriel on July 11, 1598. Later, he stopped at a Keresan-speaking village outside present day

Albuquerque and read its leaders *la toma*. He renamed the settlement Santo Domingo and followed this process at six other locales, claiming only the land. He also renamed the Tewa-speaking village pueblo of Ohkay Owingeh, calling it San Juan.[102] Had he read the *requierimiento*, a 900-word legal document, the Indians would have either accepted Spanish rule or faced war. Again, the key question is how well the Pueblos could have understood the Spaniards or their language.

Oñate may have tried to maintain the peace but like all Spanish colonizers, he was ready to use force if he deemed it necessary.[103] While he needed to keep his fellow travelers alive, Oñate also wanted to explore the surrounding area. Some party members were told to look for water, others for salt beds. The tension between the Spaniards and the Acoma began during this period. Oñate and his comrades camped at the foot of the Acoma Pueblo mesa on their way to explore what laid west. Their rest came and went without incident. Yet, on a later occasion, when Captain Gaspar Pérez Villagrá returned to San Juan from an expedition and ventured to Acoma Pueblo in search of his leader, the Acoma warriors chased him away. The Acoma resistance grew and they later killed about twelve Spaniards, including Oñate's nephew, Juan de Zaldívar.[104] In retaliation, Oñate sent seventy-two of his soldiers to the village, declaring war against them. A three-day battle ensued and the Spaniards almost completely obliterated the entire tribe. Oñate had given clear instructions: "Leave no stone on stone, so that the Indians may never be able again to inhabit it as an impregnable fortress."[105]

Weber reports that 800 Acoma were killed, including 300 women and children. Also, approximately eighty men and close to 500 women and children were captured.[106] Oñate sentenced each male warrior over the age of twenty-five to have one foot amputated as well as to provide twenty years of indentured servitude to Spanish colonists.[107] Oñate stood trial for these and other legal transgressions, resulting in his permanent removal from New Mexico, his banishment from Mexico City for four years, and his traveling to Spain seeking to rebuild his life.[108]

El Paso's fantasy heritage: Juan de Oñate as local hero

With his death Oñate slipped into historical memory. He spent only a few days in El Paso and was later convicted in Mexico City for what today would be crimes against humanity. How is it El Pasoans have adopted him as their own? This question can be answered in large part by examining local media accounts of Oñate's exploits and the local business, political, and tourism industries' efforts to convince them of Oñate's noble intentions. As we have shown elsewhere,[109] the *El Paso Times* has consistently and erroneously reported that Oñate was acting within the norms of his era. The trial and Oñate's banishment do not enter into local fantasy heritage. In fact, for years, the local media referred to the failed colonizer as "Don Juan." Only recently has the use of *Don* become less prevalent. Also, one can attend El Paso's

28 *Fantasy heritage in southwest tourism*

annual and fantastical musical show *Viva! El Paso* [110] performed each summer for tourists and locals. When Oñate takes the stage locals respond with a standing ovation. We wonder how many of them know of Oñate's role in the death of 800 people.[111] Given the fantasy heritage that has been presented to the El Paso community for more than twenty years, it is unlikely more than a handful of those in attendance have thorough knowledge of the Spanish colonial experiment.

Oñate in the contemporary Southwest

In years past, Oñate and other colonizers were vilified and shunned for their actions, at least in part because of a series of negative stereotypes of Spaniards called *La Leyenda Negra* or Black Legend.[112] This view focuses on the Spanish people's alleged violent and cruel nature.[113] Traditional scholars who focused on his Spanish background and ignored or downplayed his wife's ethnic composition facilitated converting Oñate into a fantasy heritage hero. Yet, Oñate later took on a life of his own, standing as a figurehead for all things cultural and civilized (i.e., European) in the Southwest. His legacy has allowed for the creation of heritage tourism sites throughout the Southwest (e.g., the Camino Real Historic Trail Site Visitor Center south of Socorro, NM) and this trend continues to grow. Despite the fact that no recorded image of Oñate is known to exist, statues of the colonizer stand in Alcalde, Albuquerque, Española, Ciudad Juárez, and El Paso. As a cultural icon, Oñate has become synonymous with Catholicism as well as culture and tourism. Again, a mass is held in commemoration of Oñate's arrival by none other than the El Paso area bishop each year at the First Thanksgiving Celebration in San Elizario, Texas.

Oñate's standing in El Paso has grown exponentially over the last thirty years. Initially championed by an El Paso businessman, Oñate is now a pillar in the area's tourism mythology. For example, in March 2014, the City of El Paso held its second heritage tourism symposium and Juan de Oñate was a key focus, at least among the White panelists during a town hall-themed presentation. One panelist, a local videographer claimed, "Our (El Paso's) history begins in 1598." Also on the panel was Texas State Senator José Rodríguez, a former El Paso County Attorney, who accurately added, "El Paso has centuries of history and it does not begin in 1598. Well before the Spaniards there were numerous indigenous peoples in the area." He proceeded to list a number of Indian tribes, much to his fellow panelists' amazement. Senator Rodríguez is the only El Paso area public servant we have seen with the courage to challenge the Oñate fantasy.

A number of university faculty members are also critical of the Oñate fantasy but their views are seldom presented in local media. While the exchange between Senator Rodríguez and the videographer motivates us to believe the racist tendencies in El Paso tourism may finally begin to be addressed, we were also concerned by a group of young adults at the summit. Dressed in

Spanish colonial costumes and inviting people to the 2014 First Thanksgiving, these young people displayed a passion for Oñate. Yet, we wondered how much they know about the man's legacy of brutality. Oñate sympathizers, largely composed of El Paso's White economic elites and a handful of local Hispanic businesspeople and public school personnel, are recruiting the next generation of Spanish apologists.

Of course, fantasy heritage issues transcend the El Paso area. Many New Mexicans also hold Oñate in high regard. For example, on August 16, 2009, as New Mexico Governor Bill Richardson broke ground for Space Port America, a soon to be built facility for the future launching of space tourism missions, he was surrounded by a group of young men dressed in 16th Century Spanish garb.[114] The colonial spirit lives! Spanish explorers are still seen as adventurers, replacing horses with spacecraft and seeking treasure. No Pueblo people were represented at the event. Apparently, one must be of European stock to enjoy space travel. Indians are either not welcome or not considered when planning such scientific endeavors.

A more typical representation of Oñate can be found greeting visitors entering Albuquerque's Old Town district. There a statue of the colonizer sits outside the main entryway. The Southwest is replete with examples of the pro-Spanish mindset of many internally oppressed Mexicans who reflect what Teresa Córdova has termed the *confusion of the colonized*. This term references minorities who want so badly to be part of the mainstream that they reject their very ethnicity in an effort to court favor with the White mainstream.[115]

One key machination adopted by confused individuals is to support cultural and heritage events and public monuments that deny the area's mestizo and indigenous past. These people live "in fear of the colonizer's disapproval."[116] In terms of public memory, they support a Eurocentric view of culture. Still, when one says Oñate brought culture to the region one must minimally add "European" and ask, "At what price?" Centuries of indigenous cultures predated the Spaniards' entry to northern New Mexico. While the historical record is clear, what is taught to people is an often less than complete account of the past.

Academics, fantasy heritage, and societal perceptions

As US historians developed Southwest Studies, Oñate entered the university curriculum and benefited from sympathetic representations and an Anglocentric framing of him as an intrepid explorer. Early colonizers, such as Onate, created worlds out of nothing more than "wilderness," as Frederick Jackson Turner reported in 1893.[117] Oñate moved from being an historical figure to a fantasy representation of an authentic Spanish hero. He also benefitted from popular and academic literature designed to exalt the historical experiences of Spain in the Americas. Gaspar Pérez de Villagrá's first-hand account of the colonization of New Mexico, *Historia de Nuevo Mexico*, [118]

30 *Fantasy heritage in southwest tourism*

stands as the most complete record of Oñate's colony. It is also one of the first works in the colonial literature in the New World, even if it is basically a travelogue in poetic prose. While Oñate's literary representation may have started with Villagrá, it is also tied to the historically strong anti-Mexican prejudice held by many Anglos.[119] As Rodolfo Acuña convincingly argues, many Anglos prefer people whose ethnicity is "anything but Mexican."[120] Oñate may have been part of the *mestizaje*, or cultural intermixing of Spaniard and Indian that created the Mexican people, but fantasy heritage turned him Spanish. He is thus a European, which is to say White, safe, and hegemonic.

At a recent national-level humanities conference that included a session on Oñate (with us and two colleagues among the panelists) a young woman reminded us why this work is important. During the question and answer session, she asked why people could not just forget the past. Was it necessary in the 21st Century to continue "whining" about what people did 500 years ago? Everyone looked at her in disbelief. Her question led one panelist to reply with a question: "Should we ask Jews around the world to stop examining the Holocaust because it is in the past?" The young woman sat quietly in her chair apparently wondering why she received such a strong reaction.

One possible explanation for the mindset reflected by the young woman at the conference and countless others is offered by anti-racism activist Tim Wise. He argues that Americans are glad to celebrate the glorious aspects of their nation's past, for example, the Fourth of July, but cautions that Americans also want to forget any events that show their culture in a negative manner.[121] Apparently, this desire to ignore past atrocities transcends US history, reaching back to the taking of the Americas. Conquest was brutal and ushered in the exploitation and cultural displacement of indigenous peoples.[122] It created a two-tiered society whose remnants continue to shape Southwest society.[123] This economic apartheid benefits Whites in material terms and separates them from other ethnic categories. We would add that it also relies heavily on fantasy heritage framing to hide its readily apparent effects in the contemporary Southwest and West where it appears the cultural norm.

The mythmaking that passes for academic knowledge throughout much of Western history is, at least partially, responsible for how minorities have been misunderstood by White America (and some minorities themselves). The negative framing of ethnic minorities in Western Europe gained popularity in the 19th century through the work of Cesare Lombroso, a prison physician who claimed that certain physiological features indicated a higher propensity toward criminal behavior.[124] The scholars who followed Lombroso's teachings gave way to the Italian School of Positivist Criminology. Following his logic, some late 19th and early 20th century scholars believed that the darker one's skin, the greater one's propensity to commit crime.[125] This view and others that attributed moral and intellectual flaws to dark-skinned peoples mirrored many of the negative stereotypes ascribed to Spaniards and later mestizos via the *leyenda negra* or Black Legend. Other groups have encountered similarly damaging stereotypes. The US military, for example, is replete with examples of racial segregation that were based on the views of non-Whites as unable to excel.[126] These assumptions were shaped, at least in part, by the social science of the late 1800s through the mid-1900s. These flawed "scientific" premises were widely discarded, but only in the post-World War II era.[127] Oñate's framing as a Spanish hero in the Southwest goes too far in the other direction. It turns the murderer of 800 people into a hero of the people he colonized. Fantasy heritage is a dangerous tool.

As a concept, fantasy heritage frames historical human progress as "the natural, normal, logical, and ethical flow of culture, of innovation, of human causality."[128] It extends this logic by leading some Mexican/Americans to represent themselves as a racially-pure Spaniards. Of course, Mexican/Americans are a mestizo people but many adopted a Spanish identity in reaction to Anglo entry to the Southwest. From the 1880s to the 1920s, business-class Mexicans in the region adopted a Spanish identity to gain favorable sociopolitical relationships with Anglo society elites.[129] Yet, as Monica Perales notes, even wealthy Mexican nationals, who faced much less racism than their working class brethren, were not seen as fully White by Anglo people in the Southwest during the early part of the previous century.[130]

Still, many Mexican/Americans have tried to use this rouse to enhance their social status, all the while reinforcing the area's fantasy heritage. The Spanish fantasy heritage took hold primarily in New Mexico where many Latinos continue to identify as *Hispano* or Spanish. Historian Todd Mitchell Meyers categorized the academic literature on this topic into three areas. The *functional perspective* correctly states that Chicano Studies largely denies Spanish identity, seeing it as an artificial construct, a function of Anglo encroachment into the Southwest, and the response to it adopted by Mexican elites. The *delineation perspective* asks if New Mexico culture is distinct enough from Mexican culture throughout the Southwest to count as its own category. Finally, Meyers addresses a perspective grounded in the *articulation* of Spanish identity. An excellent example of this literature is Andrew Leo Lovato's work *Santa Fe Hispanic Culture.* [131] Lovato, a native Santafean, provides an insightful critique of the impact of tourism on Fe culture from the point of view of Spanish identity. His critique is important because of its important insights and to his credit Lovato does not denigrate Mexican/Americans. Many Spanish New Mexicans view Mexican/Americans negatively.

While most who identify as Spanish in the Southwest are actually mestizos, fantasy heritage hegemony denies any ethnic intermingling between Spaniards and Indians.[132] It effectively created two ethnic categories from one population, divided by social class and political philosophy. Even Oñate's wife was mestiza.[133] The mestizaje had started in Mexico well before Oñate's party reached New Mexico and it traveled with his party. Thus, it is unlikely that many of the Spaniards' descendants maintained their racial "purity" across 400 years of geocultural isolation in New Mexico, as is claimed by fantasy heritage. This point is further complicated due to the ethnic intermingling

32 *Fantasy heritage in southwest tourism*

that occurred in Spain during centuries of Muslim control. What is racial purity, anyway? Can it even be defined outside of extremist racial discourse? The difference between Spanish and Mexican/American is semantic and a mental defense mechanism adopted by those who see Mexicans on the losing side of the Southwest's cultural divide. This view of Mexicans is tied to fantasy heritage because it omits or downplays the contributions of Mexican/Americans to Southwest culture.

Matthew F. Bokovoy explains that "the fantasy heritage was the colonial gloss for the economic development and promotion of Southern California," adding it was, "Mostly inaccurate, ahistorical, and suffused with excessive sentimentality and romanticism."[134] His point is true about California and the entire Southwest. Historian David J. Weber argues that "Anglos who glorify the region's Spanish heritage while they discriminate against Mexicans are suffering from McWilliam's fantasy heritage," adding that "Mexicans who prefer to be called Spanish, Hispano, or Latin American ... to dissociate themselves from more recent arrivals from Mexico are also deluded by the fantasy that their ancestors and heritage are Spanish."[135]

Eurocentric historical framing

Fantasy heritage frames Southwest history as one where noble Spanish colonists crossed the harsh desert, fought off dangerous Indians, and established a foothold in the region for Spain. Although Catholicism placed a great economic burden on the indigenous it was interwoven into colonial life to the point of being unescapable and thus a large influence.[136] Most incredible of all, fantasy heritage suggests that both groups voluntarily adopted a strict racial self-segregation that allowed the Spaniards to maintain their racial purity.[137] Ancient Rome used the roadways traveled heavily by its soldiers to assimilate those they colonized. The Iberian Peninsula experienced this phenomenon under imperial Rome. Later, Arab civilization spread throughout this region and lasted for approximately 700 years. Historically, cultural assimilation occurred unevenly, demanding political structures through which the invaders could maintain dominance and establish a compatibility of cultures.[138] Fantasy heritage is one such machination. It has taken on a highly politicized existence in recent years as Mexican/Americans and others challenge strong and longstanding Anglo hegemony in the Southwest.

Fantasy heritage in action

Common stereotypes of Whiteness suggest that if one is industrious and accumulates wealth, one displays the inherent elements of European character—a willingness to work hard and the ability to strategically grow one's profits for socioeconomic advancement.[139] This perception, tied to economics and skin tone, ignores the racist elements that foster and promote social marginalization. Such a view is particularly problematic in a society where

Fantasy heritage in southwest tourism 33

ethnicity and social class are nearly inseparable. In the Southwest, few, if any, of the wealthy, colloquially "established" or "old money," families in the region are Mexican American due to the racist political structures that were imposed on Mexicans by Anglos during the late 1800s and early 1900s.[140] In the US (and throughout Latin America) those non-Anglos with lighter skin tones typically gain more opportunities in school and the workplace.[141] As a result of these power dynamics, many individuals self-select labels that reflect their political views. As noted above, some mestizos in the Southwest adopted the term Spanish in an effort to curry favor with or gain acceptance from White power brokers.[142]

For example, economically affluent Americans of Mexican descent who deny the indigenous aspects of their culture often call themselves "Spanish."[143] This label is particularly popular from Socorro, New Mexico to Pueblo, Colorado, areas within the scope of this project. Similarly, "Hispanic" connotes middle-class standing, support for the status quo, and a desire to downplay one's indigenous ancestry.[144] Self-identified Hispanics tend to see Spanish representation as something positively related to their culture.[145] In general, those who identify as Spanish or Hispanic share a cultural orientation that supports the fantasy heritage of the Southwest.

In contrast, self-identified Chicanos often see themselves as members of a "historically and structurally oppressed group and advocate for social justice."[146] Those who prefer to call themselves Mexican American tend to display a less activist orientation than Chicanos, although it is important to remember that Chicanos are Mexican Americans, Mexican Americans are not necessarily Chicanos[147] and while both may have a strong sense of social justice, their approach to change may be different.[148] Yet the representation of either is the representation of the same people, viewed from different cultural perspectives. Consequently, Chicano/Mexican American representation is important to both groups. As John Nieto-Phillips notes, "To claim 'Spanish' blood [is] to declare … a European (read: racially white) heritage … to distinguish oneself from the maligned, mixed blood Mexican."[149]

Most people in the Southwest who self-identify as Spanish are in fact, mestizos,[150] but the Spanish label lightens their skin. It transforms them into heroic pioneers. Other mestizos are metaphorically darkened as flawed or villainous to explain colonial challenges or failures. These relations developed from and have been reinforced by the intellectual and perceived moral codes of the fantasy heritage. The darkened groups become one-dimensional or are erased from the historical record. The near absence of Native American voices from this essay, for example, is linked to their very limited presence in the materials we reviewed, as we have explained elsewhere.[151] Fantasy heritage allows middle- or upper-class Americans of Mexican descent to attain and/or maintain economic success at the cost of their cultural identity by claiming to be Spanish (i.e., European). The aforementioned multiple identities highlight social tensions with roots in the Spanish colonial era.

34   *Fantasy heritage in southwest tourism*

Fantasy heritage also markets Southwest history in a simplistic and romanticized way. This framing allows vendors to sell and tourists to consume without having to engage the messiness of colonial exploitation, violence, injustice, and related issues. Thus, it is viewed as the ideal marketing ploy through which to lure visitors to area historic festivals, reenactments, and memorials. Contemporary research suggests that complicating historical events can complement rather than detract from tourist experiences.[152] Yet, El Paso's heritage tourism remains focused on shallow, stereotypic representations of Spanish colonialism and the Wild West. It is logical to assume that framing El Paso sites in a complex and holistic educational manner would allow area residents, and tourists, to better understand themselves and the contributions their ancestors made to this area.

Perhaps El Paso's elites fear that Mexican Americans who learn about their past may reject much of the fantasy-filled tourism efforts. They may reclaim their history to challenge the White hegemony that continues to oppress them. A conversation between one of the authors and a community leader from Ciudad Juárez provides anecdotal evidence that some believe El Paso's White elites fear Mexican American empowerment. The community leader in question asked the author what he teaches. When the author mentioned Chicano Studies, the physician placed his arm around him and said, "That is very important work, because since your government told your people they are Hispanic, all of you [Mexican Americans] have been fucked! You have forgotten your history and your struggle." This person is correct. Politically empowered Mexican Americans, aware of the Chicano struggles of the 1960s and 1970s, continue to advocate for changes to the status quo. A political awakening in El Paso would force much more inclusive framing of the past. It would reshape local public memory. The fantasy heritage framing used in El Paso tourism not only makes historical rediscovery highly unlikely but also converts some Mexican Americans into Hispanics or as one colleague framed it into "safe Mexicans." These colonial machinations work well in a city with a low educational attainment-level and a low economic base. However, there are other ways to think about fantasy heritage, including its effects on public spaces.

Fantasy heritage and public space

Public space is a key venue for fantasy heritage elements that influence public memory, such as monuments, *kermezes* (i.e., church bazaars), museums, and the like. At one time even, the World's Fair represented an extension of the idyllic colonial world.[153] Whether advanced by festivals first popularized in the 1920s, such as *Day of the Dons* and *Mission Days*, in novels such as *Ramona*, or architecturally via the Mission Revival style, fantasy heritage was created to promote tourism and real estate development in Los Angeles.[154] Indeed, by the late 1800s, Anglos had established a two-tiered economic system in the Southwest and West where Anglos controlled and benefitted

Fantasy heritage in southwest tourism 35

from a series of strategies that ensured few, if any, Mexicans would be able to become wealthy. Mexican miners in the Southwest, for example, endured:

> a sliding pay scale based on copper prices and profits, a dual-wage system that relegated [Mexican] workers to lower-paid jobs with little chance for promotion, except on the track gangs and powder crews, limited accident and death benefits, company-controlled health plans, no retirement packages, and intolerance of unions.[155]

The Mexican community viewed these developments critically, particularly because they were denied entry to white-collar professions. However, it was in the 1930s that Anglo efforts to oust the Mexicans took full effect.[156] Racist US "repatriation" policies of that era saw thousands of Mexicans, even those born, or legally in the nation, deported to Mexico as a result of the Great Depression.[157] During World War II, Los Angeles became an ethnic battleground that pitted Mexicans against the Anglo establishment. The 1940s was a particularly hostile decade. Police harassment and the cities' anti-Mexican, anti-zoot suiter attitude led to the wrongful arrest of many Chicanas/os, including juveniles.[158] This decade witnessed the removal of much of the city's Mexican heritage. Raúl Homero Villa writes that LA's "Hispanicizing" markers of public memory led to "the neutralization or erasure of present, lived forms of expression, historical consciousness, and material iconography reflecting the city's actual Mexican legacy."[159] He attributes the loss of LA's Mexican past to the cultural uprooting of Mexicans and to the promotion of Spanish fantasy heritage in the region. We find many parallels between LA and many Southwest communities, including El Paso.

Historian Douglas Monroy recounts his experience with and the impact of cultural erasure on his community.[160] A California native, Monroy learned about the indigenous and the missions in school. He received a story-filled pastoral image where life was simple and noble Spaniards did their best to care for their indigenous neighbors. Growing up during the Chicano Movement (1965–1978),[161] Monroy came to realize that Mexican people were not part of California's official history. His research clearly demonstrates the complexity of the state's past by focusing on Mexicans, the indigenous, Anglos, and *Californios*. Other scholars have offered similar insights about the Western US.[162] The schism identified via this line of research stems from the Anglo-imposed two-tiered socioeconomic system, a political machination that continues today. Whites face much less institutional discrimination than do other ethnicities. The American psyche perceives Mexicans as criminal and Whites, simply, as good citizens. For example, communication scholars Howard Giles, Daniel Linz, Doug Bonilla, and Michelle Leah Gómez found as recently as 2012 that Los Angeles area law enforcement is more likely to stop Latino motorists than White motorists and that those perceived by officers to have an accent are more likely to be arrested.[163]

36 *Fantasy heritage in southwest tourism*

Fantasy heritage continues to tell us who is the "bad guy" and who is the "good guy." It relates to daily life in myriad other ways and begs the question: How does fantasy heritage relate to public memory and tourism in the Southwest? The answer has implications for the entire nation, as more Latinos, a majority of them Mexican, enter parts of the US where there have traditionally been few to none. As a part of popular culture, the idea of Mexican Americans, steeped in fantasy, inherits a doubly negative stereotype: "Mexican Americans are born through the racist fury of a 'Mexican' view of race that is both Spanish (think castes, Empire, Inquisition, slavery) and Mexica/Aztec (think castes, Empire, Inquisition [ask the Cholulans and the Tlaxcaltecans], slavery—oh yeah, and that little thing with the obsidian knives and victims' hearts); the Spanish merely roasted their victims' hearts over a fire."[164]

Chicanos, Mexican/Americans inherit the negative elements ascribed to their ancestral colonizers and those they colonized. Public memory artifacts rely on "language, ritual performances, communication technologies, objects, and places."[165] As we will show, negative public representations are enduring and thus difficult to alter.

World fairs and fiestas: early agents of fantasy heritage

An example of the need for public consent can be found via world fair-type festivals in the early 1900s that supported fantasy heritage on the West Coast. The Panama-California Exposition (1915–1916), the San Diego Exposition (1915–1916 and 1935–1936), and the Long Beach Pacific Southwest Exposition (1928) influenced people's perceptions of the population in the West and Southwest.[166] The Panama-California exposition "celebrated Southwestern pluralism" and helped promote future events, especially the Santa Fe Fiesta of the 1920s.[167] Similarly, the San Diego fairs offered a comprehensive description of the peoples and cultures of the Southwest that represented the region as free of social strife, supporting the fantasy heritage. "Is the reenactment of the Spanish conquest an innocent commemoration of Spanish glory, or does it serve as a public sanction of existing racial inequalities?"[168] With this question, Sarah Horton raises an important issue with respect to social and neocolonial relationships. The Santa Fe Fiesta, for example, celebrates the reconquest of Pueblo peoples who had expelled the Spaniards in 1680. Like similar dramas, the fiesta depicts the conquest of the indigenous and their forced conversion to Catholicism as a peaceful venture, focusing on the "bloodless" reconquest of 1692. This framing tradition goes back to the dawn of Latin America's colonization. Citing Ramón Gutiérrez, Horton reports that Juan de Oñate carried *Nuestra Señora de los Remedios* (literally, Our Lady of Remedies) into New Mexico, the same Marion icon Hernán Cortés carried into México-Tenochtitlán in 1519. According to Gutiérrez, "what the Indians saw and heard was but a well-choreographed political drama that was to teach them the meaning of their own defeat, of Spanish sovereignty and of the social hierarchies that would prevail under Christian rule."[169]

Fantasy heritage in southwest tourism 37

Four-hundred years later, the Santa Fe Fiesta follows this tradition, celebrating Spanish dominance over the Pueblos. The fact that fiesta supporters typically self-identify as Spanish illustrates the dominance of White hegemony in northern New Mexico. As Charles Montgomery noted, affluent Mexican families in New Mexico adopted the Spanish label in reaction to Anglo entry to the state.[170] Spanish New Mexicans are the key group celebrating this colonial victory, identifying with the European aspects of their culture and denying its mestizo elements. Thus, for many Hispanos the fiesta displays ethnic unity and cultural preservation. Many Hispanics call the fiesta their own despite what it symbolizes culturally. New Mexico history explains this irony. Fantasy heritage began here in the late 1800s, in reaction to Anglo encroachment.[171] In Socorro, elite Mexican families claimed a Spanish identity, hoping to protect their wealth and social standing. This strategy met with little success throughout the Southwest[172] but its remnants continue to permeate New Mexico's culture. "[T]hose of Spanish descent continue to play a major role"[173] in diffusing the fantasy heritage.

Fantasy heritage and tourism: marketing a neo-Spanish heritage

Over time fantasy heritage created a series of representations that would convince the population of the importance of the area's Spanish past, particularly as Mexicans and Indians disappeared from mainstream consciousness. The past became one of noble Spaniards, quickly followed by Anglo gunslingers, and culminating in the contemporary period of cultural diversity. Any inconvenient truths were omitted or turned into fantasies. Fantasy heritage met the 20th Century as a business-friendly way to characterize the past. El Paso has used this strategy since the late 1980s, like many cultural fairs and tourism entities, to make Anglo encounters with "Mexicans" (including many native-born, US citizens) in the US a safe endeavor.[174] Relatedly, William Deverall discusses how city leaders in Los Angeles proposed to "white wash" the city's early (i.e., Mexican) history and to construct a new regional history that fit the needs of an Anglo controlled city.[175] Every part of LA was included: "areas of work, landscape and environment, cultural production, city buildings, and public health."[176] Olvera Street, once the heart of Sonora Town in Los Angeles, was actually an alley in the middle of a segregated Mexican neighborhood near downtown and away from Anglo LA, for example. By the 1920s, gentrification forced the Mexicans east and what remained was converted to a quasi-Mexican town and tourist site. Restaurants, strolling musicians, and souvenirs were framed as traditional Mexican mementos and the locale as a safe place, particularly for Anglos with disposable income.

New Mexico witnessed a similar process. A refined *paisano* atmosphere, shaped by colonial history, gave the state its fantastical Spanish character. This representation originates with the Spanish-speaking leaders who separated themselves from any Mexican heritage or identity. Anglos did not take the move seriously but paid it token reference. They used it, however, to

38 *Fantasy heritage in southwest tourism*

expand their power base. New Mexicans' "Spanish heritage was [crafted] not only by Anglos and Hispanos but also by artists, journalists, politicians, novelists, city boosters, [and] educators ... united by ... the lurking image of the impoverished, footloose, and dark-complexioned Mexican."[177] Skin tone became a social marker. Mestizos, dark-skinned working-class people were never part of the fantasy heritage plan, confined as they were to daily labor, segregated schools, poor neighborhoods, and a sense of powerlessness at the nature of their own lives.[178] Once this dichotomy took effect, all things Spanish were good, all things Mexican were not. McWilliams saw this phenomenon, with roots in the 1800s, as blossoming in the 20th Century, displayed through fiestas, architecture, and historical reinvention.[179] In time, fantasy heritage also evolved into a form of pedagogy in both academic and popular practice. Literary representations operated in a similar way.

Memmi makes visible this myth to show the justification for the low wages paid to him and countless people of color. As one can see, these realities transcend economics and also speak of the myth of culture, language, and intellectual ability. These factors influence our writing about the cultural erasure of Pueblo and Mexican people. Acoma Pueblo Darva Chino notes that today's colonizers oppress Indians, just as their ancestors did. Confronting John Houser after a public lecture that was cancelled in progress because of the controversy generated by his *Equestrian* statue, Chino stated the following view on Oñate sympathizers:

> They're doing the same thing Oñate did. The only way it's different is because it's a different era and it's a different form of cruelty. They might not be cutting off our foot, like, like their ancestors did, but they are hurting our hearts. And, they're being cruel and they're digging it in some more. That's all they're doing, and they don't see that they're being like him. You know, it's really sad, because we have to be subject to that and it's cruel to us. We continue battling. We continue battling. The battles are just different. It's just a different battle ground. It's still the same thing.[180]

Chino's analysis makes a clear link to the concerns for social justice voiced by many fantasy heritage critics. Oñate sympathizers fail or choose not to see that their tourism efforts are covert attacks on the descendants of the people Oñate sought to subjugate.

Cultural erasure

To understand our opposition to fantasy heritage let us look at the evidence that contradicts its basic tenets. Much of the historical literature, academic and popular, erases or presents a fictionalized version of the indigenous and Mexican/American peoples and their cultures. Colonization and usurpation are imbued with elements of White man's burden, the flawed argument that colonization advances primitive cultures. Here, the colonizers are framed as

Fantasy heritage in southwest tourism 39

morally compelled to "uplift" the cultures of those they colonize. Ironically, this uplifting typically comes in the form of enslavement, extortion, and social marginalization. Academic research that addresses this tendency often threatens those who fear alternate interpretations of the past, negatively framing it as "revisionist."

Yet, revisionist scholarship complicates facile stories. It adds context to commonly held myths about the past and challenges Eurocentric hegemony. Revisionist work adds the voices and addresses the experiences of those whom mainstream history has erased, vilified, or otherwise marred. This research area complicates history and helps readers resist mainstream Eurocentric cultural encroachment. Still, the revisionist label is often misused or misunderstood, sometimes purposely, particularly outside academic circles. Cries of "revisionist history" fill the mainstream airwaves and digital feeds, particularly among conservative media. Pundits imply revisionist academic endeavors distort history. In truth, this research approach speaks truth to power. The backlash against it is not about accuracy or distortion, it is against the unpleasant realities and inconvenient truths revisionist history brings to the fore. It adds minority voices to long sacrosanct Anglicized versions of the past.[181] For example, the longstanding cinematic conception of cowboys as White, whether Clint Eastwood's stoic "Man with No Name" character from the Sergio Leone trilogy or Michael Landon's caring Charles Ingalls on *Little House on the Prairie*. Anglo "settlers" relied on Mexican *vaqueros* (i.e., cowboys) to learn their skills and adopted their jargon, *laso* became lasso and *riata* became lariat, for example. Revisionist views point out such realities. Many would prefer "American" cowboys to be White to the exclusion of African Americans, Mexicans, and others in the same line of work. The revisionist label is used to imply that this type of research manufactures erroneous accounts of the past. In truth, such research serves to call out the oppression hidden in mainstream fantasy heritage accounts and Eurocentric academic research. Mission architecture, fiestas, and monuments are among the veils of conceit that shift societies from a people's history, as explained by Howard Zinn,[182] toward one based on hierarchies. These ideas are evident via the land tenure struggles in New Mexico and notions surrounding the "Mexican problem" throughout the Southwest.[183]

Land tenure

Land tenure reflects how people use, live, and survive within a geographical space or region. It is an idea shaped by the practice of working the land, as well as how sociocultural relationships give direction to land use.[184] Changes in the land tenure system, such as changes to property rights, may upset a community's social and/or economic order.[185] Fantasy heritage suggests that Pueblo peoples and Spanish colonists, later Mexican/Americans, lived their lives isolated from each other. However, an examination of land tenure activities shows both groups regularly interacted with and assisted each other

40 *Fantasy heritage in southwest tourism*

to survive. The evidence challenges fantasy heritage stereotypes and the idyllic representations of Pueblo life described by heritage tourism writings of various types.

Consider Howard Lamar's views on New Mexico's Pueblo people: "In the picturesque mountain villages a simple folk culture and subsistence economy stubbornly persisted in the face of the great drive toward Americanization."[186] This stereotypic representation of the Pueblos is rightly criticized by Roxanne Dunbar-Ortiz as "statiscism," an impression that leaves the reader imagining the Pueblo living in isolation, lacking any contact with Mexicans or Whites. In Lamar's context, fiestas seem to be a daily part of life and "Spanish Americans" accepted US social institutions—fifty-four years after the US-Mexico War (1846–1848)—with open arms. Yet, Pueblos and Mexican/Americans developed their own institutions tied to their experiences as property owners and resisted US conquest. It is more correct to say that attempts to assimilate these groups did not lead them to accept capitalist institutions, even in the face of losing their own land. And there was good reason.[187] Pueblo culture "distributed to the members of the community with a system of equitable distribution of produce ... Mexican land tenure patterns in Northern New Mexico, then were [a mixture of Iberian, Mexican indigenous, and Spanish colonial] practices."[188] However, Mexicans "were not fundamentally influenced by the Indigenous Pueblos."[189] This land tenure system collapsed only after the government introduced mercantile capitalism after 1848.

One can also turn to the work of George I. Sánchez, who in 1940 profiled a group of northern New Mexican families who had, in a manner of speaking, been forgotten while modernization emerged in and around Albuquerque. The surrounding rural areas did not fit in this changing world. Sánchez visited Taos County at the end of the Great Depression to provide a social interpretation of the lives of Mexican people. A decade before McWilliams introduced fantasy heritage,[190] Sánchez observed that "the pages of history become the springboard for a fanciful imagery which obscures reality and detracts from understanding."[191] His concern focused on the residue of conquest and its longstanding social marginalization on the Mexicans of Taos. The introduction of mercantile capitalism allowed the White's allies, "Spanish" New Mexicans, to serve as the go-betweens that bridged these social categories and that allowed for the tourist-friendly framing of the "land of enchantment."

The Mexican problem

Early in the 20th Century, Mexican immigrants became a problem in the US public imagination, particularly in relation to the Great Depression.[192] Academic and governmental studies had already defined Mexican behavior as problematic by comparing it to that of the legally ostracized "Oriental" [sic].[193] The mainstream labeled Asians as Orientals, a term that later came to characterize any people under colonial rule, largely due to the impact of Edward W. Said's

Fantasy heritage in southwest tourism 41

landmark book, *Orientalism.* [194] Said explained that the Middle East (i.e., the Orient) was shaped by images and myths that colonial powers imposed on its peoples and cultures, a common theme across colonial representations of the oppressed. Viewed as less capable than their colonial masters, the idea of the Oriental or "the Other" became a useful tool in the psychological control of conquered people. Seen through cultural differences separating Americans from Mexicans, this view characterized Mexicans as "a hopeless people, entangled in a web of cultural and biological pathologies that prevented a self-generated evolution to a modern or higher national culture."[195]

As such, it should be no surprise that derogatory terms came to describe Mexicans and Native Americans.[196] The terms "peon to Americans and 'oriental' [sic] to the British meant an adult with a child's [mental] capacity."[197] Like the Black Legend, which played off British stereotypes of the Spanish, Anglo attitudes toward Mexicans justified numerous misconceptions and practices (e.g., segregation). Thus, Mexico became, in the Anglo mind, a nation of child-like individuals that required tutoring by a foreign power to help them achieve modernity. It did not end there. As Mexican immigrants increasingly entered the US to work across labor economy segments and find a place for themselves, the capitalist class and politicians developed social, economic, and legislative policies to subordinate this population.[198] Politicians turned to the literature developed by American writers in, and about Mexico to make possible the decisions to segregate Mexicans in schools, to promote Americanization programs and vocational curricula for Mexican students, as well as using a variety of means to attack those who dared to challenge the status quo.[199] These machinations developed simultaneously with the adoption of fantasy heritage in California, New Mexico, and West Texas.

The "Mexican problem" rhetoric employed by policymakers and academics of the era, led local governments to exclude Mexicans from their societies. One example of this tendency came in 1904 when Mexican families legally adopted Irish Catholic children in the Clifton-Morenci, Arizona area, only to have a posse strip them of their new charges. The "good" people of Clifton-Morenci decided that Mexicans were unfit to raise White children, and in 1905 the Arizona Supreme Court agreed, as did the US Supreme Court shortly thereafter.[200] So strong were the fantasy heritage stereotypes that they kept Mexicans at the bottom of the social order. Those who did not fit into Anglo society, such as mestizos, were slandered by mainstream academics, journalists, and popular authors, among others. This reality not only pushed some groups to the social margins, it erased them from history. It was up to the Mexicans, at least those with light skin, to assimilate, adopt the fantasy heritage, and discriminate against their own ethnic category, if they hoped to gain some sense of social acceptance. Social scientists of this era suggested assimilation as the only choice, and an easy one at that, despite the plethora of social barriers imposed by Anglos to keep Mexicans out of the mainstream.[201] In truth, the decision to assimilate is an individual choice that must be negotiated with mainstream society, at the risk of social ostracism from

42 *Fantasy heritage in southwest tourism*

one's native and adopted social categories. Some Native Americans who identify as Indians and those of Mexican origin who identify as Chicanas/os reject assimilation. This is where identity formation becomes a conflicted and conflictive process.

Deena J. González insightfully reminds us of the contradictory nature of people's individual identity. Growing up in 1950s New Mexico, she was expected to know that she was Spanish, not Mexican. Yet, her grandparents insisted on speaking "Mexican" and did not self-identify as Spanish. Her parents' generation had adopted the fantasy heritage.[202] Many who grew up in the Southwest faced similar situations. The Spanish self-designation is tied to fantasy heritage, and results from Anglo machinations geared toward social control. History, based on selected memories that explain reality, becomes the dominant mainstream knowledge and minimizes any form of counter-dialogue. [203]

Conclusions

Our assertion with this project is that while most (non)Mexicans recognize "something Mexican" about El Paso, local rhetoric is currently working to convert this group into Hispanics. Pablo Vila's work on border identity chronicles these dynamics.[204] Most of the 200-plus El Paso-area focus group interviewees consulted by Vila self-identified as Hispanic. Chicano was typically dismissed or vilified by a vast majority of those interviewed. Why is this bias so strong in a city that was a key locale for the Chicano Movement and that is 82% "Hispanic?" We argue that the forces that promote an Hispanic identity—schools, local government, local media, and others—see Mexican heritage as unworthy of promotion or preservation. As we will demonstrate later, the focus on tourism and El Paso-area missions (that are actually working churches) has eliminated the Mexican presence from much public framing of local history. It has been replaced with the fantasy of Juan de Oñate and his Christianizing and civilizing passions.

Bokovoy argues that historians view fantasy heritage as a product of false consciousness that has erased the cultural image of Mexicans and Native Americans from the Southwest. He notes that "an important set of political understandings emerged in Southwestern culture history" that both reenvisioned Indian and Mexican history and that underwrote their legal civil rights.[205] Fantasy heritage allowed for Mexicans and Native Americans to be imagined out of most people's minds, since fairs, fiestas, and plays ignore the most vivid aspects of their history.[206] This exclusion meant their eradication from area public memory and heritage tourism. Similarly, Rosa Linda Fregoso asserts that Hollywood cinema helped to rework California history in the popular imagery, thereby creating a fantasy heritage for the region.[207] Our own research led us to conclude that El Paso-area media engage in similar tactics given their friendly coverage of Juan de Oñate and Spanish-themed events throughout the 1990s and into the current era.[208] Fortunately, despite promoting the Oñate myth, the local media have helped to preserve the name

Lower Valley for a large, working-class, and predominantly Mexican American section of El Paso. Local elites have tried for over thirty years to have locals adopt the name Mission Valley for this municipal area. Thus far, it has not taken. However, El Paso is going through a large-scale and predominantly non-Mexican/American population growth. It remains to be seen how this influx alters the social order.

Fantasy heritage, as understood by Carey McWilliams, George I. Sánchez, and others served to call out the historical erasure of Native Americans and Mexicans from US popular culture. The experiences of Mexican/Americans, and Pueblo peoples throughout the Southwest have been, and continue to be, downplayed. When these groups must be acknowledged two options exist. They are vilified or stereotyped as lazy and ignorant, deserving the discriminatory practices used against them. Alternately, their experiences are turned into cartoonish representations of a mythical longstanding peace. The latter option highlights the Spaniards' heroism as colonizers and Anglos as daring frontiersmen. Here, Spanish brutalities and Anglo racism do not exist. Rather, European superiority has tried to elevate the indigenous and mestizo peoples of the region.

The management of public space is a particularly powerful fantasy heritage manifestation throughout the Southwest. It permeates the area, emphasizing the Spanish legacy and erasing Mexican/American and Indian contributions. Sonora Town in Los Angeles became Olvera Street and was converted from a working-class Mexican neighborhood to a touristy recreation of "Old Mexico." A similar strategy is used in myriad fiestas and regional celebrations throughout the Southwest, Santa Barbara's *Old Mission Days*, the *Fiesta de Santa Fe*, and the First Thanksgiving being prime examples.

A neo-Spanish fantasy heritage has merged with daily life in El Paso public memory, fostering heritage tourism endeavors that are solidly embedded in fantasy heritage. Perhaps the most troubling aspect of this phenomenon is its presence in public schools. Schoolchildren are defenseless against such a one-sided historical account, particularly in a city that has traditionally shamed schoolchildren away from speaking Spanish. Consequently, fantasy heritage and its related cultural erasure is taking hold throughout our community, and by extension US society. The following chapter addresses Juan de Oñate as the dominant icon of the contemporary assault against Mexican and Native identities in the Southwest. It will examine the First Thanksgiving Celebration and the influence of fantasy heritage in public memory vis-à-vis the controversy surrounding Spanish colonization, Juan de Oñate, and the use of fantasy heritage.

Notes

1 Thomas H. Guthrie, *Recognizing Heritage: The Politics of Multiculturalism in New Mexico* (Lincoln, NB: University of Nebraska Press, 2013).
2 Greg Dickinson, Carole Blair, and Brian L. Ott, *Places of Public Memory: The Rhetoric of Museums and Memorials* (Tuscaloosa, AL: University of Alabama Press, 2010). This definition builds on the extant literature in the field and is largely influenced by Carole Blair, Greg Dickinson, and Brian L. Ott's

44 *Fantasy heritage in southwest tourism*

exploration of the topic in the introduction to this work. Also see: Clinton David van der Merwe, "Limits of Urban Heritage Tourism in South Africa: The Case of Constitution Hill, Johannesburgh," *Urban Forum,* 24, no. 4, 573–588.

3 Throughout this work we build on Michelle A. Holling's example of using Mexican(American) to signify both Mexican nationals and Mexican Americans. However, we have substituted her use of parentheses with a slash. Mexican(s) refers to citizens of Mexico. Mexican American(s) refers to Americans of Mexican descent. Finally, Mexican/American(s) refers to both social categories. See: Michelle A. Holling. "A Dispensational Rhetoric in 'The Mexican Question in the Southwest'," in *Border Rhetorics: Charting Enactments of Citizenship and Identity on the US-Mexico Frontier,* ed. D. Robert DeChaine (Tuscaloosa, AL: University of Alabama Press, 2012), 65–85.

4 Chris Wilson, *The Myth of Santa Fe: Creating a Modern Regional Tradition* (Albuquerque, NM: University of New Mexico Press, 1997). This remains a seminal text on Santa Fe's evolution as a tourism attraction.

5 Tazim Jamal and Mike Robinson, "Introduction: The Evolution and Contemporary Positioning of Tourism as a Focus of Study," in *The Sage Handbook of Tourism Studies,* ed. Tazim Jamal and Mike Robinson (Thousand Oaks, CA: Sage, 2009), 1–16.

6 Brian Graham, G.J. Ashworth, and J.E. Tunbridge. (2000/2002), *A Geography of Heritage: Power, Culture, and Economy.* (New York: Routledge), 22.

7 Canestrini (2001), cited in Jamal and Robinson, *The Sage Handbook of Tourism Studies,* 3–4.

8 Graham, Ashworth, and Tunbridge, *A Geography of Heritage.*

9 Thrift (1989), cited in Cara Aitchison, Nicola E. MacLeod, and Stephen J. Shaw, eds. *Leisure and Tourism Landscapes: Social and Cultural Geographies* (New York: Routledge, 2000/2002), 95.

10 Hazel Tucker and John Akama, "Tourism as Postcolonialism," in *The Sage Handbook of Tourism Studies,* ed. Tazim Jamal and Mike Robinson (Thousand Oaks, CA: Sage, 2009), 505.

11 Ibid.

12 Turnbridge and Ashworth (1996, p. 21), cited in Aitchison, MacLeod, and Shaw, *Leisure and Tourism Landscapes,* 95.

13 Albert Grundlingh, "Revisiting the 'Old' South Africa: Excursions into South Africa's Tourist History under Apartheid, 1948–1990," *South African Historical Journal* 5, no. 1 (2009): 103–122.

14 Carole Blair, Greg Dickinson, and Brian L. Ott, "Introduction," in Greg Dickinson, Carole Blair, and Brian L. Ott, eds., *Places of Public Memory: The Rhetoric of Museums and Memorials* (Tuscaloosa, AL: University of Alabama Press), 1–54.

15 Marilena Alivizatou, *Intangible Heritage and the Museum: New Perspectives on Cultural Preservation,* (Walnut Creek, CA: Left Coast Press, 2012), 15.

16 Carey McWilliams *North from Mexico: The Spanish-Speaking People of the United States,* rev. ed. Alma M. García (New York: Praeger, 1948/2016).

17 David E. Stannard, *American Holocaust: The Conquest of the West* (New York: Oxford University Press, 1993). Stannard offers a detailed explanation of the brutality associated with Spanish conquistadors in the Americas. Other notable sources on the colonial experiment include: George P. Hammond and Agapito Rey, *Don Juan de Oñate: Colonizer of New Mexico, 1595–1628 Vols V & VI* (Albuquerque, NM: University of New Mexico Press, 1953); John L. Kessell, *Pueblos, Spaniards, and the Kingdom of New Mexico* (Norman, OK: University of Oklahoma Press, 2008); Marc Simmons, *The Last Conquistador: Juan de Oñate and the Settling of the Far Southwest* (Norman, OK: University of Oklahoma Press, 1993).

Fantasy heritage in southwest tourism 45

18 Examples of this tendency abound in US popular culture. For example, Thomas Jefferson is often recognized as one of the nation's most important founders. Yet, his ownership of slaves and amorous affair with Sally Hennings, one of his slaves, is often downplayed or ignored. Juan de Oñate is similarly framed as a courageous pioneer, while his atrocities at Acoma are typically ignored by those who promote his legacy. See, for example: Kessell, *Pueblos, Spaniards, and the Kingdom*; Simmons, *Last Conquistador*; or Robert McGeagh, *Juan de Oñate's Colony in the Wilderness: An Early American History of the Southwest* (Santa Fe, NM: Sunstone Press, 1990).
19 Kathleen L. McDougall, "Just Living: Geneaolgic [sic], Honesty and the Politics of Apartheid," *Anthropology Southern Africa* 37, no. 1 and 2, (2014): 19–29. See pp. 20–23. One way the nobility of colonization is addressed is via genealogical records where social shifts are framed as apolitical historical events, the colonizing culture is framed as civilized, and as simply fulfilling its destiny. Thus, the colonizers freed from any wrong doing. McDougall explains how this phenomenon happens in South Africa within this work.
20 David J. Weber, *The Spanish Frontier in North America*, (New Haven, CT: Yale University Press, 1992), 77. Citing Gibson (1978), Weber notes it was "important to the [Spanish] king that his subjects agreed voluntarily to become vassals and that their submission be recorded."
21 Tómas Almaguer, *Racial Fault Lines: The Historical Origins of White Supremacy in California* (Berkley, CA: University of California Press, 2008). Almaguer offers a detailed study of the economic impact Anglo entry had on Californios or *la gente de razón* in California. The change to a capitalist system allowed Anglos to gain much of the Californios' wealth. Similarly, the Spaniards brought with them an economic system that led to the exploitation and enslavement of many indigenous peoples, leading the Indian population into poverty and enriching the Spanish. The First Thanksgiving reenactment alludes to the "Spaniards' wealth," suggesting that Indians and Spaniards disproportionately shared in the redistribution of wealth in the West Texas region. Specifically, the narrator notes that Oñate "claimed" the region for "God and Spain" with the result that "The Native wealth became the Spanish wealth …" No mention is made of the impact this imperially imposed cultural shift had on the natives.
22 McWilliams, *North from Mexico*, 43–44. One need only consider how fantasy heritage frames the Spanish colonial era to glean insight into the idea the Spaniards' "settling" of the era was a noble and peaceful endeavor. McWillaims' recounting of the Santa Barbara Fiesta is similar to other heritage events throughout the West and Southwest, replete with representations of a noble Spanish colonizing force bent on "civilizing" the Indians.
23 Melody K. Pope, April K. Sievert, and Sheree L. Sievert, "From Pioneer to Tourist: Public Archaeology at Spring Mill State Park," *International Journal of Historical Archaeology* 15, no. 2 (2011), 206–221, see p. 208.
24 See, for example: Cristina Ibarra, *Las Marthas* (2014; PBS Video). This is a documentary that chronicles Martha Washington Day events and a related debutante ball in Laredo, Texas, and Nuevo Laredo, Nuevo León, México.
25 Adria L. Imada, "The Army Learns to Luau: Imperial Hospitality and Military Photography in Hawai'i," *Contemporary Pacific* 20, no. 2 (2008): 329–361.
26 McWilliams, *North from Mexico*.
27 Xu Zi-lin, Shen Ju-qin, Liu Bo, and Tan Liang, "Study of TOPSIS-based Evaluation of Urban Competitiveness," *Journal of Chemical and Pharmaceutical Research* 6, no. 7 (2014): 1843–1846.
28 These elements are attributed to talk TV by P. Carpignano and colleagues in "Chatter in the Age of Electronic Reproduction: Talk Television and the 'Public Mind,'" *The Phantom Public Sphere*, ed. B. Robbins (Minneapolis, MN: University of Minneapolis Press, 1993): 93–120.

46 *Fantasy heritage in southwest tourism*

29 Daniela Fiorini and Paula Socolovsky, "Argentinian Myths: Semiotics and Cultural Identity," *Society* 51, no. 1 (2014): 27–30.

30 For those visiting the First Thanksgiving, such a perception can easily develop. San Elizario's median annual household income was $25,967 in 2012, while the Texas state average for the same year was almost twice that at $50,740. Source: http://www.city-data.com/city/San-Elizario-Texas.html.

31 Fiorini and Socolovsky, "Argentinian Myths," 27–28.

32 Ibid.

33 Josiah Tucker, *Instructions for Travellers, 1757*, cited in Erve Chambers, *Native Tours: The Anthropology of Travel and Tourism*, 2nd ed (Long Grove, IL: Waveland Press, 2010), 1. Tucker uses the term traveler to mean what we define as visitor. We prefer visitor because it is more distinct from the term travel, which we use throughout the book. Our aim is to make it easy for readers to distinguish between tourist (less or uncritical traveler), travel (physically reaching a destination), and visitor (an intellectually oriented traveler).

34 Alexis Celeste Bunten, "'Sharing Culture or Selling Out?' Developing the Commodified Persona in the Heritage Industry," *American Ethnologist,* 35 no. 3 (2008): 380–395.

35 Ibid., 386

36 Duncan Light, "Dracula Tourism in Romania: Cultural Identity and the State," *Annuals of Tourism Research* 34, no. 3, 754.

37 Jonathan Culler, *Framing the Sign: Criticisms and Its Institutions.* (Norman, OK: University of Oklahoma Press, 1988), 154..

38 Edward M. Bruner, "Abraham Lincoln as Authentic Reproduction: A Critique of Postmodernism," in *The Political Nature of Cultural Heritage and Tourism: Critical Essays* Vol. 3, ed. Dallen J. Timothy (Burlington, VT: Ashgate Publishers, 2007): 19–37.

39 Jonathan Culler, *Framing the Sign*, 153.140.

40 See: https://www.santafefiesta.org.

41 Andrew L. Lovato. *Santa Fe Hispanic Culture: Preserving Identity in a Tourist Town* (Albuquerque, NM: University of New Mexico Press, 2006).

42 Media effects research has long explored the role of mass media in shaping individual and public attitudes, as well as the use of media to influence one's affective state. Among the most important examples of the power of media to shape or influence individual/social affect or perceptions are: Maxwell McCombs and Donald Shaw, "The Agenda-setting Function of Mass Media," *Public Opinion Quarterly* 36, no. 2 (1972): 176–187; George Gerbner and Larry Gross, "Living with Television: The Violence Profile," *Journal of Communication* 26 no. 2 (1976): 172–199; Walter Lippmann, *Public Opinion* (New York: Free Press, 1922/1997). For a thorough but concise overview of contemporary mass media effects research see: Jennings Bryant and Mary Beth Oliver, *Media Effects: Advances in Theory and Research.* 3rd ed. (New York: Routledge, 2009).

43 Andrea Hammer, "Memory Lines: The Plotting of New York's New Military Tract," in *Rhetoric, Remembrance, and Visual Foem: Sighting Memory*, ed. Anne Teresa Demo and Bradford Vivian. (New York: Routledge, 2012), 15–32.

44 Fan Ying, "Space, Landscape, and Memory: Chengdu's Shaocheng Park and the Historical Memory of the Railway Protection Monument," *Chinese Studies in History* 47, no. 1 (2013): 6–28.

45 Ronald L. Grimes. *Symbol and Conquest: Public Ritual and Drama in Santa Fe.* (Albuquerque, NM: University of New Mexico Press, 1976/1992): 46–50.

46 Teresa Córdova, "Power and Knowledge: Colonialism in the Academy," *Living Chicana Theory,* ed. Carla Trujillo (Berkley, CA: Third Woman Press, 1998).

47 Nestor Garcia Canclini, *Art beyond Itself: Anthropology for a Society without a Story Lien* (Durham, NC: Duke University Press, 2014).

48 John E. Badner, *Remaking America: Public Memory, Commemoration, and Patriotism in the Twentieth Century* (Princeton, NJ: Princeton University Press, 1992), 14.

49 Grimes, *Symbol and Conquest*, 46–50.

50 Lisa Maya Knauer and Daniel J. Walkowitz, "Introduction: Memory, Race, and the Nation in Public Spaces," in *Contested Histories in Public Space: Memory, Race, and Nation*, ed. Daniel J. Walkowitz and Lisa Maya Knauer (Durham, NC: Duke University Press, 2009), 2–3.

51 Benjamin Filene, "'Outsider' History-makers and What They Teach Us," *Public Historian* 34, no. 1 (2012): 11–33.

52 Ibid.

53 Ibid, 12

54 Ibid, 24

55 Frank G. Pérez and Carlos F. Ortega, "Mediated Debate, Historical Framing, and Public Art: The Juan de Oñate Controversy in El Paso," Aztlán: A Journal of Chicano Studies 33, no. 2 (2008), 121–140.

56 By "traditional high school" we mean four-year secondary education institutions with a traditional curriculum and extracurricular activities. The Ysleta Independent School District operates the Cesar Chavez Academy for at-risk teens and the El Paso Independent School District operates the Silva Magnate School. However, these and a growing number of charter schools lack open enrollment and sports teams. The latter is important because sports teams promote the school, the city, and their mascot throughout the region and the state. A number of prominent and successful Mexican Americans exist but even at the time of this writing, local school boards appear oblivious to the contributions of area heroes, such as writer Benjamin Alire Saenz, Chicano artist Luis Jimenez, astronaut John "Danny" Olivas, poet Pat Mora, and many others.

57 Monica Perales, *Smeltertown: Making and Remembering a Southwest Border Community* (Chapel Hill, NC: University of North Carolina Press, 2010), 52.

58 For example, J. Manuel Espinoza writing in 1947 refers to New Mexico natives as still living in the "stone age" when they were recolonized by Diego de Vargas in the 1690s. Espinoza claims the Franciscans who accompanied de Vargas during his "bloodless" reconquest of Santa Fe were "heroic agents of civilization." Cited in: Christopher Ross Petrakos, "'We Would Live Like Brothers: A Reexamination of Diego de Vargas' Reconquest of New Mexico and the Pueblo Indian Revolt, 1692–1696," *Delaware Review of Latin American Studies* 15, no 1 (2014): 1.

59 For a quick overview of the Chicano struggle see: José Ángel Gutiérrez, "The Chicano Movement: Paths to Power," *The Social Studies* 102 (2011): 25–32; Mario T. García, *Desert Immigrants: The Mexicans of El Paso, 1880–1920* (New Haven, CT: Yale University Press, 1982); George J. Sánchez, *Becoming Mexican American: Ethnicity, Culture, and Identity in Chicano Los Angeles, 1900–1945* (New York: Oxford University Press, 1993); Manuel G. González and Cynthia M. González, *En Aquel Entonces [In Years Gone By]: Readings in Mexican-American History* (Bloomington, IN: Indiana University Press, 2000). These sources provide a good overview of the Chicano experience across a number of eras. For the Native American struggle see: Roxanne Dunbar-Ortíz, *An Indigenous Peoples' History of the United States* (Boston, MA: Beacon Press, 2014).

60 Claudia Dolezal, "Community-based Tourism in Thailand: (Dis-)Illusions of Authenticity and the Necessity for Dynamic Concepts of Culture and Power," *Austrian Journal of South-East Asian Studies* 4, no. 2 (2011): 129–138; Jillian M. Rickly-Boyd, "Commentary – Existential Authenticity: Place Matters," *Tourism Geographies* 15, no. 4 (2013): 680–686.

61 One of the authors attended the Xcaret reenactment in July 2013 and found its framing of the Conquista much more complex and accurate than the First

48 *Fantasy heritage in southwest tourism*

Thanksgiving reenactments in San Elizario. The Xcaret event is presented in dance. Even without dialogue, or perhaps because of it, Spanish violence and its accompanying forced religious conversion of the Natives is presented in a direct manner. No effort is made to glorify or downplay the colonial era's brutality.

62 See: http://goafrica.about.com/od/legacytours. Tourism websites such as this one feature a long list of apartheid era tourist sites, for example.

63 Bernard J. Armada, "Memory's Execution: (Dis)placing the Dissident Body," in Dickinson, Blair, and Ott, *Places of Public Memory: The Rhetoric of Museums and Memorials.*

64 Dickinson, et al, *Places of public memory*; Badner, *Remaking America*; Ying, "Space, Landscape, Memory."

65 Simmons, *The Last Conquistador.*

66 Historical dates are often approximations; however, we will cite the most likely date to maintain readability.

67 James Diego Vigil. *From Indians to Chicanos: the dynamics of Mexican-American culture.* 3rd Ed. (Long Grove, IL: Waveland Press, 2012).

68 Stannard, *American Holocaust,* 4.

69 Ibid.

70 Weber, *Spanish Frontier*, 19.

71 Rodolfo Acuña, *Occupied America: A History of Chicanos* 4th ed. (New York: Longman, 2000), 3.

72 Enrique Florescano, *Memory, Myth, and Time in Mexico: From the Aztecs to Independence,* trans. Albert G. Bork (Austin, TX: University of Texas Press, 1994), 107–114.

73 In *The Last Conquistador*, Simmons states that this title was a vestige of the Middle Ages during Oñate's lifetime. However, the title is often associated by El Paso area tourism entities with those who led expeditions similar to Oñate's during that era.

74 Stan Hoig, *Came Men on Horses: The Conquistador Expeditions of Francisco Vásquez de Coronado and Don Juan de Oñate* (Boulder, CO: University of Colorado Press, 2012), 158.

75 Ibid., 159.

76 Ibid.

77 Ibid.

78 Simmons, *Last Conquistador, 40*.

79 Hoig, *Came Men on Horses*, 158.

80 Ibid., 157.

81 Ibid.

82 See Alfredo Mirandé and Evangelina Enríquez, *La Chicana: The Mexican-American Woman* (Chicago, IL: University of Chicago press, 1979), 54–55; and Weber, *Spanish Frontier*, 81. The spelling of Moctezuma is greatly debated. While the spelling used here is the widely accepted version, many Nahuatl texts use a different orthography: Motechuzoma.

83 McWilliams, *North from Mexico,* 1948/1990; Pérez and Ortega, "Mediated Debate"; Frank G. Pérez and Thomas E. Ruggiero, "Juan de Oñate as Public Art: A Case Study of Cultural Representation and Tourism," in *Communication for Development and Social Change Journal* 1, no. 3 (2007), 233–250.

84 Hoig, *Came Men on Horses*, 160.

85 Ibid.

86 Ibid., 158.

87 Ibid., 161.

88 Ibid., 158.

89 Weber, *Spanish Frontier,* 78–79.

Fantasy heritage in southwest tourism   49

90   Weber, *Spanish Frontier*, 78. Weber cites three sources in this footnote and the quotation is taken from "Ordenanzas de su Magestad hechas para los nuevos descubrimientos, conquistas, y pacificaciones," July 13, 1593, in *Colección de documentos inéditos relativos al descubrimiento, conquista, y organización de las antiguas posesiones españolas de América y Oceanía* ... (43 vols; Madrid: 1864–1884).
91   Hoig, *Came Men on Horses*, 162.
92   Ibid., 163.
93   Ibid., 165.
94   Ibid.
95   Weber, *Spanish Frontier*, 77.
96   Edward H. Spicer, *Cycles of Conquest: The Impact of Spain, Mexico, and the United States on the Indians of the Southwest, 1533–1960.* (Tucson, AZ: University of Arizona Press, 1962), 156.
97   Local tourism entities claim this as the genesis for El Paso's name. Yet, scholars Yolanda Chávez Leyva and Jeffrey Sheppard openly challenged this idea in a guest column in the *El Paso Times*. Leyva also wrote an academic essay, "Monuments of Conformity: Commemorating and Protesting Oñate on the Border," *New Mexico Historical Review* 82, no. 3 (2007): 343–367, where she decried the exclusion of Chicanas/os from El Paso's XII Travelers of the Southwest Memorial project. It includes no Mexican American historical figures.
98   Spicer, *Cycles*, 153.
99   Hoig, *Men Came on Horses*, 175.
100 Ibid., 176.
101 Ibid., 178.
102 Weber, *Spanish Frontier*, 77.
103 Ibid.
104 John Kessell, *Kiva, Cross, and Crown: The Pecos Indians and New Mexico, 1540–1840,* Washington, DC: Government Printing Office for the National Park Service, US Department of the Interior, 1979.
105 Tony Horowitz, *A Voyage Long and Strange: Rediscovering the New World.* (New York: Henry Holt and Company, 2008), 169.
106 Weber, *Spanish Frontier*, 86.
107 Horowitz, *A Voyage Long and Strange*, 169; Kessell, *Kiva, Cross, and Crown*, 86; Weber, *Spanish Frontier, 86.* It is important to note that some Oñate apologists dispute the carrying out of this sentence. To deny the Acoma's claim is an insult, particularly given the Spaniards' horrific actions and lack of credibility in framing their exploits throughout the Americas. More importantly, as illustrated here, the academic record strongly supports that this event took place. It is incorrect to allege this travesty did not occur.
108 Weber, *Spanish Frontier*, 86–87
109 Pérez and Ortega, *Mediated Debate.*
110 *Viva! El Paso* was cancelled after the 2013 season as the El Paso Association for the Performing Arts Board disbanded and ceded control to the El Paso Community Foundation, according to a KVIA-TV news report. See: http://www.kvia.com/news/viva-el-paso-suspended-for-summer-2014/26431308. Retrieved July 25, 2019. The show returned in 2015 as reported by Andrew Polk: see https://www.kvia.com/life style/viva-el-paso-set-to-reopen-this-weekend/56525327. Retrieved July 26, 2019.
111 Weber, *Spanish Frontier, 1992.*
112 The Black Legend or *Leyenda Negra* is a belief that Spaniards are a cruel, lazy, evil, greedy, treacherous, and fanatical people. Originating in the 16th Century with the Protestant Reformation and the expansion of the Spanish empire the Black Legend found many supporters in the US. We will revisit this topic in Chapter 5. For more on the Black Legend see: Benjamin Keen, "The Black

50   *Fantasy heritage in southwest tourism*

Legend Revisited: Assumptions and Realities," *The Hispanic American Historical Review* 49, no. 4 (1969): 703–719; Douglas T. Peck, "Revival of the Spanish 'Black Legend': The American Repudiation of Their Spanish Heritage," *Revista de la Historia de America* 128 (2001): 25–39.

113   María DeGuzmán suggests that the dominant or Anglo American US identity is "very much dependent on both an antagonistic and exoticizing relation with Spain and 'Spanishness.'" See: María DeGuzmán, *Spain's Long Shadow: The Black Legend, Off-Whiteness, and Anglo-American Empire* (Minneapolis, MN: University of Minnesota Press, 2005), xxvii. Anglo prejudice again Mexicans is rooted in anti-Spanish sentiment, resulting in the exotic framing of Spain and its people similar to that described by Edward W. Said against Middle Easterners. See: Edward W. Said, *Orientalism* (New York: Vintage, 1978).

114   The following links were available at the time of the writing of this chapter, April 1, 2014. Neither one has photos of the Spaniards mentioned but do provide additional context: http://www.cnn.com/2009/TECH/space/06/20/new.mexico.spaceport/index.html and http://www.spacesciencescorp.com/2009/08/space-port-america-ground-breaking.

115   Córdova, "Power and Knowledge", 33–37.

116   Ibid, 34.

117   Frederick Jackson Turner, *The Significance of the Frontier in American History*. Presentation at the American Historical Association, Chicago, IL, 1893.

118   Gaspar Pérez de Villagrá, *La Historia de Nuevo Mexico, 1610*, ed. Miguel Encinias, trans. Alfred Rodríguez (New Mexico: University of New Mexico Press, 1610/2004).

119   Arnoldo De León, *They Called Them Greasers: Anglo Attitudes Toward Mexicans in Texas, 1821–1920*. (Austin, TX: University of Texas Press, 1983); Bonilla-Silva, *Racism without Racists: Color-Blind Racism and the Persistence of Racial Inequality in the United States*, 4th ed. (New York: Rowman and Littlefield, 2014); David Montejano, *Anglos and Mexicans in the Making of Texas, 1836–1986* (Austin, TX: University of Texas Press, 1987).

120   Rodolfo F. Acuña, *Anything but Mexican: Chicanos in Contemporary Los Angeles* (New York: Verso, 1996).

121   Tim Wise, *Dear White America: Letter to a New Minority* (San Francisco, CA: City Lights Publishers, 2012).

122   Stannard, *American Holocaust*, 1992.

123   The existence of Spain's multi-tiered society during the colonial period is widely known. See: Barbara L. Voss, "Gender, Race, and Labor in Archaeology of the Spanish Colonial Americas," *Current Anthropology* 49, no. 5 (2006): 861–893. Timothy C. Parish addresses the importation and development of social categories. See: Timothy C. Parish, "Class Structure and Social Reproduction in New Spain/New Mexico," *Dialectical Anthropology* 7, no. 2 (1982): 137–153. Linda Gordon addresses the development of a two-tiered socioeconomic system that placed Anglos as superior to Mexicans during the early 1900s in the Southwest. See: Linda Gordon, *The Great Arizona Orphan Abduction* (Cambridge, MA: Harvard University Press, 1999). Lovato addresses a more contemporary manifestation of this trend in *Santa Fe Hispanic Culture*, 2004. For specific examples of this system in Texas see: David Montejano, *Anglos and Mexicans*, 1987. For the case of El Paso, Texas, see Perales, *Seltertown*; Mario T. García, *Desert Immigrants: The Mexicans of El Paso, 1880–1920* (New Haven, CT: Yale University Press, 1981); Pablo Vila, *Crossing Borders/Reinforcing Borders: Social Categories, Metaphors, and Narrative Identities on the U.S.-Mexico Border* (Austin, TX: University of Texas Press, 2000); *Border Identifications: Narratives of Religion, Gender, and Class on the U.S.-Mexico Border* (Austin, TX: University of Texas Press, 2005).

Fantasy heritage in southwest tourism   51

124   Don W. Stacks and Michael B. Salwen, "Integrating Theory and Research: Starting with Questions," in *An Integrated Approach to Communication Theory and Research*, 2nd ed., ed. Don W. Stacks and Michael B. Salwen (New York: Routledge, 1996/2009), 3–14.

125   Ricahrd Dyer, *White* (New York: Routledge, 1997).

126   For example, see: George White, Jr., "I am Teaching Some of the Boys: Chaplain Robert Boston Dokes and Army Testing of Black Soldiers in World War II," *Journal of Negro Education* 81, no. 3 (2012): 200–217.

127   J.M. Blaut, *The Colonizer's Model of the World: Geographic Diffusionism and Eurocentric History* (New York: Guilford Press, 1993).

128   Blaut, *Colonizer's Model.*

129   Charles Montgomery, "Becoming 'Spanish American': Race and Rhetoric in New Mexico Politics, 1880–1928," *Journal of American Ethnic History* 20, no. 4 (2001): 59–84.

130   Perales, *Smeltertown*, 51–52.

131   Lovato, *Santa Fe Hispanic*

132   Acuña, *Occupied America*

133   Mirandé and Enríquez, *La Chicana*, 54–55.

134   Matthew F. Bokovoy, *The San Diego World's Fairs and Southwestern Memory, 1880–1940.* (Albuquerque, NM: University of New Mexico Press, 2005), xvi.

135   David J. Weber, *Foreigners in Their Native Land: Historical Roots of the Mexican American.* 30th ann. ed. (Albuquerque, NM: University of New Mexico Press, 1973/2003), 22.

136   McWilliams, *North from Mexico,* 69.

137   Acuña, *Occupied America*; McWilliams, *North from Mexico*; Weber, *Native Land.* See also: José Rabasa, *Writing Violence on the Spanish Frontier: The Historigraphy of Sixteenth Century New Mexico and Florida and the Legacy of Conquest* (Durham, NC: Duke University Press, 2000).

138   Spicer, *Cycles of Conquest,* 1963.

139   Dyer, *White.*

140   Many of the wealthy Latino families in the Southwest are recent transplants from Mexico who fled the drug wars of the 2010s. Some are from families who fled the Mexican Revolution. However, both groups constitute a very small number in comparison to the wealthy Anglos in the region. Early on in the US entry to the Southwest, Anglos instituted policies that made wealth accumulation all but impossible for Mexican Americans, as noted by Monica Perales, *Smeltertown.* See: Acuña, *Occupied America*; Gordon, *Great Arizona Orphan Abduction*; de León, *They Called Them Greasers*; Montejano, *Anglos and Mexicans.*

141   Alastair Bonnett, "A White World? Whiteness and the Meaning of Modernity in Latin America and Japan." In *Working through Whiteness: International Perspectives*, ed. Cynthia Levine-Rasky (New York: State University of New York Press, 2002), 71.

142   Montgomery, "Becoming 'Spanish', "59–84.

143   Rodolfo Acuña, *Occupied America*; McWilliams, *North from Mexico*; Montgomery, "Becoming 'Spanish American'"; Perez and Ruggiero, "Juan de Oñate as Public Art".

144   Acuña, *Occupied America,* 408–09; Alfredo Mirandé, *The Chicano Experience: An Alternative Perspective* (Notre Dame, IN: University of Notre Dame Press, 2002), 3.

145   Lovato, *Santa Fe Hispanic Culture.*

146   Susan Rinderle, "The Mexican Diaspora: A Critical Examination of Signifiers," *Journal of Communication Inquiry* 29, no. 4 (2005): 296; Ignacio Manuel García, *Chicanismo: The Making of a Militant Ethos Among Mexican Americans* (Tucson, AZ: University of Arizona Press, 1997).

52 Fantasy heritage in southwest tourism

147 Luis Urrieta, Jr., "Identity Production in Figured Worlds: How Some Mexican Americans Become Chicana/o Activist Educators," *Urban Review* 39, no. 2 (2007).

148 John M. Nieto-Phillips, *The Language of Blood: The Making of Spanish-American Identity in New Mexico, 1880s-1930s* (Albuquerque, NM: University of New Mexico Press, 2004), 16–17.

149 Montgomery, "Becoming 'Spanish American'," 59–84

150 David Montejano, *Anglos and Mexicans*; Mario T García, *Desert Immigrants*; Manuel R. Ramirez, "El Pasoans: Life and Society in Mexican El Paso, 1920–1945," Phd Dissertation, Department of History, University of Mississippi, 2000.

151 Pérez and Ortega, "Mediated Debate," 123–124

152 Marsha Weisiger, "No More Heroes: Western History in Public Places," *Western Historical Quarterly* 42, no. 3 (Autumn 2011), 289–296.

153 Amma Y. Ghartey-Tagoe Kootin, "Lessons in Blackbody Minstrelsy: Old Plantation and the Manufacture of Black Authenticity," *TDR/The Drama Review*, 57, no. 2 (Summer 2013), 102–122.

154 Krista E. Paulsen, "Strategy and Sentiment: Mobilizing Heritage in Defense of Place," *Qualitative Sociology* 30, no. 1, (2007): 1–19.

155 Christopher J. Huggard and Terrence M. Humble, *Santa Rita del Cobre: A Copper Mining Community in New Mexico* (Boulder, CO: University Press of Colorado, 2012), 93.

156 Francisco E. Balderrama and Raymond Rodríguez, *Decade of Betrayal: Mexican Repatriation in the 1930s.* rev. ed. (Albuquerque, NM: University of New Mexico Press, 2006).

157 In addition to Balderrama and Rodriguez, *Decade of Betrayal*, see: Francisco E. Balderrama, "The Emergence of Unconstitutional Deportation and Repatriation of Mexicans and Mexican Americans as a Public Issue," *Radical History Review* 93 (2005): 107–110; R. Reynolds McKay, "The Impact of the Great Depression on Immigrant Mexican Labor: Repatriation of the Bridgeport, Texas, Coalminers," *Social Science Quarterly* 62, no. 2 (1984): 354–363.

158 See: Luis Alvarez, *The Power of the Zoot: Youth Culture and Resistance during World War II.* (Berkley, CA: University of California Press, 2008); Elizabeth R. Escobedo, *From Coveralls to Zoot Suits: The Lives of Mexican American Women on the World War II Home Front* (Chapel Hill, NC: University of North Carolina Press, 2013); Mauricio Mazón, *The Zoot Suit Riots: The Psychology of Symbolic Annihilation* (Austin, TX: University of Texas Press, 1988); Eduardo Obregón Pagán, *Murder at the Sleepy Lagoon: Zoot Suits, Race, and Riot in Wartime L.A.* (Chapel Hill, NC: University of North Carolina Press, 2003); Catherine S. Ramírez, *The Woman in the Zoot Suit: Gender, Nationalism, and the Cultural Politics of Memory* (Durham, NC: Duke University Press, 2009).

159 Raúl Homero Villa, *Barrio Logos: Space and Place in Urban Chicano Literature and Culture* (Austin, TX: University of Texas Press, 2000), 55.

160 Douglas Monroy, *Thrown Among Strangers: The Making of Mexican Culture in Frontier California* (Berkley, CA: University of California Press, 1993).

161 The dates given for the Chicano Movement vary but we agree with historian Juan Gómez-Quiñones that the Movement approximately spanned the years 1966–1978. See: Juan Gómez-Quiñones, *Chicano Politics: Reality and Promise, 1940–1990* (Albuquerque: University of New Mexico Press, 1990).

162 Acuña, *Ocuppied America*; Almaguer, *Racial Faultlines*; Montejano, *Anglos and Mexicans*; Weber, *Native Land.*

163 Howard Giles, Daniel Linz, Doug Bonilla, and Michelle Leah Gómez, "Police Stops of and Interactions with Latino and White (non-Latino) Drivers: Extensive Policing and Communication Accommodation," *Communication Monographs* 79, no. 4 (2012): 407–427.

Fantasy heritage in southwest tourism   53

164   William Anthony Nericcio, *Tex{t}-Mex: Seductive Hallucinations of the "Mexican" in America* (Austin, TX: University of Texas Press, 2007), 30.
165   Blair, Dickinson, and Ott, *Public Memory*, 10.
166   Bokovoy, *San Diego World's Fairs*
167   Ibid., xvii
168   Sarah Horton, "New Mexico's Cuarto Centario and Spanish American Nationalism: Collapsing Past Conquests and Present Dispossession," *Journal of the Southwest* 44, no. 1 (2002): 41. We researched this article but want to credit Yolanda Chavez Leyva as the scholar who led us to Horton's work. Specifically, see: Yolanda Chavez Leyva, "Monuments of Conformity: Commemorating and Protesting Oñate on the Border," *New Mexico Historical Review* 82, no. 3 (2007): 343–367. We acknowledge Leyva's important contribution to the scholarly work in this field.
169   Ramón Gutiérrez, *When Jesus Came, the Corn Mothers Went Away: Marriage, Sexuality, and Power in New Mexico, 1500–1846* (Stanford, CA: Stanford University Press, 1991).
170   Charles Montgomery, *The Spanish Redemption: Heritage, Power, and Loss on New Mexico's Upper Rio Grande*. (Berkeley, CA: University of California Press, 2002). See, also by Montgomery, "Becoming 'Spanish American'," 59–84.
171   Ibid.
172   Acuña, *Occupied America*. Also, Monica Perales explains that while wealth shielded elite *mexicanos* who fled Mexico during the revolution from much direct racism, they were never considered white. See: Perales, *Smeltertown*; Blair, Dickinson, and Ott, *Public Memory*, 10. For example, see Bokovoy, *The San Diego World's Fairs*. Horton, "New Mexico's Cuarto Centario and Spanish American Nationalism", 41; Leyva, "Monuments of Conformity," 343–367. Gutiérrez, *When Jesus Came*. Mongomery, "Becoming 'Spanish American'."
173   Jon Hunner, "Preserving Hispanic Life Ways in New Mexico," *Public Historian* 23, no. 4 (2001): 29–40.
174   Chris Wilson, *The Myth of Santa Fe: Creating a Modern Regional Tradition* (Albuquerque, NM: University of New Mexico Press, 1997).
175   William Deverell, *Whitewashed Adobe: The Rise of Los Angeles and the Removing of Its Mexican Past* (Berkley, CA: University of California Press, 2004), 251.
176   Ibid.
177   Montgomery. *The Spanish Redemption*, 16.
178   Gordon, *The Great Arizona Orphan Abduction*; Montejano, *Anglos and Mexicans*; Perales, *Smeltertown*.
179   McWilliams, *North from Mexico*.
180   John Valdez and Christine Ibarra, *The Last Conquistador* (2008; PBS Video). Chino's comments appear at 59:30–59:37. Also see, Albert Memmi, *Colonizer and the Colonized* (Boston, MA: Beacon Press, 1967).
181   See, for example: McWilliams, *North from Mexico*.
182   Howard Zinn, *A People's History of the United States: 1492 to the Present* (New York: Harper Collins, 1980/2003).
183   The "Mexican problem" is a term referencing the negative social standing Mexican immigrants encountered in the Southwest. Roberto T. Treviño recounts Reverend Esteban de Anta's laments that Mexicans found "only contempt and hatred" in Houston during the 1910s. See Robert T. Treviño, "Facing Jim Crow: Catholic Sisters and the 'Mexican Problem' in Texas," *Western Historical Quarterly* 34, no. 2 (2003): 139. This theme goes back to at least the 1830s, according to Rudolfo Acuña: "[Anglos] believed themselves morally, intellectually, and politically superior." See: Acuña, *Occupied America*, 46. In El Paso, Mario T. García's landmark *Desert Immigrants* recounts similar experiences. From this early discrimination, the Southwest has evolved into a region where large numbers of Mexican Americans, even those with

54 Fantasy heritage in southwest tourism

middle- or upper-class social status obfuscate Anglo efforts at hegemonic control of the area's versions of the past. Some Mexican Americans support mainstream views of history but many do not and are vocal in their opposition.

184 See: Willem Assies, "Land Tenure and Tenure Regimes in Mexico: An Overview," *Journal of Agrarian Change* 8, no. 1 (2008): 33–66; Maria DiGiano, Edward Ellis, and Eric Keys, "Changing Landscapes for Forest Commons: Linking Land Tenure with Forest Cover Change Following Mexico's 1992 Agrarian Counter-reforms," *Human Ecology: An Interdisciplinary Journal* 41, no. 5 (2013): 707–723.

185 Eric Jacoby, *Man and Land* (London: Andre Deutch, 1971)

186 Roxanne Dunbar-Ortiz, *Roots of Resistance: Land Tenure in New Mexico, 1680–1980* (Los Angeles, CA: Chicano Studies Research Center/American Indian Studies Center/University of California, 1980)

187 Stanley Crawford, *Mayordomo: Chronicle of an Acequia in Nothern New Mexico* (New York: Anchor Books, 1988); William de Buys, *Enchantment and Exploitation: The Life and Hard Times of a New Mexico Mountain Range* (Albuquerque, NM: University of New Mexico Press, 1985); Dunbar Ortiz, *Roots*.

188 Dunbar Ortíz, *Roots*, 4.

189 Ibid.

190 McWilliams, *North from Mexico*.

191 George I. Sánchez, *Forgotten People* (Albuquerque, NM: University of New Mexico Press, 1940/1996).

192 Balderrama and Rodríguez, *Decade of Betrayal*.

193 Eithne Luibhéid, *Entry Denied: Controlling Sexuality at the Border* (Minneapolis, MN: University of Minnesota Press, 2002), 2, 31–54; Anna Pegler-Gordon, *In Sight of America: Photography and the Development of U.S. Immigration Policy* (Los Angeles, CA: University of California Press, 2009), 57.

194 Said, *Orientalism*

195 Gilbert G. González, *Culture of Empire: American Writers, Mexico & Mexican Immigrants, 1880–1930* (Texas: University of Texas Press, 2004), 185.

196 Said, *Orientalism*. Part one of the book is especially useful for understanding the use of the term.

197 González, *Culture of Empire*, 186.

198 Almaguer, *Racial Fault Lines;* De León, *They Called Them Greasers;* Montejano, *Anglos and Mexicans;* Perales, *Smeltertown;* David J. Weber, *Myth and History of the Hispanic Southwest* (Albuquerque, NM: University of New Mexico Press, 1990).

199 Perales, *Smeltertown*, 82–85; Julie Leininger Pycior, *LBJ & Mexican Americans: The Paradox of Power* (Austin, TX: University of Texas Press, 1997), 56, 60, 78; Carlos Kevin Blanton, *The Strange Case of Bilingual Education in Texas 1836–1981* (College Station, TX: Texas A&M University Press, 2004); Guadalupe San Miguel, *'Let All of Them Take Heed': Mexican Americans and the Campaign for Educational Equality in Texas, 1910–1981* (College Station, TX: Texas A&M University Press, 2000). These authors provide a solid overview of this phenomenon in Texas. Native Americans faced similar, if not more daunting obstacles. See: David Wallace Adams, *Education for Extinction: American Indians and the Boarding School Experience, 1875–1928* (Lawrence, KS: University of Kansas Press, 1995).

200 Gordon, *Great Arizona Orphan Abduction*.

201 Alvarez, *Power of Zoot*, 17.

202 Deena J. González, *Refusing the Favor: The Spanish-Mexican Women of Santa Fe, 1820–1880* (Albuquerque, NM: University of New Mexico Press, 1999), ix.

203 Cynthia Duquette Smith and Teresa Bergman, "You Were on Indian Land: Alcatraz Island as Recalcitrant Memory Space," in *Places of Public Memory:*

Fantasy heritage in southwest tourism 55

    The Rhetoric of Museums and Memorials, eds. Greg Dickinson, Carole Blair, and
    Brian L. Ott (Tuscaloosa, AL: University of Alabama Press, 2010), 160–188.
204 Vila, *Crossing Borders*; Vila, *Border Identifications.*
205 Bokovoy, *World's Fairs,* xviii.
206 Paulsen, "Strategy and Sentiment."
207 Rosa-Linda Fregoso, *MeXicana Encounters: The Making of Social Identities on
    the Borderlands* (Berkley, CA: University of California Press, 2003), 104.
208 Perez and Ortega, "Mediated Debate."

2 San Elizario's First Thanksgiving of the Americas and the Juan de Oñate fantasy heritage

Since antiquity, communities have used fantastic stories—revealed to anyone who would care to listen—to generate tourism. To this day tourism remains an important revenue stream for municipalities throughout the globe. Marketing an area's culture, geography, history, or politics as unique attractions is a heritage tourism tradition. Amusement parks, battle sites/battle site memorials,[1] historical reenactments,[2] museums,[3] and public monuments[4] use fantasy heritage to attract visitors. The exploitation of the symbolic value of culture[5] often benefits one influential set of stakeholders over all others in a community.[6] Thus, one must consider how such an economic reality shapes collective historical or public memory—how does a community remember its past? Whose story is being told, how, and by whom? Who profits from whichever historical framing is used in a particular locale and at what artistic, cultural, or economic costs? What are the cultural implications and what effect this does have on the identity of community members?

Contemporary tourism efforts are saturated with heritage reenactments that hope to share "what happened here so long ago." Reenactments reflect fantasy heritage. They bring historical events to life by selling a reality that is grounded in a small group's beliefs about another time and place. They are "feel good" accounts of the past that generate visitors to locales and good TV ratings.[7] In truth, fantasy heritage often reflects a political vision of what happened, usually via only one dominant perspective. Too often fantasy heritage plays of this kind avoid the dark or complicated aspects of the events represented. For many Mexican/Americans, history is relegated to the stories and recollections parents and grandparents shared around the dinner table. Why are heritage reenactments so popular? For many city and county governments, tourists are seen as an economic boon. Eager to bring in tourist dollars, far too many venues perform Disney-like versions of their community's or region's past.

This chapter draws on our analysis of a video we recorded of the 2006 *First Thanksgiving of the Americas* (hereafter: First Thanksgiving) reenactment of Spanish entry into what is now San Elizario, Texas, as well as field notes from our attendance at the 2006, 2007, 2008, and 2016 reenactments. Throughout its existence, the First Thanksgiving has been economically sustained by

San Elizario's First Thanksgiving   57

business and other community leaders, providing area Mexican Americans the chance to glorify their "Spanish" roots.

Given the variations between academic accounts and fantasy heritage retellings of the past, this chapter examines the First Thanksgiving's framing of the Spanish conquest. We specifically explore how the First Thanksgiving's representations of Spaniards, Spanish women, and Indians work to legitimate the Spanish colonial experiment. We seek to understand what the First Thanksgiving suggests about colonization and its aftermath, as well as what these elements suggest about identity politics in West Texas. First, we provide a brief overview of the evolution of the Juan de Oñate/Spanish myth in the El Paso area, including a section on how attendees may perceive what they experience. This section is followed by a detailed account of the First Thanksgiving reenactment, providing readers with a summary of the play and its dialogue, explaining how this framing of the Spanish colonial experiment operates as fantasy heritage. To arrive at a conclusion, we pose four questions: How does the First Thanksgiving's retelling of history reflect fantasy heritage? How does the reenactment represent Spaniards, Spanish women, and Indians to legitimate the colonial experiment? What does the First Thanksgiving suggest about colonization and its aftermath? What do these elements collectively suggest about cultural identity in West Texas? The chapter ends with a series of suggestions for creating a more collective community memory that is likely to appeal to tourists, visitors, and locals while offering a more holistic retelling.

El Paso's Eurocentric tourism efforts, 1915–2015

For 100 years, West Texas has grappled with its colonial past and the community's desire for tourist dollars. In 1915, El Paso mayor and one-time Ku Klux Klansman[8] Thomas Calloway Lea inaugurated the idea of using local history as a tourism ploy. Thomas Calloway Lea, father of famed El Paso artist/author Tom Lea, suggested El Paso draw on its history to attract visitors using the theme of twelve travelers through history. Specifically, he wanted to identify twelve travelers who represented different eras in El Paso's past that had greatly influenced the city or surrounding area through a history motif. Mount Rushmore sculptor and KKK member Gutzon Borglum[9] thrice visited El Paso during the 1930s (1934, 1935, and 1936) hoping to carve area history into a rock formation at Hueco Tanks State Park just outside the city, according to an April 1990 XII Travelers Committee newsletter.[10] The effects of the Great Depression precluded his efforts, as funding for such a large project was unavailable. Lea's and Borglum's KKK ties imply their interest in the topic was driven by economic need, not cultural enlightenment. Lea wanted to increase tourism and Borglum sought a commissioned project. Despite the weak economy of the 1930s, El Paso's economic and political elites did not give up on their dream and it carried over into subsequent decades.

58 San Elizario's First Thanksgiving

In 1947, the El Paso Electric Company used twelve images painted by Tom Lea, son of the former mayor whose legacy is tainted by his KKK ties, in a calendar titled *Twelve Travelers through The Pass of the North* that used the travelers' concept. Although the images were originally painted for a local restaurant menu, the El Paso Electric Company's resources spread the images to a much broader audience. The Travelers theme resurfaced in the 1950s, when the *El Paso Times* addressed the historical Oñate thanksgiving in a January 13, 1952 column that referenced "perfumed Spanish dandies" and "naked savages" [sic]. That year, an El Paso Electric Company-sponsored float with a First Thanksgiving theme took second place in El Paso's Sun Carnival Parade. The Spanish fantasy lost support during the 1960s and 1970s, perhaps as a result of the Chicano Movement, but resurfaced again in the 1980s.

Since 1989, West Texas has actively grappled with its fantasy past due to the City of El Paso's funding of Sculptor John Houser's *XII Travelers of the Southwest Memorial* (hereafter: XII Travelers) concept. The project would see twelve statues of historically important individuals used to spur downtown tourism. The original proposal called for a foundry to be opened in downtown El Paso to cast the sculptures and serve as the anchor point for what was hoped to become an artist colony. Yet, the foundry idea was almost immediately dropped. An abbreviated proposal that omitted the foundry was submitted by Houser and approved by the city council, shortly after the first proposal was accepted. This change freed Houser to construct the statue in Mexico City and to have it partially assembled at the Shidoni bronze foundry in Santa Fe, New Mexico.[11] In 1989, El Paso's support of the project led nearby communities to explore Juan de Oñate's ties to the area and the use of his image to spur tourism.

El Paso and San Elizario, Texas, celebrated the inaugural First Thanksgiving commemorations on April 30, 1998 with their own respective First Thanksgiving reenactments. Each play focused on the Spaniards' arrival to the area under the leadership of Juan de Oñate, highlighted the introduction of the Catholic faith to the region (without addressing forced religious conversion), and ended with Oñate reading *La Toma* (literally: the taking), a colonial era document that claimed the Natives' lands for Spain. In both plays, the Indians and Spaniards celebrated their "union" while omitting the Spaniards' atrocities throughout the Southwest.

The late Sheldon Hall pioneered the First Thanksgiving concept and promoted the event at the national level. In 1991, he and ten other El Pasoans traveled to Massachusetts to argue before a 17th Century mock court that Oñate's thanksgiving predated the Pilgrims by twenty-three years. Hall commented, "We just want the people of the United States to realize that other things were going on before the Pilgrims ... [since it often] ignores what the Spaniards did."[12] Mock trial judge and Plymouth Schools Superintendent Bernard Sidman found Hall's evidence indecisive and suggested Plymouth representatives visit El Paso. While sincere, Hall's interest in the Spanish colonial past was fundamentally Eurocentric. It framed the Spaniards in largely sympathetic terms and callously ignored the plight of the indigenous. Yet, the publicity effort gained both cities national media attention.

Even the late Ann Richards, Texas Governor (1991–1995), supported the First Thanksgiving as good for El Paso tourism. She invited Governor William F. Weld to the 1990 reenactment; however, he declined to attend because Massachusetts officials were annoyed by the San Elizario event's claim to be first. Evident on both sides of the debate was a strong Eurocentric bias rooted in fantasy heritage. Only the Europeans' experiences were of concern to political leaders. Both parties failed to consider the mental and physical costs colonialism and cultural annihilation imposed on the indigenous peoples of what are now Massachusetts and Texas. That same year, the Texas State Legislature officially recognized the First Thanksgiving, declaring April 23 an official state holiday. Even Spain's Cónsul General Carlos Reparáz, who attended the 1991 First Thanksgiving, alluded to the controversy: "Even though Don Juan de Oñate's Thanksgiving undoubtedly happened first, I think the Pilgrims' celebration will always be the main one."[13] He too failed to display concern for indigenous suffering.

In 1995, Hall established the El Paso Mission Trail Association (EPMTA) to promote the Lower Valley's[14] three area churches, framing them as missions. In truth, the San Elizario "mission" is a chapel, a fact acknowledged in at least some El Paso Mission Trail Association (EPMTA) materials and in the San Elizario plaza.[15] By the mid-1990s, the festivities included the theft of a shipment of Spanish gold as well as fine dining events and galas that commemorated Oñate on both sides of the border. In 1996, the El Paso Independent School District (EPISD) created four scholastic regions. Students in each one were to focus on a different aspect of the Spanish quadricentennial. On February 24, 1998, the district also staged a First Thanksgiving parade in El Paso that wound its way through the downtown, ending at the first XII Travelers statue, Fray García de San Francisco. Speeches by sculptor John Houser, Sheldon Hall (dressed as a conquistador), and school board president Kathy Becker concluded the event.[16] University of Texas at El Paso Spanish professor and EPISD Quadricentennial task force member José Luis Suárez commented to the *El Paso Times*, "There is a misconception of the conquistadores ... The mixture of Spanish and Mexican is always seen as a story of power and oppression. But there are other ways of looking at it."[17] The "other way" of looking at colonization is consistent with the region's leaders' fantasy heritage framing, as Suárez suggested the Spaniards were "bringing culture to a new country."[18]

The parade romanticized the colonial experiment, misinformed school children too young to discern fantasy from fact and erased the Mexican/American reality of the city. How professor Saenz found any Mexican elements in the Spanish fantasy is anyone's guess. Even those Oñate sympathizers of color, such as the professor, who acknowledge the complexity of this time period, may display what Teresa Córdova terms the confusion of the colonized.[19] Such

Figure 3 A sign explaining the history of Presidio Chapel in San Elizario that includes the chapel's original name, San Eliceario.
Credit: Leonel Monroy

individuals fail to empathize with or to understand the indigenous tribes' experiences from the Indians' point of view. For example, while Professor Suárez noted that colonization was about more than "power and oppression," he did not elaborate. Fantasy heritage romanticizes Spanish brutality and expunges many of the Spaniards' heinous actions from any historical discourse.

The Oñate fantasy's momentum continued when Bea Bragg published a children's book, *The Very First Thanksgiving*, in 1997.[20] Local area school districts adopted it along with a coloring book for elementary schools. While these efforts may aim to promote diversity, according to those who promote their use in schools, they fail to address the historical experiences of the city's largest ethnic category. El Paso is officially eighty-two percent "Hispanic"[21] but in fact, the term masks the city's almost exclusively Mexican/American population. The city has no other measurable Latino social categories. Selling El Pasoans on the Spanish fantasy erases the realities faced by Mexican Americans in El Paso and the surrounding area, preserving its Eurocentric status quo.

Having the public schools indoctrinate children to accept the Spanish fantasy is troubling. School children lack the critical thinking skills necessary to discern for themselves what their history means to them. El Paso's Mexican Americans are taught to admire Juan de Oñate and that their history is a Spanish one. Yet, our experiences with university students suggest El Paso schools fail to educate them about Mexican American history or the city's important role during the Chicano Movement. Most of our students cannot define the term Chicano. Many do not know any of the major Chicano civil rights leaders whose struggles opened doors for students such as themselves, bilingual and first-generation college students, to enter higher education.

Keeping locals and tourists oblivious to the role Mexican Americans have played in shaping El Paso and the Southwest is a hegemonic enterprise. Mexican Americans who believe their ethnic category has played no important roles in history are likely to accept the status quo and to be content with a middle-class job. They are unlikely to advocate for social justice and will see the city's elite as hard workers who have succeeded. While no one questions the ability of elites to work hard, people need to understand the head start many White families received as a result of the area's past racist policies. Since little is done to educate locals about other aspects of the area's past, few El Pasoans are likely to learn about the discrimination that shaped their town.

The First Thanksgiving: a Mexican region's Eurocentric fantasy

Oñate's claiming of New Mexico for Spain twenty-three years before the Jamestown Pilgrims[22] held their now nationally observed day of thanks gives promoters a useful marketing ploy that has worked with varying degrees of success during the past twenty-plus years. In 1998, El Paso's reenactment of the Spaniards' arrival took place at the Chamizal Federal Park. It drew 4,000 people with two especially notable guests—Manuel Gullón y de Oñate, a Spanish banker and Oñate descendent as well as Spanish Cónsul General Ricardo Marti-Flux. *El Paso Herald-Post* columnist Alex Apostolides noted that the El Paso reenactment suffered from "poor direction, blocking, staging," and the mispronunciation of Spanish names. Although his column crassly claimed that "horses patoots" were the best items viewed at the event, Apostolides did "hope the First Thanksgiving [would] become an annual event."[23] A tradition introduced that year at the San Elizario reenactment was for the local Catholic bishop, then Raymundo Peña, to offer mass outside the chapel. The mass commemorates the 1598 arrival of Catholicism to West Texas, without mention of the Natives' forced religious indoctrination. The celebration held in San Elizario was smaller than the festivities in El Paso, but it benefitted from the support of area business leaders.

Interest in the First Thanksgiving waned at the start of the 2000s. Even Sheldon Hall admitted the El Paso "10th anniversary re-enactment was mostly for the benefit of news media and to keep the tradition alive,"[24] as paraphrased by reporter Ken Flynn. At the time of this writing, San Elizario produces the only remaining First Thanksgiving reenactment in West Texas, having produced it in two significantly different formats. The reenactment performance itself has been the work of college faculty and students (apparently ignorant of or unconcerned about Spanish brutality). Initially, El Paso Community College (EPCC) students performed a play

62　*San Elizario's First Thanksgiving*

by David Mills and Hector Serrano.[25] Beginning with the event's 25th anniversary in 2014, Opera UTEP (University of Texas at El Paso) became responsible for the reenactment performance. Later, Montwood High School took over production under the direction of teacher and Choir Director Joe Estala. Each institutions' versions were replete with fantasy heritage elements, promoting a Eurocentric hegemony that provided tourists with a sanitized version of history. That two of El Paso's most well-known institutions of higher learning have adopted the First Thanksgiving as their own strengthens the event's hegemony. Here, we will examine both versions, beginning with the original play. The event's twenty-three-year jump on the one at Plymouth has been fortuitous, particularly as San Elizario joined with the EPMTA to promote the event. The First Thanksgiving continues to be a key pillar in San Elizario's tourism efforts. But how does the reenactment promote fantasy heritage?

To find out, we examined how the following elements convey a fantasy heritage account of San Elizario's past: (1) overall stage presentation, (2) the actors' dialogue and narrator's comments, (3) the framing of the Spanish and indigenous characters within the play, and (4) issues of representation and identity. These elements allowed us to answer the questions posed at the start of the chapter. When the 2006 play began there were about seventy-five audience members, growing to approximately 150 by its conclusion.[26] The audience appeared to be composed of middle-class White and Mexican American observers and our attendance estimates suggest little, if any, additional ethnic diversity in the audience. We also attended and documented events at the 2016 First Thanksgiving reenactment, staged by Montwood High School under the guidance of Joe Estala. We estimated the audience that year at about 150; Estala estimated it at 200 during the event. Our analysis of both addresses various aspects of each, noting similarities and differences. The highlight of the First Thanksgiving play is the three-day San Elizario festival, which is staged on the entryway to the San Elizario Presidio Chapel.

The First Thanksgiving play, 2006

The 2006 event begins with a dance, performed by twenty-four members of Ballet Folklorico Paso del Norte dressed in indigenous outfits. The group dances to indigenous music composed of rattles, flutes, and drums. The song progresses from stereotypically indigenous tones to a hybrid Indian/Spanish sound. As the song ends, the narrator tells the audience that people have inhabited the area "for thousands of years" and the play shifts to a scene where a tribal chief and his two sons discuss how best to react to the Spaniards' arrival. No character is addressed by name; the dialogue and actors' movements provide the context necessary to understanding each character's role in the scene. No backdrops or props are used other than the actors' indigenous costumes.

San Elizario's First Thanksgiving 63

As the scene begins, audience members hear the chief tell his sons the Spaniards should be treated with peace and respect because they bring new technologies that will improve the tribe's living standards. The audience is not told what these technologies are or why the chief believes the Spaniards will share them. His sons object and warn their father that the Europeans "speak with forked tongues." The elder son has "heard from other villages of [the Spaniards'] cruelty." The chief cautions his sons that hearsay is dangerous because "Each time a story is told it gets further separated from the truth." The younger son warns "[T]he Spanish use hard, metal shields and strong headpieces to protect themselves ... and the four-legged beasts they ride run swiftly." The younger son is concerned the tribe will be unable to "overtake them [the Spanish forces]" on the battlefield. Apparently, the indigenous do not have horses, helmets, or metal weapons. The chief hears his sons then decrees his final decision: "[I]t would be wise to deal with these aliens in peace, since we cannot overtake them by force." His sons are dismayed. As the scene ends the elder son affirms, "Father, the decision is yours and I cannot oppose you but as next to rule, if it is within my power, I will eventually lead a revolt against their force." The chief remains steadfast, stating that his people will choose "peace, not force."

The scene ends as a group of ten Spaniards, some on horseback, approach from the left side of the audience and take the stage. As they arrive, music appropriate for a military epic fills the entire plaza. Ten women walk behind the Spanish men and two friars walk behind the women. As the actors position themselves, the narrator relates:

> almost 400 years ago, an invader burst upon the plains of Texas. The Spaniards claimed much of the land of the New World and found it safe to send their families to the Pass [of the North] (contemporary San Elizario and the surrounding area, including El Paso).

The Indians line themselves along a side of the chapel to hide from those arriving. The Spaniards then briefly discuss the hardships they faced in crossing the Chihuahua desert, before they break into a Michael Flatley-style dance. Afterward, a small group of Spanish women discuss their frustrations with the expedition. They claim the entire colonizing party is tired and that the soldiers search for a river no one can find. They are scared. Again, the audience learns few characters' names. As the discussion progresses, an unnamed woman approaches Doña Eufemia,[27] the sole female character with a name and Capitan Pérez Villagrá's alleged mistress. The unnamed woman asks Eufemia to "listen to us (the group of women). We need to talk to [the men]." A second woman echoes this view but a third passionately disagrees, stating, "We all came here willingly to improve our lives and secure our future. Our families in Spain hope to follow us here. We all agreed to lead the way ..." Some of the women on the stage begin to voice additional concerns: "We have run out of medicine!" "We have run out of everything." The third

64   *San Elizario's First Thanksgiving*

woman continues, "We have to reach [northern New Mexico] ... It is our destiny."[28]

The play's staging then shifts the audience's focus to Oñate who yells at a corporal: "If we stop, these peasants will never move again and we shall perish. ¡Vamonos! [Let's go!]. I, Don Juan, have promised us a river and by God, we'll find one." He then asks the corporal for news from a scouting party sent ahead looking for a river. Before the corporal can answer, two women approach Oñate. One woman asks if Oñate will let the group rest because they are tired: "It's rained on us for seven days and we have no water." He angrily orders the woman to "Stop your complaining." Adding, "We need to hear your prayers, woman, not your problems." As the scene ends, the narrator comments: "Holding high the red and gold banner of Spain and brandishing the cross and sword, one of the richest and most important men in Spain [sic], Don Juan de Oñate, received permission to claim this land for his king."

After a short pause in the action, Oñate reappears on horseback, reading a proclamation, *La Toma*:

> In the name of the most holy trinity, be it known that I, Don Juan de Oñate, governor, captain general, and *adelantado* of *Nuevo México*, desire to take possession of the land on this, the 30th day of April, in the year 1598. Therefore, in the name of the most Christian of kings, Don Felipe ... I take possession of this land, once, twice, thrice, as many times as I can and must ... for the lands of the said *Río del Norte* without exception ...

Oñate then dances to a flamenco style song with three women as the narrator suggests, "It was a new era, a new vision, a new world. And these men [sic] risked their lives and the fortunes of their kingdoms for the promise of a fuller, richer life." As the dance ends, a soldier informs Oñate that a river has been found. At this news, Captain Gaspar Pérez de Villagrá,[29] who documented the journey in a book-length poem, proclaims, "I can now conclude this chapter in my book on a happier note!" Oñate declares "a day of rest and thanksgiving, the very first in the Americas—well deserved by all ... who have traveled so far to ... *El Paso del Norte* [the Pass of the North]—our new home!"

Then, Oñate and a young Indian woman dance together, as the narrator explains how Oñate "in the name of God and Spain claimed the Indians' land. Native wealth became Spanish wealth and in exchange the Indian god became the Spanish god." At the back of the stage, the indigenous women from the opening dance bow before a cross and exit the play. After the dance, Oñate speaks to a friar, noting that the place where they rested (contemporary San Elizario) should be "a resting place for travelers coming up the *Camino Real* from Mexico." As the play ends, the Spaniards exit on horseback with the Indians walking behind them. The narrator closes the play: "And so, the Indians and the Spanish got together to celebrate the First

Thanksgiving in the Americas ... 400 years ago, and today we proudly reenact that encounter." As the actors exited the area, we observed several attendees leaving the plaza.

The First Thanksgiving reimagined: the 2016 high school reenactment

The 2016 Montwood High School-produced (MHS) reenactment, led by Joe Estala, presented a similar account of Oñate's arrival. The MHS play is almost exclusively sung; the narrator speaks but sings as part of the cast. The high school's involvement is important because its actors require parental permission and the project likely requires district-level administrative clearance. MHS parents who approved their children's participation are either unaware of or unconcerned about Juan de Oñate's violent legacy. The adolescents' involvement is troubling and one area school disctrict's continued support reinforces the area's Eurocentric fantasy heritage.[30] The story line and its focus are almost identical to the earlier EPCC reenactment (see below).

A female narrator, in period Spanish costume, begins the MHS play by introducing Spaniard Isador Dijaga, a colonizer who holds a notebook and quill in hand throughout the play. The events of 1598 are told from his perspective. Who this possibly fictional character is and why he guides the play is not explained. We found no information related to this name or anything similar in the academic literature. During the introduction, the narrator suggests that "Some historians say the Spanish conquistadores were just as interested in winning converts to Christianity as they were in conquering land and searching for gold and silver."

From this point, Oñate leads a Spanish man, four Spanish women, and the narrator in singing: "As we play, we may plant a cross in the name of the good king of Spain. All we ask is shelter ... may the good Lord keep us." The narrator elaborates on the Spaniards' challenges crossing the Chihuahua desert as the play moves onto the next scene, which depicts two Spanish women leaning on each other, until one finally falls. The rest of the colonizing group, also exhausted, follows them. Doña Eufemia Peñalosa, a "beautiful" and "unsung hero" encourages the group to continue their trek, claiming that "[a]lmighty God would not abandon such brave and noble people." She then asks the Spanish deity for help via a song that refers to the colonizers as "your [God's] children." The cast sits on the floor before Doña Eufemia as she sings. Immediately after the song, the sound of rain comes across the PA system and the Spaniards rejoice at the sudden rain.

In the next scene, two Indians talk amongst themselves. Regrettably, external noise, the actors' low voices, and poor amplification made their comments inaudible. As the two Indians exit the stage, the Spaniards depict a long journey by walking in large, oblong circles along the church's front area. Just then, a soldier returns to the colonizing party with news that a river has been found. The narrator informs viewers that at that this point Oñate claimed the land for Spain. Oñate sends a group of soldiers to find a place to ford the river and the scouts encounter a group of four Indians. The Indians sing a song that simultaneously appears to be an indigenous language and stereotypic "Indian speak" from a Hollywood western. The Indians then shake the Spaniards' hands and return with them to the colonizer's campsite. At this point, an Indian woman brings a large bowl of fruit to a Spanish woman, followed by another Indian woman who brings a gourd to the Spaniards. Two Spanish women accept the gifts and a Spanish soldier gives thanks. Once the gifts are accepted Oñate questions his ability to lead. He sings "it was my dream [to colonize] a new land, adding ... on this road I will stand," referencing the *Camino Real*. The end of the song leads a Spanish couple to engage in a dance routine where the man acts as a bullfighter and the woman as the bull, while the other actors shout, "Ole!"

After the bullfight dance, the narrator claims the Spaniards held a mass of thanks for their successful crossing of the Chihuahua desert. Oñate then claims the San Elizario region for Spain by singing *La Toma*. The narrator explains that the expedition went on to colonize other lands—"but it all began in El Paso." The cast of Indians and Spaniards then conclude the play by singing a song that says: "and as we face tomorrow, there'll be tons of sorrow [nevertheless] on this rock we will stand." The Spaniards and Indians then walk offstage in pairs.

After the performance, Estala addressed the audience and estimated attendance at 200, claiming "We should have the entire city of El Paso backing this event," noting, "We're [he and his students] here to tell you a story and to

Figure 4 The 2016 First Thanksgiving cast outside the San Elizario Chapel. Credit: Leonel Monroy

entertain you." He then asked attendees for a round of applause for his students. EPMTA Board Member Suki Ramos then delivered a brief message:

> [W]e are all one people, the human race [sic] ... Do not let history die here, today ... promote the mission trail association ... When you hear us go [mimics Indian cry from an old Hollywood film] or 'Ajua!' you know where we come from.

She then invited EPMTA President George Córdova to present the San Elizario chapel with a $1,712.50 donation from funds raised through a Texas Department of Transportation license plates charity program. No one from the El Paso Catholic Diocese was in attendance. However, the chapel's priest happened to be outside talking with parishioners. With no previous notice, he accepted a poster-sized ceremonial check after concluding his conversation. The priest thanked Córdova for the donation and noted his recent arrival to the area, promising to learn more about local history. No one announced the end of the play. The actors and their teacher posed for group photos in front of the chapel entry. The audience stood, confused. After a few minutes, as at the end of the 2016 play, the plaza was empty.

The First Thanksgiving and Eurocentric fantasies on the border

The EPCC First Thanksgiving reenactments celebrate the colonial past from a heavily Eurocentric perspective. As we have argued, fantasy heritage is replete with rhetorical elements sympathetic to the colonizers while downplaying the plight of the indigenous. Fantasy heritage framing and dialogue operate to represent "heroic" Spaniards via a storyline that all but ignores the indigenous peoples of West Texas as we will show below.

Fantasy heritage requires a Christ-like hero driven by noble goals and Juan de Oñate's persona fulfills this requirement. His representation frames the Spanish colonial experience in sympathetic terms and neutralizes any oppositional framing through the First Thanksgiving's dialogue and framing of the past. To support this contention, we relied on a semiotic analysis[31] to create a framework for the interpretation of images as a series of interrelated social constructs. Each character in the play and the elements surrounding the event are related and collectively offer attendees a way to understand the past. However, sociologist Orrin E. Klapp cautions that heroes are "the poetical creations of dramatists, story-tellers, and writers."[32] The First Thanksgiving storyline, the product of a performing arts professional and a local theater professor as story-tellers, illustrates this point.[33] The play ignores most, if not all, of Oñate's shortcomings, focusing on dramatic elements aimed at engaging the audience.

In truth, Juan de Oñate's life ended in failure. His desire to colonize New Mexico led to his financial ruin, made him a criminal, and turned him into a social pariah.[34] The play omits these important historical details and completely misrepresents others. For example, the narrator claims Oñate was one

68 *San Elizario's First Thanksgiving*

of the richest and most powerful men in Spain, when Oñate was actually born in or close to Zacatecas. His wealth was acquired using Indian slaves to work silver mines in and around Zacatecas—not Spain.[35] Still the image created in the play is one of Oñate as a powerful, successful, and entrepreneurial commandant. Oñate is converted from a barbarous criminal and weak leader into the proverbial American "self-made man."

The First Thanksgiving dialogue as historical guide

Many who attend the First Thanksgiving or who learn about the event via local media receive and may internalize an incomplete understanding of the Spanish colonial past. The play's characters are a key element to this fantastical retelling of events. While attendees to the reenactment may believe they are seeing the past brought to life, the characters are simple representations that advance the fantasy of noble Spaniards settling an area. These representations are such that the play's authors gave names to only a few characters. No Indian is addressed by name and only three Spaniards are named: Juan de Oñate, Gaspar Pérez de Villagrá, and Doña Eufemia.

The Indians frame the Spaniards as a powerful military force and as the audience later learns in the play, they are led by Oñate. The chieftains fear the Spaniards' military superiority and reputation for cruelty and treachery. The Chief, however, represents the voice of experience, leading his people from violence. He cautions his sons to ignore hearsay. Instead, the Chief wants to pursue a peaceful strategy because the Spaniards bring technology. The Chief's attitude also recognizes the Spaniards' military force. The tribe "cannot overtake them by force." In this way, Oñate becomes a powerful leader prior to his taking the stage.

The MHS play represents the Spaniards similarly but links them more closely to religion. The play's songs feature multiple references to God and to the Spanish destiny to colonize the region. For example, Oñate sings about his uncertainty to lead and his faith, referring to religion as "on this rock I will stand." A song performed by Doña Eufemia proclaims that God will not abandon his children. Consistent with fantasy heritage this framing softens the Spaniards' image. The Church's sanction of colonialism and its violence is ignored. The Spaniards are portrayed as people of God. The main character, Dijaga, carries a journal and quill throughout much of the play, signifying the Spaniards' literacy and alleged superior knowledge. The Indians appear much later in the MHS reenactment than in the EPCC version. Strong winds and a weak PA system precluded our ability to analyze the lyrics to the one song where the Indians express themselves. The Indians' song's lyrics sounded somewhere between a Native language and Hollywoodesque "Indian" intonations, reducing an entire civilization to pop culture caricatures. After the song, the Indians shake hands with the Spaniards, any reference to conflict between the two groups is avoided. The stereotype of the passive Indian is represented when the Indian women

San Elizario's First Thanksgiving 69

arrive at the Spanish camp bearing gifts of food. As the play ends, the Spaniards and Indians walk side-by-side down steps outside the chapel and off the stage area. In truth, the Spanish colonial experiment was marked by violence and forced religious conversion.[36] Yet, the MHS narrator claims "some historians" believe the Spaniards were more interested in proselytizing than land, gold, or silver. We found no academic historians who espouse such views and are confident few, if any, contemporary historians would share such naïve views. Fantasy heritage gains support by merely making preposterous claims, as seen here. It is worrisome that some attendees may view this misinformation as accurate and then share it with others.

The female characters also help the audience see Oñate in heroic terms. Although they talk amongst themselves about being tired and running out of supplies, this conversation omits any men. When a woman approaches him in the 2006 reenactment saying, "It's rained on us for seven days and we have no water," Oñate appears to be both an unsympathetically forceful leader and a man of faith. He responds that the convoy needs to hear "your prayers ... not your problems." Here, the 2006 play shows the audience an arrogant leader with the conviction to place his faith in the Judeo-Christian god. Oñate "knows" God will provide what the colonists need if they keep moving. He tells the corporal that allowing "these peasants" (i.e., the colonists) to stop will lead to the convoy's inability to keep moving. He also predicts that stopping will lead to the Spaniards' deaths. Oñate appears a capable, if strict leader who leads his people. He gets his group to the Promised Land and unlike Moses, Oñate survives the trip. However, Hoig contends that Oñate was perceived as a poor leader as well as easily agitated.[37] Still, the women's concerns change when one of them approaches Oñate. The woman makes mention only of rain and a lack of water. Granted, water is vital to survival but she makes no mention of the colonizers' many other problems. Water's symbolic value is tied to religion, for example, within the practice of baptism or in biblical verses that center on forgiveness or renewal. Although the play fails to directly address the Moses parallel, Oñate is imbued with heroic characteristics that are inspired by the Judeo-Christian deity. His sense of purpose, though morally flawed, drives him as did Moses' quest to free his people. He is both loyal Spanish subject and pious religious pilgrim.

When Oñate takes possession of the land, he invokes "the most holy trinity" and "the most Christian of kings, Don Felipe." Strengthening this element is the narrator's comment that "[I]n the name of God and Spain," Oñate "claimed the Indians' land." Spanish imperialism is transformed into a noble act. The Spaniards are represented not as stealing, so much as claiming. Plus, the indigenous are given a god in exchange for their wealth. Oñate heroically leads his people along the "Camino Real" without supplies but, guided by God (the one given to the Indians), he finds water and a fertile locale for rest.

The Spaniards will use this area as a rest stop for future travelers. No concern is expressed that the territory is inhabited by Indians. The fantasy

70 *San Elizario's First Thanksgiving*

element of settlement, as opposed to conquering, is present in Oñate's suggestion to the friar in the 2006 reenactment that the San Elizario region will make a good place for travelers to rest. At another point, a friar jokes about making "communion wine" in the fertile soil near the river. No one mentions the Natives or questions the Spaniards' right to settle on indigenous territory. This framing overlaps with the fantasy heritage tendency to ignore complexities unique to a particular era or period. The play indirectly alludes to the imposition of a new social order. The Indians kneel before a cross as they exit the stage at the play's conclusion, signaling their conversion to Catholicism and the imposition of a new social order.

The 2016 MHS play allows for Indian/Spanish interactions but the indigenous are merely simple people bearing gifts. The Indians' roles require almost no dialogue and their interaction with Spanish characters is brief, non-verbal, and subservient. After he dances with the three women and is told the river was found, Oñate proclaims a day of thanks, "the very first" in the Americas. The notion that this is the first thanksgiving is troubling. Spectators are asked to believe no indigenous tribes ever held a similar ceremony. People have inhabited the Americas for thousands of years, if not millennia. To suggest that only Europeans have the mental acumen to show gratitude is, at best, presumptive. We find it morally offensive to espouse such pretence.

Thus, we can see the First Thanksgiving reenactments promote an incomplete and romanticized view of the past. As Jeff White explains: "British romantics ... valorize[d] the English provincial worker as the essential English character ... Rousseau extended this sentimentalism to non-Western cultures ... by referring to the 'Noble Savage,'... by modernization."[38] According to White, these Romantic-era ideals combine well with contemporary commercial pursuits. For example, Matthew Arnold saw culture as a concept that "... seeks to do away with classes; to make the best that has been thought and known in the world current everywhere."[39] White's point ties into the Spanish fantasy in the post-World War II period where best thoughts are still deemed to be exclusively European.[40] This tendency is well-established in the academic literature, public memory, and in contemporary heritage tourism, with one caveat. Heritage tourism has expanded the British character into a European character. When community leaders unite to support fantasy heritage across multiple sectors, tourists will likely see it as legitimate, while critics may find it erroneous and off-putting. Either way, fantasy heritage benefits from a network of practices that preserve the status quo. As we noted in our earlier work, critics, at least in far West Texas, are often ignored or ridiculed by local media and elites.[41]

The implications of a fantasy past: fantasy heritage and identity politics

The First Thanksgiving performance has taken on a mythic quality in the El Paso area, even with multiple entities producing different reenactments. The Oñate myth permeates much of this region and New Mexico. In economic terms, the myth has deep-rooted support from those who stand to benefit

San Elizario's First Thanksgiving 71

from the growing tourism industry in far West Texas. The event also has strong effects on the cultural representation of the area in terms of identity politics. The colonial legacy continues to affect Southwest society. A small number of Hispanics are protected by the Spanish fantasy but Whites continue to enjoy even greater social status locally and throughout the United States.[42] Heritage is one key area in the preservation of White privilege and in the stereotyping of all non-White groups as culturally or intellectually deficient.[43]

Returning to our preliminary questions, how does the First Thanksgiving's past reflect fantasy heritage? How does the reenactment represent Spaniards, Spanish women, and Indians to legitimate the colonial experiment? As noted above, West Texas' civic leaders have an interest in promoting the Spanish conquest as a tourism endeavor. Tourist dollars have long been a desire for the community. Again, in the 1910s, El Paso Mayor, and later Ku Klux Klansman,[44] Thomas Lea introduced the idea of celebrating the area's colonial past, and Klansman sculptor Gutzon Borglum promoted the same idea during the 1930s. While the plan did not materialize, Oñate's legend continued. The 1940s saw artist Thomas Lea promote Oñate's legacy in union with the El Paso Electric Company. During the 1950s, El Paso community leaders and the local media promoted the Spanish fantasy through various endeavors. The idea was revived in the late 1980s by sculptor John Houser, who was commissioned by the El Paso city council to create statues of historically important personalities as part of the XII Travelers of the Southwest Memorial. The list of proposed statues has changed over the last three decades but not a single Mexican American has ever been included among the Travelers. Sheldon Hall's efforts to bring awareness of the area's past led to national publicity via an El Paso-Plymouth "Who was first?" debate. Texas politicians responded by making the First Thanksgiving a state holiday, unconcerned for the First Thanksgiving's omission of the indigenous and mestizo peoples. No El Paso community leader has seriously considered that omitting a Mexican American from a twelve-piece project in a community that is eighty-two percent Mexican American is reprehensible. Indian and Mexican American community leaders' voices are notably absent from these pro-memorial efforts. Maintaining the old Eurocentric tourism events will see El Paso leaders continue to ignore the large number of Mexicans who either visit or pass through El Paso throughout the year. Local power brokers do not consider the Indian and Mexican American communities sufficiently important to consider likely because many Indians and Mexican Americans view the colonial era differently than those who support the Spanish colonial fantasy. Since at least the 1950s, and into the present, the local media, particularly newsprint outlets, have continued to support the Spanish fantasy as a tourism ploy.

A majority of those committed to the Oñate fantasy have been White and few supporters show any concern for the plight of the indigenous or mestizos. Indians

72   *San Elizario's First Thanksgiving*

and Mexican Americans have very limited cultural, economic, or political influence in the region. As such, their views have been largely ignored. This assertion is substantiated when one considers the claims made by El Paso Independent School District officials that the First Thanksgiving teaches students "who they are,"[45] Spanish descendants in the minds of many area leaders. The First Thanksgiving as a vehicle for learning one's identity excises the importance of mestizaje, a central element of border identity. Traditionally, mestizaje defines the Mexican cultural hybridity first popularized by José Vasconcelos in his classic essay, *La Raza Cosmica*. [46] Early 20th century social thought saw racial purity as superior to racial hybridity.[47] In the early part of the 20th Century, Brazil and Venezuela went so far as to create political policies to breed out the Black, Indian, and mestizo characteristics of its people.[48] Yet, Vasconcelos argued that racial mixing resulted in a bronze race that was superior to all others in the same way a metal alloy is superior to the two pure elements used to create it. In fact, the Mexican population on both sides of the US-Mexico border is the result of the racial mixing that took place after the Spaniards conquered Mexico in 1521. Mestizaje also reflects multiple social experiences—racial, economic, and legal injustice, for example. In contrast, fantasy heritage forms a subjectivity that shames Mexican identity. Ignoring cultural, ethnic, and historical complexity creates confusion in terms of identity issues for those of Indian and Spanish mixed ancestry.[49]

The affective impact of historical reenactments vis-à-vis the artifacts used in them also influences people to think they are in, or are witnessing the past.[50] The danger here is that Disneyfied historical representations like the First Thanksgiving are thus able to create strong and historically inaccurate, hegemonic understandings for their actors.[51] It is logical to assume a similar phenomenon also exists for locals who are constantly exposed to the Spanish myth, and to tourists as well.

The First Thanksgiving celebrates the Spanish conquest as a praiseworthy effort via manifested and veiled latent forms of framing to make its case. The Indian men in the first dance routine wear skirts and the Indian women carry tall ornaments on their heads. The skirts are emasculating, even if they are period-correct, and we are not convinced they are. The Spaniards' costumes appear more masculine since they wear armor and pants. The women's head ornaments suggest a lack of sophistication. Carrying large ornaments on one's head is physically challenging and makes one easy to target at a distance. The Spaniards do not use such forms of dress. The music reinforces the idea the Indians intellectually trail their European subjugators. The dance begins with indigenous drumming but ends as a Spanish-style number. The song's progression suggests the indigenous will "evolve" as they become assimilated into the colonizers' cultural framework. The song's structure hints at assimilation rather than cultural hybridity. The indigenous will advance their culture only under Spanish tutelage. This view is central to Eurocentric conceptions of the colonial experiment, Whiteness is the supreme human form[52]

San Elizario's First Thanksgiving   73

and European forces simply sought to enlighten their colonial subjects. Oppression was a tool for the oppressed people's cultural benefit, according to this view.

In terms of gender, Oñate's interactions with Spanish and indigenous women reflects both the sexism of the colonial era and the manner in which fantasy heritage naturalizes such discrimination. Antonia Castañeda points out that in the early 18th Century, Spanish soldiers routinely raped and violated Amerindian women, despite criticisms from Spanish friars. She notes that Spanish behavior reflected the politically installed low value of indigenous women based on political actions rooted in conflict, subjugation, and the installation of European economic, political, and social structures over the Indians.[53] The Spanish men who appear in the play are hyper-masculine and unconcerned about the Indians as a potential military threat, much less as the rightful inhabitants of the region. The women's discussion reveals that many colonists are ill, tired, and forcibly driven by their leader—elements absent from the Spanish men's dialogues. While the women fear "The Natives do not want us here," such concerns are absent from the Spanish men's reality. Sexism is evident in Oñate's dismissal of the woman who asks for rest. He denies her appeals and asks for her prayers instead. The Indians have even less power. They are invisible to Oñate and his soldiers and are thus emasculated. They pose less a threat than the women in the play. At least the women can petition for rest, even if it the request is denied. A male God and King have sanctioned Oñate to bring a "new land" into the empire. Thus, he garners souls and territory through conquest. The Spanish women are able only to offer supportive prayers.

Masculinity also appears as a central theme via the narrator's erroneous description of Oñate as "one of the richest and most important men in Spain." In truth, Oñate was born in Zacatecas, Mexico[54] and was considered a criollo,[55] not a Spaniard. He married the great granddaughter of Aztec ruler Motechuzoma II, and their children were mestizos.[56] Yet, the First Thanksgiving provides an exclusively Eurocentric framing of events. This information about Oñate's life is absent and the play operates as a cultural binary, a story of two cultures coming together to praise a Judeo-Christian deity. The play focuses on Oñate as the Spaniards' visionary leader. Once the river is found, Oñate festively invites his fellow Spaniards to celebrate reaching their new home. He is vindicated. No mention is made of the indigenous' suffering under colonial rule. Oñate's slaughter of the Acoma Pueblo and his standing trial for multiple offenses, including what would today be considered crimes against humanity, is ignored. Instead, the 2006 reenactment's narrator tells the audience the Spaniards and Indians celebrated "the First Thanksgiving in the Americas ... 400 years ago," adding the event is now being "proudly reenact[ed]." As the play ends, the indigenous bow before a crucifix, their assimilation completed. The 2016 version ends with a nearly identical framing. The focus on masculinity is an important heritage tourism element in many fantasy contexts (see Case study 2.1).

Case study 2.1 How men become "real Alaskans"

Maureen Hogan and Timothy Pursell explored the link between nostalgia and rural masculinity in Alaska, being told by one man that an Alaskan man needed to: "(1) pee in the Yukon River, (2) shoot a grizzly, and (3) fuck [sic] an Eskimo" (p. 2). Hogan and Pursell note these criteria seek to dominate nature, including Alaska's indigenous people who are equated with wildlife. Hogan and Pursell explain that masculinity in a post-structuralist sense refers to "a set of social performances and practices ... [that] arise in various cultural, social, and geographic contexts and at different historical moments." Masculinity is fluid and in a continual stage of negotiation. While dominant forms of masculine behavior are seen as "common sense" by most people (Belsey, 1980, cited in Hogan and Pursell, 2008), men must define their masculinity as rural (e.g., farming, fishing, hunting) or urban (e.g., consumerist, cultural). Given the dominance of urban hegemony, men in rural contexts focus on physical strength and toughness, and having "mastery of high-tech farming machinery" (cited in Hogan and Pursell, 2008). Crucially, "Alaskan-ness" remains coded as being a "White male." Alaskan masculinity is partially linked to romanticized versions of the past (i.e., one that never existed). Alaskans "must buy the appearance of it to pacify [their] postmodern anxiety." Claims of Alaskan-ness preclude birth in the state but are tied to interactions with the Alaskan economy, climate, and/or landscape. The view is held by many presumably White Alaskans that they "are more connected to the land then other Americans [and the view is] endangered when not every Alaskan can be guaranteed access to the wilderness, wild fish, and game." This nostalgic link to landscape and nature (i.e., fantasy heritage) ignores the Native American peoples who have inhabited this region for far longer than Whites. In fact, Native Alaskan peoples claim they have always lived in the region and argue against the "myth" that their ancestors crossed the Bearing Strait. Yet, Whites use the Bearing Strait explanation to suggest that Whites and Natives are all regional pioneers.

To illustrate these dynamics, Hogan and Pursell analyze Pioneer [Amusement] Park, previously Alaskaland. They find the new name erases Native links to Alaska. Only one section, Native Village, acknowledges them and it is located at the farthest point in the park. Another section, Pioneer Park continues in a tradition where the park's focus on pioneers (e.g., "gold miners, entrepreneurs, and scoundrels") suggests that "real" Alaskan men should think of themselves in masculine terms. Hogan and Pursell note that "in nostalgia re-creations, [such as] the gold rush (as a conflation of several events into one trope) ... plucky male gold panners become the state's upright citizens." They add that these ideals are embodied in literary texts readily available at Alaska bookstores, for example, Jack London's *The Call of the Wild*, which suggests that to rediscover their masculinity men must tame nature. Another common trope relates to dangers in the wild. Susan Kollin (2001, cited in Hogan and Pursell, 2008) argues that "psychologically,

Americans ... need to know that there is a place in the United States where it is impossible to be alienated from nature." Thus Alaska as a place where men from the rest of the nation can go to prove their manhood. Alaska frees men to "freely act on sexual instincts, and escape the industrial metropolis ... [it] is a place free from church tyranny where a man could explore alternative modes of morality." This framing is grounded in male privilege and even White women's roles are defined via their relationship to men, whose identity needs precede all others'.

Discussion questions

1. Susan Kollins' (2001) analysis of Alaska as the "last frontier" leads Hogan and Pursell to note:

   if we Americans fail to see that Alaska is not the nature state of the nostalgic imagination, we will misrecognize and misunderstand the social, cultural, and political nature of the environmental problems Alaska has and thus buy into misguided solutions (cited in Hogan and Pursell, 2008).

   How do you think this analysis relates to the consequences or effects fantasy heritage may have on locations? Do you see parallels between Kollins's comment and the perceptions one may have of other places, for example, Paris, France as the "city of lights" or Los Angeles as the "entertainment capital of the world"?
2. Discuss the ways your hometown is typically framed in popular culture and how such framing influences life in that community. What effect, if any, do you believe this framing has on masculinity in your hometown? What about femininity? Sexual identity? Social class? Ethnicity?

   Source: Hogan, Maureen P., & Pursell, Timothy. (October 1, 2008). The "real Alaskan": Nostalgia and rural masculinity in the "last frontier." *Men and Masculinities*, 1–23.

Interestingly, there is no scene in the First Thanksgiving where the Spaniards and Indians actually share a meal; perhaps such an interaction would suggest equal social standing. Overall, the costumes, music, dance routines, and dialogue reposition the Indians as *foreigners in their native land*, to borrow from historian David J. Weber.[57] Creating a Eurocentric hegemony is a key fantasy heritage element and the First Thanksgiving, striving to please tourists as opposed to visitors, retains this feature to sell a Spanish fantasy. The Indians become the Other and are unable to fight off the European interlopers. They choose peace, hoping Spanish technology will help them improve their lives. Europeans being posited as purveyors of technological innovations is a common fantasy heritage theme that assimilates non-European progress into a marketable, Eurocentric myth. Other than "hard metal shields" and horses, no examples are offered of Spanish technologies. To be sure, the Spaniards did bring useful technology, but they also imposed an economic system that enslaved the indigenous and exploited their land's natural resources.[58]

76 *San Elizario's First Thanksgiving*

The Chief's comment that "each time a story gets told it gets further separated from the truth" is important. It suggests that even academic accounts of colonial violence are exaggerated, at least in the mind of Oñate sympathizers. For example, historian John L. Kessell reports finding only one document referencing the chopping off of Indian men's feet after the battle of Acoma and argues that the paucity of documents "raises doubts" the Spanish "followed through [with the sentence]."[59] Oral cultures do not document their past in written form. More importantly, the historical record shows Oñate's brutality and poor leadership led to a formal trial where he was found guilty of numerous crimes, including the Acoma tragedy.[60] Oñate's cruelty against the Acoma, his own soldiers, colonists, and soldiers was recognized by Spanish institutions and led to his being barred from New Mexico for the rest of his life. These results suggest that those who are in doubt of Oñate's actions should reconsider their interpretation.

The First Thanksgiving, colonization, and its aftermath

Both First Thanksgivings suggest the Indians were weak, willingly accepted Christianity, and lived in peace with the Spaniards. Oñate sympathizers contend the indigenous benefitted from this arrangement and minimized the events at Acoma. One must consider how the First Thanksgiving fantasy creates these perceptions. If the Indians were militarily weaker than the Spaniards, it is likely because Europeans have a conflictive past. Their superior weaponry reflects their violent past and conflictive orientation. The Spanish generation of 1492 had just completed the reconquest of the Iberian Peninsula. By driving out Islamic people who had occupied southern Spain from the 9th Century, as well as Jews through the Inquisition, the Catholic kingdom of Isabella and Ferdinand was secured. Those who participated in the struggle not only embraced warfare but also the elimination of non-Catholics. These violent perspectives towards conquest were soon brought to the Americas. For example, during the Age of Discovery, "much of Europe … was the scene of fratricidal wars, Church-sponsored violence, and peasant rebellions."[61] Yet, fantasy heritage frames this reality as reflective of a superior European intellect. The Indians are shamed for their supposedly feeble minds. The Indians' peaceful outlook was such an anomaly to the Spaniards that they mistook the name Manso to mean meek.[62]

The First Thanksgiving's use of fantasy heritage also suggests the Indians voluntarily abandoned their religious orientations, adopting Catholicism out of a sense of its evident righteousness. Such framing erases the violence associated with the forced religious conversion the Spaniards imposed upon the Indians throughout the Americas. As Kathleen Deagan reminds us, "Spain's imperial expansion into the 16th-Century Americas was simultaneously an invasion, a colonization effort, a social experiment, a religious crusade, and a highly structured enterprise."[63] Those indigenous peoples and mestizos who adapted to their marginalization and accepted the Spanish god as their own

San Elizario's First Thanksgiving 77

became "good" Indians. Those Indians and mestizos who defied the Spaniards' brutal tactics became "bad" Indians and faced extreme censure, including death. Spanish cruelty was viewed by the British of the era as having been a key obstacle to more successful Indian conversions to Christianity. This view was an effect of the Black Legend, according to Gregory Murray.[64]

Identity labels and debates in the Southwest

The current state of identity politics in the Southwest are reflective of the continuing conflict between those who sympathize with the Spanish colonial experiment and those who oppose such Eurocentric fantasies. How people navigate their relationship with these competing social ideologies reflects their sociopolitical orientation. Unsurprisingly, sociologist Pablo Vila finds that social identities in the El Paso/Ciudad Juárez area can be categorized along socioeconomic and ethnic lines.[65] Those with power in the community, as well as most of the local middle-class, prefer to frame the area's Spanish-speakers as Hispanic. This is not surprising since the term Hispanic refers to assimilated, middle-class Spanish-speakers who deny or downplay their indigenous roots.[66] We have also noted that many of our students claim a Hispanic identity because it is the term they have been given since entering grade school. It is also very much a mindset that is promoted in the schools and on countless government forms and official documents. The Hispanic social category is analogous to the "good Indians" addressed above.

Spanish or Hispanic framing makes El Paso "safe" for any tourists who may potentially hold negative views on Mexican/Americans. Yet, the Spanish and Hispanic labels have strong cultural repercussions for those sensitive to issues of social justice, since they imply an exclusively European background for a mixed-race population. The Hispanic label implies a White identity and a light skin tone. Fair skin in Latin cultures often translates to greater economic opportunity and better social standing.[67] Thus, assimilation becomes for some a strategy through which to seek out greater social acceptance. For others, the Spanish/Hispanic frame is a lasting remnant of the colonial era. The mestizo descendants of those who resisted Spanish colonialism remain a symbol of defiance and are viewed with suspicion or contempt. Many of this defiant progeny self-identify as Chicano, Mexican, or Mexican American rather than a more socially acceptable identity.[68] The colonial focus on skin tone and degrees of assimilation permeate the region.

Our own research suggests that six labels are commonly used in the academic literature to reference to the Spanish-speaking people of the Southwest: (1) Chicana/o, (2) Hispanic, (3) Latina/o, (4) Mexican, (5) Mexican American, and (6) Spanish.[69] The extant academic literature suggests a Chicana/o is a politically aware and socially active American of Mexican descent concerned with the promotion of social justice. Hispanic refers to assimilated, middle-class Americans of Mexican (or other Latin) descent who are content with the status quo

78 *San Elizario's First Thanksgiving*

and who downplay the indigenous aspects of their culture. Latina/o is a term used in an effort to unite people in the US of Spanish- and Portuguese-speaking cultural backgrounds. Mexican refers to a Mexican national, a citizen of Mexico. Mexican Americans are proud of their indigenous/mestizo background, less socially activist than Chicanas/os, but more critical of the status quo than Hispanics. Spanish refers to those individuals who profess a completely Spanish cultural background, denying any indigenous or mestizo "blood." While Hispanic and Mexican American are the mostly used common labels, the plethora of available labels demonstrates the volatile cultural context that has shaped the largest ethnic population in the Southwest (and the largest ethnic minority category in the US). Heritage tourism efforts to homogenize these categories into a safe and marketable Spanish fantasy are thus problematic. A majority of the region's people identify with their Mexican roots, while tourism business entities insist that the people of the Southwest are, indeed, Spanish.

The First Thanksgiving fantasy suggests Spanish-speakers in West Texas are Spanish. Few in the city self-identify as Spanish. However, many have been socialized to self-identify as Hispanic first, and as Mexican or Mexican American second.[70] Those who identify as Spanish in El Paso are often transplants from New Mexico or highly assimilated Mexican-origin people who likely use the label to identify with the dominant group.[71] These individuals are often ashamed of their mestizo roots and believe social acceptance and upward economic mobility are tied to the fantasy heritage. Here, we again see Teresa Córdova's concept of the "confusion of the colonized" in full effect.[72] Concerned with profits and unwilling to adopt a more contemporary social view, First Thanksgiving organizers in San Elizario present a simple version of the past for tourist consumption. They produce an annual fantasy heritage event analogous to a Disney or Warner Brothers cartoon. However, their audience varies widely in age and the tourism events do briefly imply some of the violence that characterized the region's earlier periods. This and related fantasy heritage events, monuments, and places may influence more locals to identify as Hispanic or Spanish.

Yet, those who adopt the Spanish label will also likely encounter strong cultural repercussions. Why are their ancestors' actions so vilified by other non-Spanish Latino identities? Why do people fail to see their ancestors as positive historical figures who overcame great odds to bring Hispanic culture to the region? Without a thorough and complex understanding of the past, such individuals may grow frustrated and misinterpret critics' arguments as racist attacks. John J. Valadez and Cristina Ibarra's documentary *The Last Conquistador*[73] explores how Chicano/Mexican American, Indian, and Spanish identities clashed in El Paso and New Mexico when the world's tallest equestrian statue—thirty-six feet tall—was installed at the El Paso International Airport, highlighting many of these tensions in action.

Those of Mexican origin who benefit from the status quo tend to adopt either the Hispanic or Spanish label. It appears as though sociocultural and economic inclusion is more important to them than acknowledging their

San Elizario's First Thanksgiving 79

mestizo heritage. Hispanics and Spanish people in the region tend to support a Eurocentric framing of familial, personal, and regional history, even if most of them are mestizos.[74] However, this label and its Eurocentric ideals are vital to people of Mexican origin who wish to associate with the Whites who continue to hold a disproportionately large amount of economic and political power in the region. More importantly, the adoption of Spanish and Hispanic ethnic labels furthers the racist attitudes many people hold against Chicanos, Mexicans, and/or Mexican Americans, ethnic labels that reflect varying degrees of cultural hybridity and social activism.[75] The Spanish fantasy heritage supports a Eurocentric view of self and of Southwest history where Europeans were benevolent entrants to the sparsely populated region, establishing a "civil" society.

The First Thanksgiving encourages attendees to see the Native and the Spanish culture in very specific ways. The storyline discourages readings of history that challenge the fantasy heritage. Tourists and visitors alike are encouraged to see Europeans as naturally superior to the Indians. The implication is that mestizos should identify with the European aspects of their culture. The First Thanksgiving play suggests that (1) colonial era violence was minimal, if not entirely hearsay; (2) the Spaniards ushered an era of innovation that benefitted the Indians; (3) Indians, regardless of sex, and Spanish women, are weak; and (4) Juan de Oñate was a powerful and wealthy Spaniard who, driven by God, settled the region. The implications of this fantasy are troubling.

Tourists will likely share what they "learned" with family, friends, and colleagues. Locals may internalize the information, believing it to be an accurate account of the area's past when such is not the case. The fantasy will potentially grow if event attendance improves. However, it appears that far more people from San Elizario and the surrounding area attend more organic and traditional community events, such as the annual church bazaars in the region. In the words of one San Elizario resident, "The community does not believe it has a place in the First Thanksgiving because it is controlled by a few and produced for tourists."[76] This situation suggests that the El Paso Mission Trail Association and other promoters may be failing to reach locals or is perceived as out of touch with the San Elizario community. It is also possible that the event means little to local residents. Annual area church bazaars at the Presidio Chapel in San Elizario and at nearby San Lorenzo Catholic Church typically draw thousands of people over their respective three-day weekend runs. The San Lorenzo parish celebrated its 100th anniversary in Clint, Texas, a small community three miles east of San Elizario, in 2014. The authors had to wait in line for ten minutes simply to enter the churchyard that houses the bazaar. It was filled with a few hundred people. In contrast, they have never faced any delays entering the San Elizario plaza to witness the First Thanksgiving. Both the event in the Presidio Chapel and San Lorenzo Church are grounded at the community-level.

80 *San Elizario's First Thanksgiving*

Business interests brought the First Thanksgiving to San Elizario; the bazaar is a longstanding religious community generated event. Even if monuments and other initiatives continue to promote the failed Spaniard, attention to the First Thanksgiving has remained miniscule in the El Paso region. San Elizario remains the only city in the area that has a yearly First Thanksgiving reenactment. The event's fantasy inspired tradition and other efforts to make the Lower Valley region appealing to tourists have been largely ineffective. For example, former city council representative Eddie Holguin, Jr. referred to the Lower Valley as the Mission Valley throughout his time as a city representative (2005–2014). In an economic summit during his initial term, the city council and mayor formally adopted Mission Valley as the name of what had traditionally been, and largely continues to be, called the Lower Valley. Holguin's replacement and current city council representative Claudia Ordaz also refers to the area as the Mission Valley. El Paso county commissioner Vincent Pérez refers to District 3 as the Mission Valley. Yet, one of the authors is a lifelong Lower Valley resident and has yet to hear its residents using the Mission Valley name.

The Mission Valley label speaks to the fantasy heritage of Spaniards bringing Catholicism to the area out of altruistic desire. In reality, the Spaniards used religion as part of their conquest strategy.[77] However, local politicians see the name as fostering a more positive image of one of El Paso's most economically depressed areas. This area needs new schools, roadways, healthcare professionals/facilities, and myriad other forms of investment before it needs a new name. Still, the desire by some to rename the region alludes to the important cultural repercussions the Spanish fantasy holds for West Texas tourism. We think it important to note that the idea of tourism for this depressed region as one of economic develop is also problematic. Tourism brings in few full-time jobs and even fewer that offer a healthy income.

The First Thanksgiving's fantasy heritage has important repercussions for local cultural identity. Given the play's framing, many will see the actual events as nothing more than a meal shared peaceably by two groups. They will misunderstand the community's origins and politics, assuming the area's conquest was one of mutual respect and benefit. It was not. Chicanos and other progressives will likely resent the festival, believing their history has again been woven into a sanitized version suitable for economic exploitation, a kind of cultural whoring. Sympathizers to the cause will continue to fail to understand why the opposition rejects these community-building efforts. As anthropologist Edward T. Hall reminds us, intercultural exchange requires respect, a desire to learn about others, interaction, and knowledge gathering.[78] How can intercultural communication occur when those with the socioeconomic wherewithal to impose their version of the community's past onto the entire region ignore the rest of the community? Community members have spoken against the First Thanksgiving and the Spanish fantasy for decades but West Texas elites continue to focus only on what they believe will draw tourists to the area—a simplistic retelling of the past.

The First Thanksgiving operates to create only one positive community identity for tourists, the Spanish identity. Returning to the play, we can see these machinations at work. The Spaniards first take the stage against a backdrop of military music similar to that used in Hollywood war epics. The use of Wagner's *Ride of the Valkyries* in *Apocalypse Now* (1979) is one example. Heroic music helps audiences identify the protagonist and antagonist. These aural cues are offset by the narrator's description of Spanish "invaders" who are here to claim the land. Certainly, the play's dialogue converts the invaders into peaceful settlers by the time the story ends. No discussion takes place to address the immoral act of stealing an entire people's territory. The Indian's framing suggests an Otherness to the tribe. The interrelationships between the play's music, narration, framing, script, and visual elements reinforce notions of Spanish grandeur.

Fantasy heritage naturalizes a Eurocentric view of history as it neutralizes critics. The emphasis on one perspective of the past creates a myth, a fantasy that spreads to school curricula, political symbolism, and other social contexts. Economic resources, mass media access, and social capital facilitate efforts to advance the Spanish fantasy to attract tourists. The support from local elites and a near-monopolistic local media point of view lend credibility as well. In short, fantasy heritage benefits from a network of practices that defends the status quo. Criticism of this framing is largely ignored by local leaders and is made to appear trivial by the local hegemony.[79] For twenty years, West Texans and New Mexicans opposed the *Equestrian/Juan de Oñate* statue that was finally installed at the El Paso International Airport. Several mayors and city councils ignored their pleas. The name change of the Oñate statue as the *Equestrian* and its installation at the airport angered many who support El Paso's fantasy heritage, believing the council and mayor had unnecessarily bowed to political pressure.

Conclusions

The First Thanksgiving allows one to explore the role of fantasy heritage in cultural identity struggles and as hegemonic devices in tourism. Within the reenactment, cultural issues suggest Europeans are naturally superior to the Indians. The Spaniards have better weapons and horses, a god who grants them victory, and they "settle" the region. The warring nature of the Spanish culture is absent from the play. Europe's war-filled and violent past allowed the Spaniards to develop advanced weapons. The Spaniards provide the Indians with a new deity that they appear to accept without question. The Chief's wisdom allows him to choose peace over his sons' pleas for war, reinforcing the concept of the peaceful or noble savage [sic]. As part of a local hegemonic system, the event fits well with the Juan de Oñate Trail, the *Equestrian* statue, and numerous other pro-Oñate tourism elements throughout the region.

82　*San Elizario's First Thanksgiving*

This hegemony converts a largely Mexican/American region into a Hispanic one. The dearth of knowledge of the area's racist past leads many individuals to adopt a nonchalant attitude toward ethnicity. Others desire to be more widely accepted by the White power structure that controls the city and develop an attitude of internalized oppression, seeking to be "anything but Mexican," as suggested by Rodolfo Acuña.[80] As such, they promote a safe identity that supports the status quo, unlike a Chicano, Mexican, or Mexican American identity. Any of these latter terms suggests a mestizo identity and, to varying degrees, an orientation toward social justice. These different sociopolitical orientations create a dynamic set of competing social identities in the border region.

Fantasy heritage complicates this discourse by making the Eurocentric appear normal. It erases colonial violence, naturalizes the status quo, and fosters a negative view against Mexican/Americans. El Paso's history is replete with racist policies used to subjugate its largely Mexican-origin population. However, the Spanish fantasy suggests El Paso has European roots (ignoring the Natives who predate 1598), moves quickly to remind us of John Wesley Hardin and other gunfighters, and then sells us an image of El Paso today as an interethnic paradise. In this way, fantasy heritage works to maintain the privileged status of Whites in the region.

With the exception of State Senator José Rodríguez, no area civic leader has acknowledged that the Indians and their communities predate the Spaniards' entry to the region by centuries. In our research, we found no evidence to suggest any influential El Pasoan has publicly acknowledged that the Indians likely held Thanksgiving celebrations here prior to the Spaniards. One need only participate in a sweat lodge ceremony to understand how Indigenous people regularly gave thanks for their good fortune, even after colonization. Where does one draw the line? The problem for tourism vendors is not who first celebrated thanks along the banks of the Río Grande but how to profit from the First Thanksgiving holiday. It is not our intention to sound like cynical academics. On the contrary, our point is that El Paso tourism must move from a fantasy heritage rubric to one that fits contemporary social mores. At a minimum, the First Thanksgiving (and related tourism attractions) needs to accommodate a broad spectrum of community views and peoples.

We offer three suggestions: First, address the brutality of the colonial experiment and make the First Thanksgiving a more complete educational experience. Second, solicit much more minority input to create an event that better reflects the community. Finally, acknowledge that the history of the Americas does not begin and end with Europeans. Providing background on local cultures prior to Spanish colonization would likely draw tourists, with or without the Spanish legacy. Only through such efforts will the city develop a positive image of its past. Historical complexity and greater ethnic inclusion would truly be something for which thanks could be given.

Notes

1 John Barnes, "The Struggle to Control the Past: Commemoration, Memory, and the Bear River Massacre of 1863," *The Public Historian* 30, no. 1 (2008): 81–104.

2 Andrew Leo Lovato, *Santa Fe Hispanic Culture: Preserving Identity in a Tourist Town* (Albuquerque, NM: University of New Mexico Press, 2006).

3 Greg Dickinson, Brian L. Ott, and Eric Aoki, "Memory and Myth at the Buffalo Bill Museum," *Western Journal of Communication* 69, no. 2 (2005): 85–108.

4 Frank Pérez and Carlos Ortega, "Mediated Debate, Historical Framing, and Public Art: The Juan de Oñate Controversy in El Paso," *Aztlán: A Journal of Chicano Studies* 33, no. 2 (2008): 121–140.

5 Mike Robinson and Melanie Smith, "Politics, Power and Play: The Shifting Contexts of Cultural Tourism," in *Cultural Tourism in a Changing World: Politics, Participation and (re)Presentation* (2006): 1–17, citing Rojek & Urry, (1997): 4.

6 Bob McKercher, Karin Weber, and Hilary Du Cros, "Rationalizing Inappropriate Behavior at Contested Sights," *Journal of Sustainable Tourism* 16, no. 4 (2008): 369–385.

7 Vanessa Agnew. "Introduction: What is Reenactment?" *Criticism* 46, no. 3, (Summer 2004), 327–339.

8 Shawn Lay, "Imperial Outpost on the Border: El Paso's Frontier Klan 100," in *The Invisible Empire in the West: Toward a New Historical Appraisal of the Ku Klux Klan in the 1920s*, Shawn Lay, ed. (Urbana, IL: University of Illinois Press, 2004); Shawn Lay, *War, Revolution, and the Ku Klux Klan: A Study of Intolerance in a Border City* (El Paso, TX: Texas Western Press, 1985). Lea's KKK power base is important because it shows the degree of influence and racism that permeated El Paso politics early in the history of the Twelve Travelers' concept. Contemporary critics continue to allege the project remains a discriminatory public arts project. This point is hard to deny when one considers El Paso is 82% Mexican American but no single standing or proposed Traveler statue represents a member of this ethnic category.

9 Howard Shaff and Audrey Karl Shaff, *Six Wars at a Time: The Life and Times of Gutzon Borglum, Sculptor of Mount Rushmore* (Sioux Falls, SD: Augustana College, Center for Western Studies, 1985); Albert Boime, "Patriarch Fixed in Stone: Gutzon Borglum's Mount Rushmore," *American Art* 5, no. 1 and 2 (1991): 143–167. Building on Shaff and Shaff, Boime reports that Borglum found the Klan's perspective "congenial" and that Borglum hoped to see the Klan "become a major political force that would put a member in the White House and influence national polity" (p. 165).

10 XII Travelers. XII Travelers Memorial of the Southwest, "A Monument to Principles" [newsletter], El Paso, TX, 1995.

11 The foundry's official address is a PO Box in Tesuque and its website states the foundry is "five miles north of Santa Fe" (http://www.shidoni.com/html/home.asp). Yet, 1508 Bishops Lodge Road and the surrounding landmarks on this street (i.e., North of the Border, Santa Fe Mountain Center, Tesuque Glass Works) list Santa Fe as their city. Nearby San Ysidro Church also lists Santa Fe as its city. See: http s://www.google.com/maps/@35.7546623,-105.9276994,16.5z.

12 Robert Moore, "El Paso's Planning to Rock Plymouth on Thanksgiving," *El Paso Times*, August 18, 1991, A1.

13 David Bennett, "Wind, Pig, Media Were Stars of Thanksgiving," *El Paso Herald-Post*, April 29, 1991, B1.

14 The Lower Valley is a large, predominantly Mexican American working-class/ lower middle-class district in Southeast El Paso. Due in large part to Hall's efforts, the city has tried for over a decade to get locals to refer to this zone as the Mission Valley. The name was officially changed to Mission Valley circa 2005. An El Paso Police Department substation is called the Mission Valley Regional Command and

84 *San Elizario's First Thanksgiving*

the El Paso Community College System has a Mission Valley campus. Wikipedia entries for both El Paso (https://en.wikipedia.org/wiki/El_Paso,_Texas) and for Mission Valley (El Paso) (https://en.wikipedia.org/wiki/Mission_Valley_(El_Paso)) downplay the Lower Valley name. Despite these efforts, the name remains Lower Valley for a vast majority of El Pasoans. Apparently, hegemony, even in El Paso, has its limits.

15 On Hall, see *El Paso Herald-Post*, 1995, April 27.

16 Charles Edgren, "Youngsters Re-enact Thanksgiving Trek," *El Paso Times*, February 25, 1998.

17 Charles Edgren, "Students Capture Spanish History," *El Paso Times*, February 23, 1998, B3.

18 Ibid

19 Teresa Córdova, "Power and knowledge: Colonialism in the academy," in *Living Chicana Theory*, Carla Trujillo, ed. (Berkley, CA: Third Woman Press, 1998): 17–45.

20 Bea Bragg, *The Very First Thanksgiving: Pioneers on the Rio Grande* (Niwot, CO: Roberts Rinehart, 1991). Printed in cooperation with the El Paso Mission Trail Association.

21 Source: https://www.elpasotexas.gov/economic-development/business-services/data -and-statistics/population.

22 While San Elizario can convincingly argue that their thanksgiving predates the one in Plymouth, other venues have also made claim to being the first locale to have a thanksgiving. In our research we uncovered no venue that acknowledges that the Native Americans held celebrations of thanks in the Americas for centuries, if not millennia, before the Europeans' arrival.

23 Alex Apostolides, "Best View of Thanksgiving was Horses' Patoots," *El Paso Herald-Post,* May 4, 1989, C2.

24 Ken Flynn, "El Pasoans Mark 401st Anniversary," *El Paso Times,* May 1, 1999, B1.

25 John Hall, "First Thanksgiving: 1598 Oñate Arrival Celebrated." *El Paso Times*, May 1, 2011.

26 EPMTA Vice President Mike Lewis claimed "thousands of people" attended the 2013 event on April 20, 2014, in an interview on KVIA TV's *Xtra* news program. Journalist and host Maria García shared she had seen estimates of 5,000 participants each year at the event. However, the accuracy of such estimates is open to question. The San Elizario plaza is small and 5,000 attendees over three days equals 1,667 people per day. How many attend the First Thanksgiving play is unknown, as is the number of unique visitors versus the number of people who attend multiple times or days. See: http://www.kvia.com/video/ABC-7-Xtra-First-Thanksgiving-History-or-Marketing-Ploy/25581100. Lewis's comments appear from 15:10 to 15:30.

27 Marc Simmons, *The Last Conquistador: Juan de Oñate and the Settling of the Far Southwest* Vol. 2 (Norman, OK: University of Oklahoma Press, 1993). Doña Eufemia references Francisco de Sosa Peñalosa.

28 The video recording is inaudible in parts of this scene. However, the scene takes place in 1598 and Santa Fe was not founded until 1610. We could not determine what word was used to denote northern New Mexico.

29 Gaspar Pérez de Villagrá, *History of New Mexico,* trans. Gilberto Espinoza (New York: Arno Press, 1933). This edition is a facsimile of Espinoza's 1933 publication of the same title published by Quivira Society in Los Angeles.

30 Pérez and Ortega, "Mediated Debate."

31 For readers new to semiotics we suggest: Arthur Asa Berger "Semiotics and Society," *Society* 51, no. 1 (2014): 22–26.

32 Orrin E. Klapp, "The Creation of Popular Heroes," *American Journal of Sociology* 54, no. 2 (1948): 135.

San Elizario's First Thanksgiving   85

33 Mills lists his profession as "Independent Performing Arts Professional" on his Linkedin profile. See: https://www.linkedin.com/pub/david-mills/12/ab8/123.

34 The details of Oñate's life are provided in Chapter 1. For further reading see Simmons, *Last Conquistador.*

35 Stan Hoig, *Came Men on Horses: The Conquistador Expeditions of Francisco Vásquez de Coronado and Don Juan de Oñate* (Boulder, CO: University Press of Colorado, 2012.)

36 Ramón A. Gutiérrez, *When Jesus Came, the Corn Mothers Went Away: Marriage, Sexuality, and Power in New Mexico, 1500–1846* (Stanford, CA: Stanford University Press, 1991).

37 Hoig, *Came Men on Horses.*

38 Jeff Lewis, *Cultural Studies: The Basics* (London: Sage, 2002), 120–121.

39 Matthew Arnold, cited in Cornel West, "The New Cultural Politics of Difference," *The Humanities as Social Technology* 53 (1990): 93–109.

40 James Morris Blaut, *The Colonizer's Model of the World: Geographical Diffusionism and Eurocentric History* (New York: Guilford Press, 1993).

41 Pérez and Ortega, "Mediated Debate."

42 Eduardo Bonilla-Silva, *Racism Without Racists: Color-blind Racism and the Persistence of Racial Inequality in the United States*, 4th ed. (New York: Rowman & Littlefield Publishers, 2014)

43 Thomas H. Guthrie, *Recognizing Heritage: The Politics of Multiculturalism in New Mexico* (Lincoln, NB: University of Nebraska Press, 2013).

44 Shawn Lay, *War, Revolution, and the Ku Klux Klan: A Study of Intolerance in a Border City* (El Paso, TX: Texas Western Press, 1985).

45 Charlie Edgren, "Youngster Re-enact Thanksgiving Trek," *El Paso Times,* April 25, 1998, B1.

46 José Vasconcelos, *The Cosmic Race/La Raza Cósmica,* trans. Didier T. Jaén (Baltimore, MD: Johns Hopkins Press, 1979/1997). First published in 1925, the essay argues that Mexico will rise to be a world power after the revolution of 1910–1920, largely because of its people's ethnic composition. This essay is credited with ushering in the concept of *raza*, a term adopted by Chicanos and other Mexican-origin categories to foster interethnic unity.

47 Blaut, *Colonizer's Model*; Ella Shohat and Robert Stam, *Unthinking Eurocentricism: Multiculturalism and the Media* (New York: Routledge, 1994/2004).

48 Alastair Bonnett, "A White World? Whiteness and the Meaning of Modernity in Latin America and Japan," in *Working through Whiteness: International Perspectives,* ed. Cynthia Levine-Rasky (Albany, NY: State University of New York, 2002), 79–80.

49 Rafael Pérez-Torres, *Mestizaje: Critical Uses of Race in Chicano Culture* (Minneapolis, MN: University of Minnesota Press, 2006).

50 Mark Auslander, "Touching the Past: Materializing Time in Traumatic 'Living History' Reenactments," *Signs and Society* 1, no.1 (2013): 161–183.

51 An example of this tendency is found in Christopher Bates, "Oh, I'm a Good Rebel: Reenactment, Racism, and the Lost Cause" in Lawrence A. Kreiser and Randall Allred, Eds., *The Civil War in Popular Culture: Memory and Meaning* (Lexington, KY: University of Kentucky Press, 2014), 191–221. Bates, for example, reports on Captain Vern Padgett, a Confederate Civil War reenactor, who has developed "a lengthy and highly polished lecture on [the Civil War]" (p. 191). Although Padgett's work is filled with flawed mathematics and historical fallacies, he stands by its validity and argues that academic historians "can't be trusted and are inclined to hide information that doesn't fit their preconceived notions" (p. 192). Padgett argues that as many as 200,000 Confederate soldiers were Black.

52 See Richard Dyer, *White* (New York: Routledge), 1–40.

86 San Elizario's First Thanksgiving

53 Antonia I. Castañeda, "Sexual Violence in the Politics and Policies of Conquest: Amerindian Women and the Spanish Conquest of Alta California." In *Between Conquests: The Early Chicano Historical Experience*. Ed. Michael R. Ornelas. 4th Ed (Dubuque, IA: Kendall-Hunt, 2004).

54 David J. Weber, *The Spanish Frontier in North America* (New Haven, CT: Yale University Press, 1992).

55 Criollo refers to a person born in the New World to Spanish parents born in Spain. See: James Diego Vigil, *From Indians to Chicanos: The Dynamics of Mexican-American Culture*. 3rd Ed. (Long Grove, IL: Waveland Press, 2012).

56 Alfredo Mirandé and Evengalina Enríquez, *La Chicana: The Mexican-American Woman* (Chicago, IL: University of Chicago Press, 1979).

57 David J. Weber, *Foreigners in Their Native Land: Historical Roots of the Mexican Americans*. Rev. ed. (Albuquerque, NM: University of New Mexico Press, 1973/2004).

58 David E. Stannard, *American Holocaust: The Conquest of the New World*(New York: Oxford University Press, 1993).

59 John L. Kessell, *Spain in the Southwest: A Narrative History of Colonial New Mexico, Arizona, Texas, and California* (Norman, OK: University of Oklahoma Press, 2002), 84.

60 Weber, *Spanish Frontier*, 86–87.

61 Ella Shohat and Robert Stam, *Unthinking Eurocentrism: Multiculturalism and the Media* (New York: Routledge, 1994/2004), 58–59. Building on Ronald Wright, *Stolen Continents: The Americas through Indian Eyes since 1942* (Boston, MA: Houghton-Mifflin, 1992), 12; and Milton Meltzer, *Columbus and the World Around Him* (New York: Franklin Watts, 1990), 31.

62 Simmons, *Last Conquistador*, 101.

63 Kathleen Deagan, "Colonial Origins and Colonial Transformations in Spanish America," *Historical Archaeology* 37. no. 4 (2003): 3–13.

64 Gregory Murray, "'Tears of the Indians' or Superficial Conversion? José de Acosta, the Black Legend, and Spanish Evangelization in the New World," *Catholic Historical Review* 99, no 1 (2013): 29–51.

65 Pablo Vila, *Crossing Borders, Reinforcing Borders: Social Categories, Metaphors, and Narrative Identities on the U.S.-Mexico Border* (Austin, TX: University of Texas Press, 2000); Pablo Vila, *Border Identifications: Narratives of Religion, Gender, and Class on the U.S.-Mexico Border* (Austin, TX: University of Texas Press, 2005).

66 Alfredo Mirandé, *The Chicano Experience: An Alternative Perspective* (Notre Dame, IN: University of Notre Dame Press, 1985).

67 Alastair Bonnett, "A White World?", 69–105.

68 Pérez and Ortega, "Mediated Debate," 123.

69 Ibid.

70 Vila, *Crossing Borders*. Vila illustrates how Spanish speakers find benefits in an Hispanic identity, in comparison with other ethnic labels. This point is illustrated in his conversations with "Alejandro," see pp. 30–31 and p. 105.

71 In conducting our research we attended numerous First Thanksgiving and pro-Oñate events for a number of years. During this time we met only one native El Pasoan who self-identified as Spanish.

72 Córdova, "Power and Knowledge," 33–37.

73 John Valdez and Christine Ibarra, *The Last Conquistador* (2008; PBS Video).

74 Rodolfo F. Acuña, *Occupied America: A History of Chicanos*. 4th Ed. (New York: Longman, 2000).

75 Pérez and Ortega, "Mediated Debate."

76 This comment was made by a local San Elizario small business operator to us and one of our research assistants as we waited for the 2006 First Thanksgiving play to begin. The man claimed he was pressured to move his business from a location in

the plaza to a peripheral space after local business leaders, involved with the First Thanksgiving, learned the man had hung a Mexican flag in his store. He claimed First Thanksgiving supporters became upset with him because they want to promote a Spanish identity for San Elizario, a predominantly Mexican/Mexican American area.

77 Robert Ricard, *Spiritual Conquest of Mexico: An Essay on the Apostolate and the Evangelizing Methods of the Mendicant Orders in New Spain, 1523–1572,* trans. Lesley Byrd Simpson (Berkley, CA: University of California Press, 1974).

78 Edward T. Hall, *The Silent Language* (New York: Anchor Books, 1959).

79 This point is based on our experiences dealing with local elites and media. There is no support for complicating the First Thanksgiving story at the level of those who could most effectively do so. The local media disproportionately report on the First Thanksgiving from a positive angle. However, some criticism has been addressed via television news programs, such as KVIA's Xtra, and a handful of guest newspaper columns in the *El Paso Times*.

80 Acuña references Los Angeles in the mid-1990s when he uses this term. We adopt it because the same mindset appears to permeate many segments of West Texas and New Mexico.

3 Mediated debate, historical framing, and public art

The Juan de Oñate controversy in El Paso[1]

Public art links aesthetics to city planning and the formation of civic identity. Artists, designers, planners, and city leaders involved in such projects must balance a number of interests in weighing community impact. Media also influence the process, reporting on artistic events and shaping debates regarding public art.[2,3] This media framing is important because public art can be read in multiple ways and may influence widespread community support or rejection.[4] If public art should represent and reaffirm a community's "sense of self,"[5] who determines what that is? Who decides whom such monuments will honor?

Beginning in 1998, a debate over public art gripped the community of El Paso, Texas. At the center of the controversy was a thirty-six-foot statue of Spanish colonizer, Juan de Oñate, which formed the centerpiece of the XII Travelers Memorial of the Southwest.

We draw on articles, opinion pieces, letters in local newspapers, and an open letter to the El Paso mayor to analyze the civic debate that erupted among residents of El Paso who favored or opposed the statue. This debate illustrates how competing insights of identity affect community views about public art. We argue that as a work of public art, the Oñate statue distorts El Paso history and exemplifies the Eurocentric framing of southwest colonization, which Carey McWilliams called the region's "fantasy heritage."[6] This fantasy ignores the brutality of the colonial experiment, offering images of a peaceful, if racially segregated society in which Spaniards and indigenous cultures intermingled. It is our contention, that in their efforts to create a marketable history, El Paso authorities ended up promoting a fantasy heritage misrepresenting people and events focusing on the idyllic images of Spanish colonization and thus contributes to the continuing exclusion of the city's Chicano and indigenous population.

Hegemony and the history of the Southwest

The Southwest saw numerous colonial Spanish incursions into indigenous territory. Spanish victory over indigenous people provides the basis for the assimilationist framing of the region's culture. This framing is an aspect

The Juan de Oñate controversy in El Paso 89

of the mainstream hegemonic worldview that influences contemporary understanding of the region and its people.[7] Through a network of practices involving the late artist, John Houser, the XII Travelers organization, the City of El Paso, and the media, a worldview leaning towards a Spanish image of cultural development, set the stage for a statue of Juan de Oñate.

In April 1598, Juan de Oñate and approximately 500 colonists arrived at the Río Grande in West Texas, east of current-day El Paso. There the party met Manso Indians and held a thanksgiving celebration that included *La Toma* (literally, the taking), in which Oñate claimed the region for the Spanish Crown.[8] In June Oñate's party reached northern New Mexico and subjugated the Pueblo people of that region. They established a head-quarters in Ohkay Owingeh Pueblo and renamed it San Juan. The Spanish occupied the villager's houses and refused to work. That winter, the Acoma Pueblo rebelled against the Spanish and killed eleven of Oñate's soldiers, including his nephew, Juan de Zaldivar. In a three-day battle, seventy-two Spaniards destroyed the pueblo and murdered 500 Acoma men and 300 women and children.[9]

After the battle, the Spaniards staged trials of eighty Acoma men and 500 women and children. Upon adjudication, male prisoners older than twenty-five had one foot severed and were sentenced to twenty years of servitude. Males between twelve and twenty-five and females over twelve years of age also received twenty-year sentences of servitude. Children younger than twelve were placed under the supervision of colonial families.[10] Oñate's purpose was to send a message to Indians, essentially "outlawing acts of rebellion," particularly to those "who had already pledged obedience to the Crown."[11]

When news of these, and other actions reached Mexico City, Oñate was dismissed from his position as first colonial governor of New Mexico and placed on trial. Found guilty of cruel "abuses against Indians, ill treatment of some of his own officers, colonists, and priests; and adultery,"[12] he was banished permanently from New Mexico. Oñate left for Spain, hoping to reestablish his social position and finances. He died in 1626 after working for a short time as a mining inspector.[13]

In El Paso, critics of the Oñate statue focus on the colonist's atrocities and his violation of colonial law. Statue supporters call attention to the creation of a Southwest Hispanic culture they attribute in part to him while they ignore or downplay colonial strife. Thus, different interpretations of Oñate's social relevance continue to divide the peoples of the Southwest. The coercive nature of power relations in El Paso frames the Spanish conquest of the Southwest as a righteous endeavor. Since hegemony breeds consent among members of the local community, it leads people from Spanish-speaking cultures to adopt different ethnic labels that reflect various political perspectives on the region's history, as discussed in Chapter 1 and in our previous work.[14]

90 *The Juan de Oñate controversy in El Paso*

Chicano competition for public space

The El Paso-Ciudad Juárez area has a long history of conflict between Mexicans and Whites. Ciudad Juárez previously included El Paso, on the north side of the river when it was Mexican territory. The separation between the two nations began in earnest with the 1836 Texas Revolt and was solidified after the US-Mexico War (1846–1848). David Montejano describes race relations in Texas history as racially charged and driven by Anglos' systematic discrimination against Mexicans. On the other hand, Mexicans in El Paso played key roles in the city's progress, but persistent racism and segregation, denied them upward mobility or inclusion in the historical record.[15] This systematic exclusion led to competition between Mexicans and Whites for representation in public spaces.

The potency of El Paso government and Anglo elites, kept both the US-born and immigrant Mexican population on the fringes of El Paso society. While "colonialism, slavery, immigration, and exile" have defined the Chicano experience, traditional historians "have justified these conditions and events in the name of reason, progress, and freedom."[16] Despite discrimination, Mexicans in El Paso have not passively accepted their place. The 1877 Salt War is an early illustration of Mexican attempts to counter White power struggles in El Paso's public domain.[17] When a group headed by W.W. Mills usurped the local salt flats that had for generations been used by individuals from El Paso and Ciudad Juárez, the residents of nearby San Elizario launched an armed revolt against local business interests who wanted to charge for using salt. The melee demonstrated the potential strength of the Mexican community and forced a congressional investigation. The counterhegemonic action against White reinvention of public space led to the recommissioning of Fort Bliss to monitor border conflicts.

A century later, expression of Mexican and Chicano identity through art is an important part of the contest over representation. In the 1970s, El Paso's Chicano Movement pushed for greater local representation of Raza culture through various means, including public art. The Chicano murals of that decade reflected counterhegemonic messages of social resistance and cultural affirmation. They reminded people that although Chicanos lacked formal power, their historical roots, social contributions, and future place could not be denied. Creation of El Paso's Chicano murals continued,[18] and in 1990 the Junior League of El Paso formed Los Murales Project.[19] This effort allowed for greater Chicano cultural inclusion in area public art, for example, the murals at Lincoln Center in South Central El Paso. Located on freeway pillars that sit in front of the center represent a long history with numerous artists and community members who made use of the freeway pillars to establish images of the Chicano Movement.

However, the El Paso Museum of Art remained resistant to exhibiting Chicano art. In 1992, when the *Chicano Art: Resistance and Affirmation* (CARA) exhibit reached the museum, its presence should have signaled that Chicanos were finally recognized in El Paso's art community. Nevertheless,

Figure 5 Murals at Lincoln Park beneath Interstate 10, possibly El Paso's most visible Chicano artwork.
Credit: Leonel Monroy

the museum, a self-appointed guardian of high culture, downplayed CARA's Chicano essence. Notably, the exhibit brochure used the term *Hispanic* in place of Chicano—it headlined the exhibit "Interpretations of Hispanic Reality—and did not display the CARA logo."[20] Alicia Gaspar de Alba claims that this action deprived the exhibit of its "political and resistance ethos." The museum's framing suggested that while El Paso reflects a Chicano/Mexican culture, some part of the population still prefers a safer, Hispanic identity. Indeed, as recently as 2002, local public relations professionals reported that *Hispanic* was the preferred ethnic label in the city.[21] Chicano cultural representation in El Paso has been coopted.

Chicanos experienced an important cultural victory when Cheech Marin's *Chicano Visions* was exhibited at the newly renamed El Paso International Museum of Art in 2003. Everyone, including the museum's administration, understood that this was an exhibition of Chicana/o art, and the show had a strong counterhegemonic impact. Other Chicana/o-themed exhibits have followed. But art housed in museums is limited in its reach, above all in the border area; several faculty members at the University of Texas at El Paso, found that some of their students had never been to a museum, making it likely that many other community members had not been to a museum either. Public art and heritage events in public space, on the other hand, have potentially a much wider reach. It is in this context of history and Chicano public art that the debate on Juan de Oñate emerges.

92 *The Juan de Oñate controversy in El Paso*

The XII Travelers project and the selection of Oñate

In 1998, sculptor John Houser approached the El Paso city council with a proposal to create twelve statues of important Southwestern historical figures as part of an effort to revitalize the downtown area. His inspiration came from a calendar called "XII Travelers Through the Pass of the North," created by local painter, Tom Lea, Jr. and published by the El Paso Electric Company in 1947.[22] The painter's father, Tom Lea, Sr., who was mayor of El Paso from 1915 to 1917 and later a Ku Klux Klan member, introduced the XII Travelers idea in 1915.[23] Twenty years later, Mount Rushmore sculptor and Klansman,[24] Gutzon Borglum, expressed interest in "carving 400 years of history, beginning with Cabeza de Vaca, on the granite walls of Hueco Tanks," a geological formation outside El Paso.[25] He failed to garner support for his concept. However, city officials accepted Houser's proposal in April 1988 and set aside $1 million in project funding that June.

Houser's proposal stated that XII Travelers supporters would independently raise an additional $2.7 million in funding for the memorial. The city's acceptance caused concern, in part because some people questioned Houser's artistic abilities. Supporters claimed that Houser was world renowned, yet the University of Arizona had initially declined a Houser statue donated by an alumnus. It was eventually installed near a university library at the request of the university president, according to Betty Ligon in the weekly periodical, *Accent.*[26] Ligon interviewed university museum director, Peter Birmingham, who verified this account and added that to label Houser as a renowned artist was "hyperbole."

Despite the controversy, Mayor Suzanne Azar supported the project. She created a XII Travelers Committee to guide the selection process. Sculptor Houser, the mayor, and each member of the city council was allowed to appoint a person to the committee. A downtown Tax Increment Finance Board was created to raise project revenue, according to Gary Schroeder writing for the *El Paso Scene* newspaper in June 1995. Azar later withdrew her support for the project because of contractual disagreements between the city and the artist. In 1992, the city approved the first phase of the project, partially funding the creation of two XII Traveler statues in the amount of $275,000.[27]

As Houser was laying the groundwork for the Oñate statue, the first Traveler statue capturing, Fray Garcia de San Francisco took in downtown El Paso on September 26, 1996. Fray Garcia was a priest credited with bringing Catholicism to the area. And while the installation occurred without controversy, the selection of Juan de Oñate for the second statue was far more contested. Oñate's image is ubiquitous in the El Paso area, going beyond the realm of public art. Although his role in public history was short-lived, tourist-oriented references to Oñate pervade the city, painting him as a heroic and noble explorer. A central El Paso roadway is called the Don Juan de Oñate Trail; it encapsulates a section of road formally designated the César Chávez Border Highway. Neighboring Las Cruces, New Mexico, is home to Oñate High School and another Oñate statue can be found at *Parque Municipal Cuatro Siglos* (Four Centuries Municipal Park) in Ciudad Juárez, which sits adjacent to El Paso, across the Río Grande. There is also the *El Camino Real de Tierra Adentro National Historic Trail*, thirty-five miles south of Socorro, New Mexico. These elements and similar ones are part of a hegemonic network of practices sympathetic toward Spanish colonization.

For example, naming a roadway after Oñate represents how local governing elites utilize their power to commemorate his legacy. However, public commemoration of a figure normally indicates positive social contributions, not brutal slaughter. The use of the word *trail* in the Don Juan de Oñate Trail roadway implies that Oñate is from the distant colonial past and that his crimes against the Acoma were in accordance with colonial-era standards. This naming is a strong metaphor for the historical road from the colonial past to the neocolonial present. The section named after Chávez, linked to the idea of a border highway, evokes Chávez's bicultural heritage. The road, like Chávez's background, straddles the line between the US and Mexico. Naming the highway in honor of both Oñate and Chávez may lead some to see Oñate through the fantasy heritage that links his brutality to Chávez's humanitarian legacy. Such machinations influence the community's

Figure 6 A photo of the Juan de Oñate/César Chávez Memorial Highway with US border fencing and the Ciudad Juárez "X" (equis) statue in the background.
Credit: Leonel Monroy

94 *The Juan de Oñate controversy in El Paso*

civic discourse, and like Chicano art's struggle for public space, they lead some people to select sides that reflect their views.

Oñate's selection for the second statue made transparent the power relations surrounding the discourses and iconography associated with the XII Travelers. From 1998 to 2003, Oñate's torso and his horse's head were displayed at a local shopping center, Sunland Park Mall. This display created a discursive link between the future statue and economic activity, implying Oñate would be good for commerce and tourism. Placing the uncompleted statue here possibly led some shoppers to form positive mental associations between it and their shopping experiences. Such people most likely overlooked the statue's political significance. This display and similar local references sought to naturalize Oñate as part of El Paso history and as a central element in the local economy. Displaying the statue also allowed supporters to claim that it would generate economic growth simply through its association with area commerce.

A maquette of the Oñate statue was also displayed inside the El Paso International Airport. This model showed how the design of the proposed statue would ascribe moral authority to Oñate, showing him as a noble explorer influenced by the Catholic faith. One side of Oñate's helmet features a kneeling figure before a crucified Christ, placing Oñate under the auspices of the Roman Catholic Church. Although Catholicism remains a central element in Chicano culture,[28] Spanish colonial forces imposed it upon the indigenous peoples they conquered. Nevertheless, the image on the helmet figures Oñate as a pious individual. The statue's right arm extends skyward and holds a scroll representative of *La Toma*, emphasizing that written documents legitimated colonial ownership of previously inhabited lands.[29] The scroll also represents Oñate as an *adelantado*, a colonizer authorized by the Spanish Crown to claim a territory and its riches.[30] Despite protests against the project, the El Paso airport funded the statue's completion.

On November 4, 2003, the *El Paso Times* reported that the city council had renamed the Oñate statue *The Equestrian* [31] in an effort to placate the opposition. Social struggle is often aimed at contesting "the interlocking relation between corporate, financial, and political elites [that have] access to a disproportionate amount of resources, power, prestige, and status in society."[32] In El Paso, these powerful elements promote a network of practices that frame El Paso's history as a fantasy heritage. History and art are political, and when examined critically they always reveal relationships of power.[33] The social politics associated with a public art sculpture such as the Oñate statue illustrates this point. Media coverage of events and representations of Oñate, his detractors, and his supporters also has important influence on fantasy heritage and tourism (See Case study 3.1).

Figure 7 El Paso leaders celebrate the unveiling of the Equestrian statue in April 2007; protestors were forced to remain across the street.
Credit: Leonel Monroy

Case study 3.1 South Africa, the 2010 World Cup, and media representations

South Africa hosted the 2010 FIFA World Cup and gained much international media attention. Initially seen as way to prop up the nation's image, South Africa soon found itself framed "as exotic and alluring, but also dangerous and pre-modern" (p. 63). The nation state learned first-hand the powerful ability of various mass mediated representations to "support or resist 'official' ideologies and ... geopolitical perceptions of people, places, and identities" (p. 64). South African leaders promoted "the World Cup as a Pan-African unifier" (Myers & Smith, 2010, cited in Hammett, 2011). They emphasized their nation's transition from a racially divided apartheid state to a united nation with a thriving democracy eager to take its place in the global community. Yet, British newspaper coverage provided a strong xenophobic and Eurocentric hegemonic framing unfriendly to South Africa. Newspapers juxtaposed the nation's touristic allure against stories of fear and danger. Hammett found that tabloids focused on South Africa's alleged "primitivism and exoticism" (p. 68), for example, the *Daily Star* focused on such things as the threats to tourist safety by African wildlife, specifically reporting on a baboon attack faced by soccer player Peter Crouch's family. There was also a focus on President Jacob Zuma's polygamous lifestyle that compared it to morally superior, non-animalistic British instincts. The hypersexualization of Africans (and people of color) is a commonly used representation that speaks to colonial era notions of "White man's burden." Hammett suggested this trope framed African men as sexually rapacious and given to their baser instincts. He also argued that such framing pandered to British readers, reinforcing their self-image as a people superior to Africans. Another common trope was crime and its effects on tourists, while in South Africa (e.g., pickpockets) and at the World Cup (e.g., crowd control issues). He notes that while there were 267 such articles only sixty-eight addressed race, suggesting representations of the "dangerous African was mobilized through more nuanced and subtle ... 'othering' than overt racism" (p. 69). Mainstream broadsheet papers fared no better, focusing on the economically marginal status of South Africa and its Black population as "savage native[s]" (p. 70). FIFA and the South African government viewed such negative and stereotypic framing as a key reason the 2010 World Cup failed to attract as many soccer fans as initially projected. Tragically, many British media sources and their personnel responded that this claim was "'Brit-bashing' by outsiders jealous of British success and values" (p. 71). In the end, many negative stereotypes of South Africa were reinforced by the British media and its effects potentially impacted readers from across the British socioeconomic spectrum.

Discussion questions

1. Can you think of examples of places you have lived or visited where a similar claim can be levied against the media? Do you think such a comparison is a fair one? Why or why not?
2. Almost a century of mass media research suggests that some media affect some people some of the time. In the 1920s, the Payne Fund Studies discovered that the mass media have a limited ability to alter or influence one's perceptions. In 1963, political scientist Bernard Cohen suggested that the media may not tell us what to think but are very good at telling us what to think about. Later that decade and throughout the rest of the previous century, communication scholar George Gerbner noted that the media influence perceptions of self and other. How do you think these academic findings relate to the case study above?
3. What might South Africa and similar places do to resist or possibly alter such negative media representations?
    Source: Hammett, Daniel. (2011). British media representations of South Africa and the 2010 FIFA World Cup. *South African Geographical Journal, 93(1)*, 63–74.

The civic debate: media and expert commentary

The local print media provided a major forum for the Oñate statue controversy. The *El Paso Times* and the now defunct *El Paso Herald-Post* provided much news coverage of—and editorial support for—the statue. It is not surprising that the El Paso newspapers covered the XII Travelers project in a generally supportive tone, given that the mainstream media in most places reflect elite interests.[34] In addition to reporters and editorial writers, academic historians writing in the local press contributed to shaping the debate. If academics have license to create truth,[35] media interventions in civic debate likely have a similar credibility with many readers. This idea is reinforced when statue proponents had their comments published in the newspaper. Such coverage implies a degree of expertise. We touch on the role of the mainstream press and look more closely at the arguments of two academic historians and one writer of popular history as they addressed the Oñate controversy.

In 1998, the *El Paso Times* published a booklet titled *El Paso Quadricentennial: Celebration of the First Thanksgiving.*[36] It references the "Spaniard Don Juan de Oñate." In Latino cultures, the honorific "Don" denotes high social status or respectability. Most XII Travelers materials of the time refer to "Don Juan de Oñate," and the local El Paso press has generally followed suit. The quadricentennial booklet cover features a color drawing of Spanish soldiers, priests, and Indians praying in thanksgiving. The image is a hegemonic device that reinforces the idea of "Don Juan" as a moral leader who peaceably brought two cultures together, despite historical evidence to

98 *The Juan de Oñate controversy in El Paso*

the contrary. On the other hand, *El Paso Times* reporter Leonard Martínez covered a one-day teacher's workshop, organized by Frank G. Pérez and Marc Thompson, director of the El Paso Museum of Archeology in 2002. The workshop title, "Juan de Oñate: The Man, Myth, and Mestizaje," omitted "Don", however, the *El Paso Times* added the honorific title in its coverage of the event.[37]

Also writing in the booklet was sports writer Joe Muench who reduces Oñate's expedition to a tourism parody:

> Don [Oñate], as most are aware, was one of the world's first captains who dared to go where no man had gone before ... The expedition was really en route to San Antonio by way of the Laredo port of entry. Don [Oñate] wanted his ancestors [sic] to have an NBA team and a big fish aquarium ... until [Oñate] heard tales about El Paso having the best Mexican food in the world.[38]

In this heritage account, Oñate did no harm to the indigenous people. Indeed, there is no reference to them at all. Rather, readers are led to picture Oñate as seeking to provide a good quality of life for his charges. Apparently, El Paso's gastronomic excellence should lead people, as it did Oñate, to see it as a premier Texas destination. There is no explanation as to why a sportswriter would write a column about a historical expedition. Muench's apparent lack of expertise was of no apparent concern to the *El Paso Times.*

As debate intensified over the proposed statue, academics and other non-journalists weighed in. Of particular interest are comments by three historians that appeared in the El Paso media and in an open letter to the Mayor. Marc Simmons is an independent scholar who has published works on New Mexico history, most notably, *The Last Conquistador: Juan de Oñate and the Settling of the Southwest* (1991). Popular historian Leon Metz is regarded by the *El Paso Times* as the city's resident expert on local history. Oscar J. Martínez is Professor of History at the University of Arizona and a former faculty member in history at the University of Texas at El Paso. Simmons' and Metz's pro-statue discourse displayed a mainstream hegemony sympathetic to Spanish colonization and grounded in the fantasy heritage; they received considerable access to the local media. In contrast, Martínez's counter-hegemonic framing raised questions about contemporary mores in historical interpretation and received little attention.

Writing in the *El Paso Times,* [39] Simmons provided a biographical account of Oñate's life that omitted mention of the Acoma tragedy. Ironically, he covers this topic in his aforementioned book.[40] He did however, comment on Oñate's previous lack of notoriety: "Until now, the poor fellow [Oñate] has been pretty well neglected." In a later interview with the *New York Times,* [41] Simmons claimed that statue critics have a "Hollywood" image of the West and noted that the precolonial Americas were not a "Garden of Eden." The implication was that statue opponents were incapable of grasping more than

The Juan de Oñate controversy in El Paso   99

superficial elements of the Oñate discourse. Yet his argument can be inverted to suggest that Simmons himself has a Hollywood perspective. Indigenous suffering, for Simmons, is as imaginary as the deaths of Indians in a low budget Western. His view is consistent with Hollywood's mainstream hegemony, where good guys wear white cowboy hats and kill "savage" Indians.

Simmons' comparison between the precolonial period and the Garden of Eden is Eurocentric, reinforcing the Judeo-Christian aspects of the Oñate discourse. Under the auspices of the Roman Catholic Church, Spanish forces subjugated indigenous people, and their cruelty remains a bitter reminder of colonialization. Therefore, it is not surprising that in January 1998, a then unknown person or group sawed off the right foot of an Oñate statue in Alcalde, New Mexico, as a counterhegemonic reaction to the celebration of the Spanish role in the southwest. A note published in the *Albuquerque Journal*, [42] purportedly from the vandals, states, "Foot removed on behalf of Acoma Pueblo who suffered at the hands of the Spaniards." On October 2, 2017, the *New York Times* conducted an interview with an anonymous man who claimed to have been part of a group called "Friends of Acoma" and to have been the foot's remover. The man stated the goal was to "focus attention on Oñate's atrocities" against the Acoma, and, as reported by Simon Romero, it appears the strategy worked. The topic gained public recognition at the time and resurfaces from time to time, as evidenced by this article. [43]

Metz also attacks those who oppose the Oñate statue. In a newspaper column, he describes the critics as "local and regional naysayers [who] rant about as they dance around their sacrificial fires." He mocks calls for cultural sensitivity, suggesting that the XII Travelers committee nominate 1,000 historical figures so that "every political group in town could be comforted." [44] Simmons and Metz defend the Oñate statue with culturally insensitive arguments that reduce the colonial experiment to a Hollywood film or a pagan ritual. The *El Paso Times* supported the statue, and publication of these columns constituted another element of the network of practices reflecting a hegemonic worldview embracing the fantasy heritage. The fact that the columns were written by "expert" historians gave them added credibility. Yet, one of these experts, Simmons, was quite capable of eliding an event as large as the Acoma tragedy. He was dismissive of the colonial experiment's negative impact on indigenous people, comparing their plight to a Hollywood image. Metz framed critics as "naysayers" who dance around a sacrificial fire. Rather than engage their argument, Metz suggests that the statue's critics are primitive and superstitious. To Simmons and Metz, Oñate is a victim in his own time and the present.

Martínez, by contrast garnered comparatively little public attention when he sent an open letter to then El Paso Mayor, Raymond Caballero, on August 6, 2001, [45] voicing concern about the statue and its impact on the city. Martínez notes that those who support the statue include "many well-meaning and dedicated people" who "love El Paso and see the statue as a positive thing." But he raises the questions about the appropriateness of the statue in light of Oñate's violence against the Acoma. He argues, "The horse and rider icon

100 *The Juan de Oñate controversy in El Paso*

will be seen as an 'in your face' affront by all who value human rights and sympathize with Native Americans." For this reason, Martínez equates the statue with "racist symbols, such as the Ku Klux Klan hood, the swastika, and the confederate flag." Although the XII Travelers project seeks to boost tourism, Martínez warns of boycotts against the city for its support of the statue, particularly by academic societies. Finally, he compares Oñate's actions to those of Nazis who also directed genocidal campaigns, some of whom were tried for war crimes. He asks, "Who would ever consider building a statue to some Nazi personage and placing it in a town square?"

Martínez's arguments counter those of Simmons and Metz in perspective and tone. Rather than attack statue supporters, Martínez acknowledges that both sides want what they think is best for El Paso. He provides well-supported arguments to explain why the statue is a flawed symbol for the city. The apparent lack of media coverage of Martínez's letter to the Mayor underscores its counterhegemonic nature. In public form, the letter was published only on the stanstonstreet.com website, which featured local news and politics. It also circulated as an e-mail among an undetermined number of individuals. One can speculate that the local hegemonic network of practices silenced this counterhegemonic account through omission. As a result, relatively few people in the community read the letter.

Martínez frames the controversy as a difference of historical memory and suggests that public art memorials should reflect contemporary values. Analyzing past events through the lens of contemporary values is a counterhegemonic act that complicates historical interpretation, challenging the fantasy heritage. While Simmons and Metz acknowledge the brutality of Pre-Columbian and colonial life, they appear dismissive of indigenous suffering in those eras and the present. Martínez suggests that people and contemporary public art should acknowledge the suffering ushered in by the colonialization of the Southwest. He points that the project may end up an economic failure if the statue fails to attract tourists or even drives them away.

Simmons and Metz suggest that their expertise as historians places them above the general public and, especially, it is implied, the primitive and superstitious Chicano masses. Both claim to be in possession of the "truth." For example, Simmons tells the *New York Times,* "The truth is those times were rough and bloody," But what truth and whose truth? Simmons' comments ignore the fact that Europeans recorded most Western historical accounts.[46] Similarly, *El Paso Times* editorial writer Charles Edgren defended Oñate's actions at Acoma, naming him "Juanito" and erroneously claiming that amputation "was accepted practice" in that era.

The media role is important because of the strong correlation between media consumption and individual attitudes.[47] Writing in the local press illustrates the mainstream hegemony that surrounds El Paso's statue. In reference to hegemony, Gramsci noted that subordinated classes hold potential energy but are held in check by dominant groups using sophisticated strategies that transcend brute coercion: "Central to any long-term domination is gaining the 'consent' of the dominated."[48] Thus, the local media supported the statue and used their influence to frame the debate, leading many local residents to support the statue as well. More broadly, the press promoted the fantasy heritage understanding of history contributing to what Córdova termed the confusion of the colonized.[49] In this case, consent of the dominated is secured through the machinations of elite actors with social influence. Martínez, an accomplished scholar who opposes the statue, was deprived of the media access given to those who support it. He is outside the network of practices that promotes El Paso's fantasy heritage.

Assessing benefits and costs

The Oñate sculpture was installed at the El Paso International Airport in November 2006. It was officially unveiled the following April once the initial oppositional uproar had died down. The statue sits at the central artery used to enter or exit the airport, a hub of El Paso's tourist industry. This insures that tourists passing though the airport's main terminal engage Oñate's legacy as a fantasy heritage.

Fantasy heritage of one sort or another plays a central role in tourist promotions in many communities. In El Paso, the Oñate's statue's civic backers claimed it would boost tourism and generate revenue, and this expectation underlay the city government's determination to complete the project. Critics,

Figure 8 An Oñate protestor holds an effigy of an amputated foot, a reminder of Oñate's brutality against the Acoma Pueblo peoples.
Credit: Leonel Monroy

102   *The Juan de Oñate controversy in El Paso*

however, contested the notion, and we found no evidence to indicate that the statue, once installed, benefited either commerce or tourism in El Paso.

The costs, on the other hand, are of concern. Business leader Moises Bujanda noted in the *El Paso Herald-Post* that "a feasibility study has never been done to determine the economic potential" of the project. He added that the $1 million cost "is a lot of money in [El Paso]," particularly because only one artist was involved.[50] On November 4, 2007, *Los Angeles Times* writer T.J. Simers ridiculed the statue, fearing the University of Southern California Trojans would play in the Sun Bowl rather than in a more prestigious game:

> They've got a 42-foot-high statue at the El Paso Airport honoring some guy who decreed every male over the age of 25 should have a foot amputated. I guess he wanted to make it tough on anyone looking to escape the dump.[51]

While Simer's attack was in poor taste, his comments suggest the statue lacks the appeal that its supporters had counted on. This is true even though Simers, like Oñate sympathizers, trivialize the plight of the Acoma. For those who support the statue and even for some who oppose it, the project promotes a fantasy heritage that foreshadows the role of the Spanish colonizers. To the extent that El Pasoans see themselves as Spanish and their culture as European, the contributions of their mestizo ancestry may be framed negatively, even by them, or lost completely.

Hegemony hinders the ability of subaltern people to produce "coherent accounts of the world they live in,"[52] and while those seeking to counter hegemony have been rewriting existing accounts to create more complete representations, their insights do not necessarily mean hegemonic practices will crumple. Social action, education, and persistence will make the difference. Chicano writers have been rewriting the impact of hegemonic practices on the Mexican American community for some time and have demonstrated that the community has responded with activist practices to counter power relations.[53] Despite these efforts, demands for historical representation in public art has been particularly difficult. So long as El Paso's elite promote and benefit from the region's fantasy heritage, a distorted image of the Chicano and Mexican American community—termed Hispanic—will remain.

Case study 3.2 Marketing unpopular tourism destinations

Not all popular tourist destinations began as such and many locales that desire tourist dollars face complex challenges in luring people to them. Avraham and Ketter suggest that unexpected crises, (e.g., natural disasters or terrorism) negatively impact tourism as do long-term problems related to political or social dynamics (e.g., high crime rates). Tourism's international scope and intense competition for visitors make countering negative stereotypes and/or prejudices imperative for locales, particularly those with longstanding negative public perceptions. Avraham and Ketter offer a model to help communities facing such difficulties using either of two strategies. They begin by focusing on place marketing and branding as "two sides of the same coin" (p. 146). Marketing references how a locale is perceived, and branding refers to how a locale is promoted via marketers. The authors suggest that tourism sites use either a cosmetic approach that seeks to restore a positive public image for a locale, while a strategic approach works to change the site itself using marketing to improve public perceptions. Currently, many locales focus on place marketing and attempt to improve their "media image and their public perception" (p. 147). One such category for this strategy relates to places with a longstanding negative image. Such locales have three media message strategies at their disposal: (1) focus on the message source; (2) focus on the particular message and its intended audience; and (3) focus on the perceptions and values of audiences the message targets. The greater number of items used to improve a locale's reputation, the more likely they are to be in attracting tourists, according to this approach.

Avraham and Ketter's review of the literature led them to create two categories of media strategies for improved public perceptions, cosmetic and strategic approaches. The first category relates to marketing or branding strategies and the latter references an approach that also enhances local conditions (e.g., efforts to lower crime, improve infrastructure) and uses sporting or cultural events to lure tourists. This strategic approach works only when communities provide visitors with a better than expected experience, particularly if the tourists had previously visited the community. Building on Baker (2007), Avraham and Ketter conclude that "destinations that take care of both image and reality are involved in a greater extent of change than destinations that focus only on their image" (p. 151).

Using the cosmetic approach some community leaders may ignore the reality of their locale's negative image and find that a public relations campaign does little to change perceptions. Other locales seek to "disassociate" themselves from problematic geographic locations. For example, Madagascar focused on items other than its close physical proximity to the African continent. The reverse strategy is employed when locales link themselves to other, well-established, and positively regarded destinations. The example here is Kansas City adopting the KC moniker to imply commonalities with DC (Washington, DC), LA (Los Angeles), and NY (New York). Acknowledging that a locale has improved from past challenges (e.g., limited tourism activities) works when it has genuinely improved its tourism experiences. Counter-messages help other locales to market themselves. Avraham and Ketter cite, for example the slogan of Gambia, an African nation state, "closer than you think," to entice European tourists. Sometimes locales work to convert the negative image into a positive one by spinning it around. Here we see underdeveloped destinations marketing themselves as

104   *The Juan de Oñate controversy in El Paso*

natural, rural, of rustic. The final cosmetic approach is to ridicule the ste-reotype and occurs when marketers represent the negative image at its extreme in a humorous manner. Israel used this strategy in an advertisement where a woman stares at an attractive man on the beach and is so taken by his looks that she walks into a pole. The ad's narrator then states, "Indeed, Israel can be a dangerous place," alluding to some common perceptions held by many at the time.

The strategic approach consists of both image and changes to a locale's actual state or reality. Here, greater changes produce results. The strategies entailed include spotlight events (e.g., festivals) or events that counter per-ceptions and branding efforts to counter negative perceptions. Citing the extant literature, Avraham and Ketter note that the strategic approach also relies on the "inclusion of residents, vision formation, strategy design, defining long-and short-term goals, enhancing local pride, employing research tools, and target audience analysis" (p. 156). In the end, a suc-cessful campaign will include a variety of factors.

Discussion questions

1. Identify three elements that you think are likely to help promote an area with a longstanding negative public view. How might you use them to help alter such perceptions?
2. Can you think of a place you have lived in or visited that faced this type of challenge? If so, what did that community do to change public per-ceptions? Where they successful? If so, what do you think helped the most. If not, why do you think their efforts failed?

    Source: Avraham, Eli, and Eran Ketter. "Marketing Destinations with Prolonged Negative Images: Towards a Theoretical Model." *Tourism Geographies* 15, no. 1 (March 2012): 145–164.

In El Paso, the network of hegemonic practices prevents, or at least dissuades, most residents of Mexican descent from becoming politically active. The work-ing class are forced to spend the bulk of their time earning a living at the cost of their activism. The statue is a central symbol of this tendency. It separates both local residents and tourists from a more thorough understanding of the region's past. Until El Paso elites engage in a more complex civic debate with Chicanos and Mexican Americans, the current status will remain unchanged. While one can argue Oñate's legacy *ad infinitum,* perhaps a more effective strategy would be to use this case to begin a dialogue with community members on questions of fantasy heritage. Why was Oñate so central to the XII Travelers project? What could have been done to better research the personalities selected for the statues? How can the city broaden community input into the public art process?

The city council's insistence on completing the statue illustrates how El Paso's Chicanos and Mexican Americans continue to struggle for recognition in public spaces. The selection of a Chicano or Mexican American personality as the next Traveler statue, if the project continues, would be an ideal first step toward remedying the situation. None of the suggested sculptures honors a Chicano or Mexican American. The cut-off date set by the XII Travelers committee may partially explain this omission. The sculptures are to be of individuals who lived prior to 1910, according to the *El Paso Times.*[54] It is not clear if those chosen to be memorialized must have died by 1910 or been born before that year. In 2012, a third Traveler statue was unveiled of Susan Magoffin and as of this writing, a statue of Mexican President, Benito Juárez is in the works. Proposed names for future statues include: Spanish explorer, Cabeza de Vaca; Moroccan explorer, Estebanico; Tigua tribal governor, Juan Moro and War Captain Bartolo Pique; Spanish explorer, Juan Bautista de Anza; and, first African American West Point graduate, Henry Flipper.[55] All lived before 1910; however, one proposed Traveler, Pancho Villa (1878–1923), died in the 1920s.

The 1910 cut-off date comes sixty-two years after the signing of the Treaty of Guadalupe Hidalgo.[56] Several positive Mexican American role models lived during this period. The best candidate may well be a Mexican-born resident of El Paso named Marcelino Serna (1896–1992), the most highly decorated World War I veteran from Texas. Another possibility is Mexican-born religious healer Teresa Urrea (1873–1906), who lived in El Paso for a time and was an inspiration to many during the Mexican Revolution. Although Serna and Urrea were born in Mexico, they lived in the city for different periods and reflected many social justice ideals consistent with those of today's Chicano community. Tejano Gregorio Cortéz (1875–1916) would also be a good choice, particularly as the literary figure celebrated in Américo Paredes' *With His Pistol in His Hand* (1955); although the likelihood of Cortéz being chosen is small because he lived in central Texas, and the debate would focus on his being a hero or bandit. Any of these individuals would add a Chicano dimension to the XII Travelers project.

Chicano and Mexican contributions to El Paso history deserve recognition. Chris Wilson contends that the framing of New Mexican history for the benefit of tourists will lead the region to "lose sight of its own needs and lack the intellectual, political, and spiritual will to address the pressing social, economic, and environmental problems."[57] A focus on New Mexico's Hispano identity that ignores its Mexican past supports a "perverse status quo."[58] El Paso must avoid falling into this trap. Other localities have generated tourism despite a history of ethnic conflict and growing ethnic diversity in the contemporary period.[59] Without equal representation for Chicanos, El Paso's official history will remain tourist-friendly fantasy heritage, supporting a mainstream hegemony that encourages a distorted view of the past. A more complete history is being cast aside in the pursuit of tourist dollars that may or may not ever materialize in El Paso.

Notes

1 An earlier version of this chapter appeared in the Fall 2008 issue of *Aztlán: A Journal of Chicano Studies* (vol. 33, no. 2), and we thank the editors for permission to republish the essay here. We have made slight changes to the original and added new material regarding the controversy over Juan de Oñate.

2 Maria Luisa de Herrera, Kathleen Garcia, and Gail Goldman, "Public Art as a Planning Tool," Paper presented at Contrasts and Transitions: National Planning Conference of the American Planning Association, San Diego, CA, April 5–9, 1997. http://www.design.asu.edu/apa/proceedings97/herrera.html.

3 Joanne Sharp, Venda Pollack, and Ronan Paddison, "Just Art for a Just City: Public Art and Social Inclusion in Urban Regeneration," *Urban Studies* 42, nos. 5–6 (2005): 1001–23.

4 Eva Sperling-Cockcroft and Holly Barnet-Sanchez, "Introduction," *Signs from the Heart: California Chicano Murals* (Venice, CA: Social and Public Art Resource Center, 1990): 5.

5 Carey McWilliams. *North from Mexico: The Spanish-speaking People of the United States.* Rev. Ed. by Alma M. García. (Santa Barbara, CA: Praeger, 1948/2016).

6 Carey McWilliams. *North from Mexico.*

7 Andrew Leo Lovato. *Santa Fe Hispanic Culture: Preserving Identity in a Tourist Town* (Albuquerque, NM: University of New Mexico Press, 2004).

8 Oscar Martínez. *The First Peoples: A History of Native Americans at the Pass of the North* (El Paso, TX: El Paso Community Foundation, 2000).

9 David J. Weber. *The Spanish Frontier in North America* (New Haven, CT: Yale University Press, 1992).

10 Martha Menchaca. *Recovering History, Constructing Race: The Indian, Black, and White Roots of Mexican Americans* (Austin, TX: University of Texas Press, 2001).

11 José Rabasa. *Writing Violence on the Northern Frontier: The Historiography of New Mexico and Florida and the Legacy of Conquest* (Durham, NC: Duke University Press, 2000): 106.

12 Weber, *The Spanish Frontier,* 86.

13 Joseph P. Sanchez, "Introduction: Juan de Oñate and the Founding of New Mexico, 1598–1609," *Colonial Latin American Review* 7, no. 2, (1998): 89–107.

14 Frank G. Pérez and Carlos F. Ortega. "Mediated Debate, Historical Framing, and Public Art: The Juan de Oñate Controversy in El Paso." *Aztlán: A Journal of Chicano Studies,* 33, no. 2, 121–140.

15 Victor Zamudio-Taylor, quoted in Amalia Mesa-Bains, "Chicano Bodily Aesthetics," in *Body/Culture: Chicano Figuration.* Eds. Richard Kubiak, Elizabeth Partch, Amalia Mesa Bains, and V.A. Sorell (Sonoma, CA: University Art Gallery, Sonoma State University, 1990): 12.

16 Mary Romero, "El Paso Salt War: Mob Action or Political Struggle?" *Aztlán: A Journal of Chicano Studies* 16, nos. 1–2 (1985): 119–143.

17 Mary Romero, "El Paso Salt War".

18 George Vargas, "Border Artists in the Contemporary El Paso Mural Movement: Painting the Frontier." In *Chicano Studies: Survey and Analysis,* 3rd Ed. Eds. Dennis J. Bixler-Marquez, Carlos F. Ortega, Rosalia Solorzano, and Lorenzo G. LaFarelle (Dubuque, IA: Kendall-Hunt, 2007).

19 Los Murales Project, "An Art of Conscience: A Guide to Selected El Paso Murals," EL Paso, TX: (The Junior League of El Paso, 1996).

20 Alicia Gaspar de Alba, *Chicano Art Inside/Outside the Master's House: Cultural Politics and the CARA Exhibition* (Austin, TX: University of Texas Press, 1998): 219–220.

21 Frank G. Pérez, "Effectively Targeting Hispanics in the southwest: Views from Public Relations Professionals in a Border City," *Public Relations Quarterly,* 47, no. 1 (2002): 18–21.

The Juan de Oñate controversy in El Paso   107

22 XII Travelers, *Travelers Memorial of the Southwest* (newsletter), April, 1990.
23 Shawn Lay, *War, Revolution, and the Ku Klux Klan: A Study of Intolerance in a Border City,* (El Paso, TX: Texas Western Press, 1985).
24 Albert Boime, "Patriarchy Fixed in Stone: Gutzon Borglum's Mount Rushmore," *American Art* 5, nos. 1–2 (1991): 142–167.
25 XII Travelers, *Travelers Memorial,* 1.
26 Betty Ligon, "XII Travelers Decisions Not Yet Set in Stone," *Accent, El Paso Herald-Post,* September 27, 1990: 2.
27 Gary Schroeder, "Taking form: XII Travelers Project Gives Hope for New Era of Public Sculpture," *El Paso Scene,* June 13–15, 1995 and Joe Olvera, "Twelve Travelers Project Mired in Confusion," *El Paso Times,* June 17, 1990: B1–B2.
28 Lara Medina, "Los Espiritus Siguen Hablando Chicana Spiritualities." In *Living Chicana Theory,* ed. Carla Trujillo (Berkeley, CA: Third Woman Press, 1998): 189–213; and Carla Trujillo, "La Virgen de Guadalupe and Her Reconstruction in Chicana Lesbian Desire." In *Living Chicana Theory* ed. Carla Trujillo (Berkeley, CA: Third Woman Press, 1998): 214–31.
29 James Morris Blaut, *The Colonizer's Model of the World: Geographic Diffusionism and Eurocentric History* (New York: Guilford Press, 1993).
30 Alfredo Mirandé and Evangélina Enríquez, *La Chicana: The Mexican-American Woman* (Chicago, IL: University of Chicago Press, 1979).
31 Moises Bujanda, "Larger-Than-Life Statues and Larger-Than-Life Price Tag," *El Paso Herald-Post,* March 22, 1991: B3.
32 Cornel West, "The Indispensability Yet Insufficiency of Marxist Theory." In *The Cornel West Reader,* (New York: Basic Civitas Books, 1999b): 213–30.
33 Michel Foucault, *The Archeology of Knowledge and the Discourse on Language,* Trans. A.M. Sheridan Smith, (London: Tavistock, 1972); and Chon A. Noriega, "Editor's Commentary: Preservation Matters," *Aztlán: A Journal of Chicano Studies,* 30 no. 1 (2005): 1–20.
34 Catherine E. Crawley, "Localized Debates of Agricultural Biotechnology in Community Newspapers: A Quantitative Analysis of Media Frames and Sources," *Science Communication* 28, no. 3 (2007): 314–346.
35 Teresa Córdova, "Power and Knowledge: Colonialism in the Academy." In Living Chicana Theory, ed. Carla Trujillo. (Berkeley, CA: Third Woman Press, 1998): 17–45."
36 "El Paso's Quadricentennial: Celebration of the First Thanksgiving," *El Paso Times,* Special Sunday Supplement, March 29, 1998.
37 Leonard Martínez, "Workshop Explores Real Oñate," *El Paso Times,* April 21, 2002, B1.
38 Joe Muench, "There's More to Oñate's Journey then Once Thought," in "El Paso's Quadricentennial," March 29, 1998: 13.
39 Marc Simmons, "New Mexico's Father Remains a Mystery," *El Paso Times,* March 12, 1989, B2.
40 Marc Simmons, *The Last Conquistador:* Juan de Oñate and the Settling of the Far Southwest. (Norman, OK: University of Oklahoma Press, 1991).
41 Ginger Thompson, "As a Sculpture Takes Shape in Mexico, Opposition Takes Shape in the U.S.," *New York Times,* January 17, 2002, A12.
42 *Albuquerque Journal,* January 3, 1998, 3.
43 Simon Romero, "It Takes a Foot Thief," *New York Times,* October 2, 2017, online: https://www.nytimes.com/2017/10/02/insider/new-mexico-statue-conquistador-foot-thief.html. Retrieved January 15, 2019.
44 Leon Metz, "Without Oñate El Paso Might Not Exist," *El Paso Times,* August 27, 2001, A6; and Leon Metz, "Statue Fury Puts Attention on History," *El Paso Times,* December 1, 1997, A10.

108 *The Juan de Oñate controversy in El Paso*

45 One of the authors received a copy of the letter from a colleague; it is no longer online and we uncovered no evidence to suggest that Martínez's comments were ever presented in the local mainstream media.

46 Blaut, *The Colonizer's Model.* Also, Charlie Edgren, "Oñate Belongs at Cleveland Square," *El Paso Times,* August 25, 2001, A12.

47 George Gerbner and Larry Gross, "Living with Television: The Violence Profile," *Journal of Communication,* 26, no. 2, (1976): 173–99 and George Gerbner, Larry Gross, Michael Morgan, Nancy Signorielli and James Shanahan, "Growing Up with Television: Cultivation Processes." In *Media Effects: Advances in Theory and Research,* eds. Jennings Bryant and Dolf Zillman, (Mahwah, NJ: Lawrence Erlbaum Associates, 2002): 43–67.

48 Kate Crehan, *Gramsci, Culture, and Anthropology,* (Berkeley, CA: University of California Press, 2002): 101.

49 Córdova, "Power and Knowledge."

50 Bujanda, "Larger-Than-Life-Statues, B3.

51 T.J. Simers, "Trojans Would Ruin the Day for Folks in Old El Paso," *Los Angeles Times,* November 4, 2007.

52 Crehan, *Gramsci, Culture and Anthropology,* 104.

53 See for example, Rodolfo Acuña, *Sometimes There is No Other Side: Chicanos and the Myth of Equality,* (Notre Dame, ID: University of Notre Dame Press, 1998); Córdova, "Power and Knowledge"; Ignacio Manuel García, *Chicanismo: The Forging of a Militant Ethos Among Mexican Americans,* (Tucson, AZ: University of Arizona Press, 1997); and, Menchaca, *Recovering History.*

54 M.M. Davis, "Sculptor's Daughter Comes to Sun City to Budge Travelers Project," *El Paso Times,* January 13, 1991, F1.

55 The current list of statues is available on the XII Travelers Memorial of the Southwest webpage: http://xiitravelers.org.

56 Richard Griswold del Castillo, *The Treaty of Guadalupe Hidalgo: A Legacy of Conflict* (Norman, OK: University of Oklahoma Press, 1990).

57 Chris Wilson, *The Myth of Santa Fe: Creating a Modern Regional Tradition* (Albuquerque, NM: University of New Mexico Press, 1997).

58 Ibid., 313.

59 Gustave Visser, "Social Justice, Integrated Development Planning and Post-Apartheid Urban Reconstruction," *Urban Studies* 38, no. 10 (2001): 1673–1699; and Jeffery Hou and Michael Ríos, "Community-Driven Place Making: The Social Practice and Participatory Design in the Making of Union Point Park," *Journal of Architectural Education* 57, no. 1 (2003): 19–27.

4 Inclusive tourism and public memory

For much of the 20th Century, tourism flourished on both sides of the US-Mexico border, fueling economic activity for Mexican and US citizens. During Prohibition, for example, US citizens would cross to cities such as Ciudad Juárez and Tijuana to pursue entertainment, whether food, drink, or sometimes vice, while Mexican tourists crossed to El Paso or San Diego for shopping, food, drink, and, in some cases, vice.[1] During the Prohibition Era, San Diego garnered an "unsavory ... reputation as a wide open town among Mexican tourists."[2] Yet, heavy tourist visits continued throughout World War II and into the present, making periodic reinvention a necessity because authenticity has a limited shelf life. Thus, tourist destinations will periodically work to reinvent themselves, straddling the line between novelty and retaining elements that speak to tourists' perceptions of heritage. Since the 1960s, for example, Mexico has worked to reinvent its tourism industries to lure Americans to five economically depressed coastal areas.[3] A newer trend toward medical tourism has also impacted the cross-border tourist markets of both nations.[4] Related to our work here, however, is the idea that tourism relies on "the construction of fictive pasts packaged for consumption [and that it negates] the fundamentally opposed interests of laborers, tourist consumers, and multinational conglomerates."[5] Our work documents how border region tourism efforts have kept pace with these trends by increasingly promulgating Spanish colonization stories. The promotion of fantasy heritage stretches from Ciudad Juárez, Mexico, to Santa Fe, New Mexico, and other locales. Ciudad Juárez has engaged in the Oñate fantasy, installing a statue of him at *Parque Municipal Cuatro Siglos* (Four Centuries Municipal Park) and a historical marker with information about Spanish colonization sits just south of the Ciudad Juárez city limits. The State of New Mexico renamed its *El Camino Real International Heritage Center*, which opened in 2005, the *El Camino Real Historic Trail Site* in 2015, with the apparent goal of garnering more visitors to the building south of Socorro, New Mexico.[6] These efforts show the region's current fantasy heritage efforts but they date back several decades. For example, in the 1990s, elites on both sides of the US-Mexico border held galas that celebrated Oñate's arrival to the region. Though short-lived, these events highlighted the desire of borderlands elites to sell this tourism ploy.

Figure 9 A sign that directs visitors to the Oñate historical marker.
Credit: Leonel Monroy

The Oñate fantasy heritage in El Paso

Some local organizations and people are very publicly linked with the fantasy heritage. For example, the El Paso Mission Trail Association (EPMTA) and its founder, the late Sheldon Hall, as well as the late sculptor John Houser have become synonymous with the Oñate fantasy. Each worked diligently to promote the area's fantasy heritage. Hall chartered the EPMTA in 1986[7] to promote the Spanish fantasy. In 1991, Hall took an entourage of El Paso leaders to Plymouth, Massachusetts, for a mock trial to determine whose Thanksgiving was first.[8] El Paso historian Leon Metz recalled how the "visionary [and] enterprising ... Sheldon Hall recognized the significance of what had occurred [in El Paso] 400 years earlier" and worked for twenty years to promote the First Thanksgiving. Metz claimed Hall's efforts "brought El Paso reams of exceptionally favorable national and international publicity."[9] Hall spent much time attempting to get El Pasoans interested in the Spanish fantasy from about this time until his passing in November 2012. Hall was the catalyst that brought this myth to the fore and his legacy continues. In 2007, sculptor John Houser also claimed his efforts were to get "these people," presumably Mexican/American El Pasoans, to develop an interest in their history.[10] Houser's perspective is offensive because it implies that Mexican/Americans are unaware of their history and must rely on Whites to explain it to them. Yet, it was largely Chicana/o activists and

Inclusive tourism and public memory 111

Figure 10 The historical marker that commemorates the approximate location where Oñate's colonizing party may have crossed the Rio Grande.
Credit: Leonel Monroy

cultural workers who led and organized the protests against Houser's work. People ignorant of their own history would likely accept the fantasy heritage.

In 2014 KVIA-TV's *Xtra* news show interviewed EPMTA Vice President Mike Lewis as a guest panelist. Lewis claimed that 5,000 people attended the 2013 First Thanksgiving. His description suggested throngs of tourists piled on top of each other waiting to see the thirty-minute reenactment. While Lewis' attendance estimate seems overly optimistic, we found no publicly available figures to support or challenge his assertion. Since we were not present at the 2013 First Thanksgiving, we cannot speak to Lewis' claim. However, we attended the First Thanksgiving reenactment five times over a twelve-year period (2006, 2007, 2008, 2016, and 2017) and estimated the crowd at about 150 people each year. A key First Thanksgiving organizer, teacher Joe Estala estimated 200 people were in attendance at the 2016 event when he addressed that year's First Thanksgiving audience. El Paso heritage tourism is driven by political and economic considerations, presenting a Eurocentric and sanitized historical frame that erases the Spaniards' moral failings. For many years, the main tourism narrative was centered on the First Thanksgiving and the Equestrian/Juan de Oñate monument; nothing else seemed to matter. Yet, El Paso has many non-Spanish fantasy tourist options, for example, Hueco Tanks State Park, nearby White Sands National Monument in New Mexico, among others. Economic maneuvering by the City of El Paso and some business leaders fueled the Spanish fantasy narrative because it was assumed these icons would generate tourist dollars. We say

112 *Inclusive tourism and public memory*

"assume" because it appears that a feasibility study was never conducted to determine the fantasy heritage's potential economic impact.

Although the First Thanksgiving and the Equestrian monument still generate outcries from supporters and detractors, recent tourism developments overshadow them. Designed to bring people and spending into El Paso's downtown area, the local city hall was demolished to make room for a minor league baseball park. The decision to demolish a thirty-year old building was politically charged and led many to protest against the city's actions. How will this focus on Triple-A baseball affect the First Thanksgiving and Equestrian monument as tourism sites or fantasy heritage tourism in general? It may be too early to tell but both seem to have been lost in the tourist shuffle. This shift makes sense in some ways. For one, the First Thanksgiving is twenty miles from downtown El Paso in neighboring San Elizario, Texas. While some residents there support the annual reenactment, when we have attended, it seems that most people leave immediately after the play's conclusion. The economic payout is questionable. Also, many San Elizario residents believe the project excludes locals and thus they do not attend.[11] As a result, organizers do what they can to attract tourists. The event is free, people come and go as they please and may or may not spend their money in San Elizario. As for the Equestrian statue, the city council decided, and the El Paso International Airport management agreed, to place the four-story statue on a small parcel of land with few parking spaces. It sits adjacent to a major roadway, Airway Boulevard, and the airport itself, surrounded by trees. People may or may not see the statue as they drive by. It is uncertain how many stop. What we often hear from our students is, "We don't know who that is." For a decade, one of the authors taught classes at Fort Bliss for our institution. He reports that many service members, particularly those who fly into El Paso at night, say they did not see the statue when they first arrived. Perhaps El Paso's marketing efforts need to be reworked at a more basic level beyond cultural inclusion. People will not support tourism sites and events they do not know exist.

The city and county of El Paso must partner with education and cultural organizations to develop a culturally inclusive and economically viable heritage tourism program. Countless examples of what can be done exist outside the immediate area (e.g., Ireland,[12] and South Africa[13]). The relatively weak link between the El Paso, Las Cruces, and Ciudad Juárez metro areas can be strengthened to provide a foundation for a three-city heritage tourism effort. These cities are linked via a handful of Oñate fantasy heritage elements. El Paso is home to the four-story Oñate/Equestrian statue and some gunslinger myths. The Las Cruces area has Oñate High School and promotes its ties to Billy the Kid. Finally, Ciudad Juárez has the aforementioned Oñate statue at *Cuatro Siglos Park* and a sign with information about the Camino Real at a rest area south of the city. However, tri-city coordination is weak to nonexistent. Worse, at least from our perspective, these efforts promote the Oñate fantasy heritage, rather than recognize the contributions of the area's primary

Inclusive tourism and public memory 113

ethnic groups. This tendency is troubling particularly because heritage tourism can be used to celebrate the border's diversity and cultural richness. It is preposterous to assume that the identity of this region resides solely in the presence of Juan de Oñate. If one embraces the Oñate fantasy, one must erase the contributions of the area's Mexican/Americans, Native Americans (i.e., Tiguas), African Americans, Asian Americans, and even Whites.

Rather than promote the region as a laboratory for diversity, as a model for the rest of the US, local economic and political elites cling to a Spanish fantasy heritage. They prefer to embrace a colonizer who stood trial for what are now crimes against humanity.[14] No large-scale events exist to celebrate El Paso's cultural diversity. The right heritage tourism project might bring together the area's various ethnic populations under the banner of diversity. However, diversity is just an empty promise if attempts at inclusiveness are not promoted by city leaders. To that end, we next provide an overview of our findings and then offer a comparative look at Santa Fe, New Mexico, and El Paso. The following section explains our eight-step framework to foster greater respect for cultural diversity and inclusion in heritage tourism events and related public projects.

The double-edged sword of fantasy heritage

Our research began as a response to the controversy over the thirty-six-foot tall statue of Juan de Oñate and the fantasy heritage-driven and historically incomplete framing of the Spanish colonial experiment in El Paso.[15] The 1998 announcement that the Oñate statue would be the second piece of the XII Travelers Memorial of the Southwest was supported by many local elites. They wanted it placed in the downtown area. All thirty-six-feet of it! Oñate sympathizers and opponents quickly filled local newspapers' editorial pages. Local television news outlets provided reports chronicling the statue's development and the accompanying protests. These events allowed us to scan and analyze newsprint columns, editorials, news stories, as well as other Oñate and First Thanksgiving activities[16] for our research on the current topic.

By the time the City of El Paso announced in 1998 that John Houser's second XII Travelers' statue would be of Juan de Oñate, civic discord had already erupted in New Mexico as the state celebrated the quadricentennial of Spaniard's arrival to the region. In January of the same year, a statue of Oñate in Alcalde, New Mexico had its right foot sawed off at the ankle.[17] The act was followed by a letter claiming credit for a faction of "Native Americans and native New Mexicans" who saw no reason to celebrate Oñate's violence and the dishonest framing (i.e., fantasy heritage) it promoted.[18]

We initially examined the issues surrounding the thirty-six-foot tall Oñate statue. Upon closer inspection other issues arose and we began to see a much larger web. As we expanded our scope to include the First Thanksgiving and the role schools took in advancing the Oñate fantasy we decided to examine these areas also. Oñate sympathizers repeated the mantra that the First

114 *Inclusive tourism and public memory*

Thanksgiving attracted tourists to El Paso (actually, the township of San Elizario, the site where Oñate and his party are thought to have stopped to rest in 1598). We note that to our knowledge no Oñate critic wanted him erased from the historical record, an erroneous claim made by some Oñate sympathizers. However, we were among the academic and cultural workers who criticized the absence of Native Americans and Mexican/Americans from the mainstream Spanish colonial narrative and related topics.

A strong Eurocentric sentiment permeated many of the different authors' points of view and the local media covered many Eurocentric events and people who believe Oñate deserved a place in the city.[19] After all, he stopped just outside El Paso in 1598, created the First Thanksgiving, and brought "civilization" to the area. We also observed that the statue would not only tower over all local monuments but would also render invisible other forms of public art as evidenced in the Native Tigua and Chicano communities. For example, murals in and around the *Segundo Barrio* as well as those at the Chamizal National Park, and work at the Tigua Cultural Center fell into disrepair with little to no effort made by the city, county, or federal government to save them. This lack of Mexican/American inclusion is also present in the El Paso city council's decision of the early 2000s, to rename the Oñate statue "The Equestrian" in response to public outcry. Still, many Oñate sympathizers held onto the idea that the statue would give visibility to El Paso as an important historical city. After three decades promoting the area's Spanish colonial "glory" with little to no apparent economic impact one must question this belief.

As we discovered, there was more to the Oñate fantasy than just a statue. This reality led us to turn our attention to the annual First Thanksgiving Celebration reenactment in San Elizario, Texas. In it Oñate and his party are portrayed as a group of noble explorers (as opposed as violent colonizers) who stopped in the local area to rest and claim the land for Spain. For thirty years (1989–2019), the Mission Trail and others have sponsored the reenactment with the goal of attracting tourists and locals to San Elizario to witness a piece of history. At the heart of the First Thanksgiving events is its thirty-minute reenactment. Three versions have been written by different, presumably El Pasoan, authors. Over the years, we have observed the reenactment and related activities, finding little historical accuracy or complexity. In only a half-hour, the play shows the area's indigenous people adopt Christianity and accept, nay, celebrate their colonized status under Spanish overlords. To be sure, there is no evidence that local indigenous people rebelled or sought to use violence against the Spaniards, unlike their New Mexican brethren. The pacifist or "noble savage" portrayal fits well with the First Thanksgiving's fantasy and leaves the colonizers free to continue their journey to what became New Mexico as the reenactment ends.

We attended five reenactments during the execution of this research, speaking with San Elizario residents, educators, and tourists. We noted an obvious Eurocentric framing of the reenactment, attended by relatively small audiences. While some community residents enjoyed the festivities, others never felt welcomed. In recent years, some business leaders began to publicly question the embrace of the colonial past at the expense of Mexican/American identity. After thirty years, we wondered if it were ever possible to draw a large crowd from El Paso proper to this small hamlet to celebrate the First Thanksgiving. While this appears doubtful, the promotional materials for the 2017 event show the EPMTA has picked up some new and economically powerful local sponsors. What effect, if any, this will have remains to be seen.

Our next turn examined public school curricula from throughout the US, focusing on Texas and New Mexico where possible. The policies in both these states changed over time; however, those curricula we analyzed glorified Spanish exploration and colonization. While the role of Native Americans, Mexicans, and European immigration to Texas and New Mexico are present, the Spanish surface with great frequency. While teachers had the space to examine the consequences of Spanish colonialism, there was no way to determine from the literature the myriad ways they might choose to examine those consequences. One can take religious conversion as an example. From a Spanish perspective, conversion to Christianity can be viewed positively. From a Native perspective, it may be seen as the destruction of traditional religions. Either way, most students, are apparently taught to view Spanish colonialism in the positive. The perspectives of Native Americans, Mexican/Americans and others are omitted or downplayed in the curricula we examined.

Linking the curriculum, public art, memorials, and historical reenactments, substantiates our premise about the regional overrepresentation of the Spanish fantasy heritage. Oñate's high profile in El Paso is only one example of this tendency. Thomas Guthrie's[20] study of Española, New Mexico, a town established only in the 1880s, shows how the desire for tourist dollars has worked there to create a pseudohistorical link to the colonizer. We suspect a desire to be European (i.e., White) on the part of some Mexican/Americans throughout the region may also be at work.[21] The Spanish presence in the American Southwest has long been a subject of university curricula, although it too changes to reflect social mores. Early on, the Black Legend shaped academic perspectives of Spain as a cruel and violent nation. This British interpretation made its way into the US, becoming popular in the 1800s. Near the end of the 19th Century, scholars began to rethink views on Spanish culture, economics, and politics. The reconsideration of Spain's history shaped university students and had great social impact. Historical interpretations, in California, for example, saw Mission-style architecture become both influential and profitable.

Abundant literature exists on tourism and interest in the topic continues to grow. Tourism's impact in developing countries or other regions (e.g., New Mexico and West Texas) is important on multiple levels. At a minimum it affects local economies and how places see themselves via marketing. Interestingly, places anchored in heritage tourism with few to no additional tourist

116 *Inclusive tourism and public memory*

attractions (e.g., restaurants, golf courses, shopping) benefit little. Ashworth suggests "the tourist experience of local heritage is short, with visits to particular towns measured in hours and to a particular site or exhibit better measured in minutes or even seconds."[22] Valerie Smith notes that discretionary income enables one to step outside one's daily routine and thereby become a tourist.[23] Denison Nash claims that "only in industrial societies [does] tourism becom[e] a 'pervasive social phenomenon.'"[24] Furthermore, Dean Mac-Connell suggests that "the tourist industry rhetoric about fostering goodwill and understanding between cultures parallels colonial discourse focusing on the 'civilizing nature of empire.'"[25] Our research supports these views, as the First Thanksgiving, the Oñate/Equestrian statue, and the Mission Trail fail to foster greater cultural understanding. Such ideas are crucial when El Paso's political leaders fail to conduct a feasibility study on the economic impact of their efforts to romanticized colonization. Coupled with the San Elizario elite's refusal to replace the First Thanksgiving with a more culturally inclusive festival, one can see that fantasy heritage remains entrenched in far West Texas, one of the poorest regions in the nation. Their fantasy of victimless colonization breeds greater misunderstanding via the omission of the Tiguas, Mexicans/Americans, and mestizos from the tourist narrative.

Contemporary tourism issues in El Paso

In recent years, the city's tourism attention has focused on luring locals and others to spend their money in the downtown region. El Paso's political and business leaders embrace the idea of what downtown might become. Their position has led to a push toward downtown revitalization that includes the recent completion of a Triple-A baseball stadium, complete with a new team, the El Paso Chihuahuas.[26] The team's arrival led to controversy as El Paso's thirty year-old city hall and the local science museum were demolished to create a downtown baseball stadium. Despite this situation, the local community has embraced the ball park. The Chihuahuas enjoy what appear to be excellent ticket sales and one can spot many locals wearing the tee-shirts and ball caps with the team's logo throughout the city on any given day. The success of this effort is one of the factors that shifted the tourism focus from the Lower Valley to the downtown area.

In 2017, the city moved to build a new, $180 million "multipurpose" arena aimed at attracting touring acts that typically bypass the city. However, like many other city initiatives, community leaders encountered much community opposition, facing allegations of gentrification and cultural erasure. At the time of this writing, community leaders remain focused on toppling the city's oldest neighborhood, *Duranguito* (Little Durango), to build the arena in the downtown area. This downtown focus pitted city leaders against the neighborhood's low-income residents. The newly elected mayor, businessman Dee Margo, supports building in *Duranguito*. During the 2017 mayoral election, then-candidate Margo voiced his support stating that, "The city sold bonds.

We need to get the job done." Margo is an experienced politician with experience as a state representative and service on a local school board. Another candidate, former City Representative Emma Acosta, also supported this effort. Only candidate David Saucedo, yet another local businessman, opposed the site, noting that "Tourism is a $6 billion industry in the state of Texas and we [El Paso] only take two percent of it because we don't champion our heritage."[27] In the end, Margo won the election.[28] At the time of this writing, District Judge Amy Clark Meachum has issued an explanation to an earlier ruling she made prohibiting a sports arena being built in the Duranguito neighborhood. The *El Paso Times* reported that: "The proposed $180 million arena in Downtown El Paso cannot have basketball courts, ice skating rinks or other sports structures."[29] Meachum stated, "A sports arena does not comport with the quality-of-life purpose [El Paso] voters approved."[30] In 2012, El Pasoans voted in support of a quality-of-life bond that was to fund the creation of a Mexican American Cultural Center (MACC) and a children's museum. After a series of lawsuits, in August 2018, the Texas Supreme Court sided with the city's claim that a petition with 4,600 signatures in opposition to the demolition plan did not necessitate a city vote. Coincidentally, the same business people that own the Chihuahuas recently brought a minor league soccer team to El Paso, the Locomotive FC. Having the team play in a new downtown arena would surely be a boon to the city and the team's owners. The team's inaugural season began with a pre-season game against Texas United (Houston) on January 26, 2019. To date, about four games have been played and local support seems strong, even if the team's record is not particularly successful thus far. As the residents of El Paso wait to see what happens with the arena and new United Soccer League team, former El Paso mayor and businessman Oscar Leesar announced his intention to run against Margo, making a resolution to "solve" the Duranguito crisis with minimal impact on the historic neighborhood.

The biggest current concerns with the pending Mexican American Cultural Center thus far were in choosing Mexican American over Hispanic or Latina/o for its name and its future location. One key city council member, Lily Limón, organized a committee of local experts and cultural workers to help answer the name question. She championed what we view as the most correct name; however, she lost to retired El Paso police officer Henry Rivera in her 2017 reelection bid. The coincidental nature of her supporting a politically aware label and of her losing reelection in a lower middle- and working-class district leads one to ponder how much support she had from district elites, if any. Finally, a planned children's museum appears to be the sole hope elected leaders have for launching a local venue that may possibly avoid a strong backlash. No matter the outcome, interest in heritage has waned, posing a problem for First Thanksgiving and other similar efforts. The Equestrian/Oñate statue stands outside the airport, eight miles from the city center. The Mission Trail is twenty miles east of downtown. Only three of the twelve statues (in 20 years) have been installed and only one in downtown. Furthermore, the

118 *Inclusive tourism and public memory*

downtown tourism focus led a number of new businesses to sprout up in the area. Fine dining, upscale bars, and other venues are banking on current revitalization efforts to eventually deliver a tidy profit. El Paso's tourism efforts led us to consider what lessons might be learned by comparing the city with Santa Fe, perhaps the most successful tourism area in the Southwest. It is also a city with a predominantly Hispanic (i.e., *Hispano* or Spanish) population that seeks to attract tourists via fantasy heritage.

Santa Fe, New Mexico: a fantasy tourism mecca

Will city politics remain the central element shaping El Paso's celebration of its colonial and neocolonial legacies? How can the dialogue expand to widen any possibilities for greater ethnic inclusion? Is there a cultural space for those excluded from current tourism efforts? To answer these questions, we first address the complexity of heritage issues by comparing tourism in Santa Fe, New Mexico, with El Paso's efforts to become a tourist destination. Santa Fe has completely transformed its culture and physical area into a tourism mecca, while driving locals out of the city due to the resultant increased cost of living.[31] El Paso is currently transforming its downtown area and while the stated goal is to drive more locals and tourists to the area, its success or failure remains to be seen. Many recent developments, framed as quality of life enhancements, have yielded great public controversy.

The Oñate expedition came north to colonize the frontier and to look for riches.[32] The first permanent Spanish colony in New Mexico was established at Ohkay Owingeh Pueblo, which Oñate renamed San Juan.[33] His permanent headquarters, however, were across the Río Grande at San Gabriel. Together these pueblos constituted "two dwelling units of a single Tewa-speaking village."[34] In 1610, Oñate was replaced as governor over allegations of brutality brought by Pedro de Peralta. The remaining colonists and those accompanying Peralta moved south and founded Santa Fe.[35]

The entry of the railroad initiated an era whereby northern New Mexico was characterized by a "delineation of Spanish and Indian" racial tropes to attract White tourists and immigrants to the region.[36] Yet, the railroad did not help bring New Mexico into the Union.[37] The biracial trope helped to dispel the fear among Easterners that New Mexico was filled with violent and "savage Indians, mongrel Mexican illiterates, and idol worshipers."[38] Instead, one would find two civilizations: indigenous and European. Racial bifurcation helped to sanitize the landscape from the legacy of miscegenation by clarifying the Spanish-Indian racial boundary. These elements led to the romanticizing of conquistadores to hide a region characterized by "peonage, poverty, undereducation, dispossession, and migratory wage labor."[39]

At the start of the 20th Century debates emerged addressing the move to consolidate New Mexico and Arizona as the regions moved toward statehood. Among the key political debates was how to draw the map in a manner that ensured Anglos would dominate Mexicans, particularly their economic and political interests. Although New Mexico was more tolerant of its Mexican/American population, Arizona's state constitutional conventioneers sought to legally marginalize this social category.[40] Many capitalists and entrepreneurs wanted to exoticize and exploit both regions for tourist consumption, going so far as to suggest renaming the region "Montezuma or Acoma" to cement the desire for a land of enchantment.[41] These efforts show that the use of fantasy heritage was important early on in the history of the Southwest.[42]

Beginning in the 1920s, the Museum of New Mexico became a key actor in luring tourists to "the city different" (i.e., Santa Fe).[43] Less than two decades later the state of New Mexico formed the Coronado Cuarto Centennial Commission to plan for celebrations of Coronado's exploits in the region. The federal government created a similar commission to cover the costs of these efforts with plans for a large event in 1940.[44] Although not an overwhelming success, the Centennial laid a foundation for future Santa Fe commemoration celebrations. By 1957, Santa Fe began enforcing an adobe-style architectural ordinance in the downtown area, pushed by novelist Oliver La Farge.[45] Work carried out by Alfred Bandelier and Frank Cushing influenced early romantic tourism narratives of Santa Fe. Nieto-Phillips calls their work as associates of the Bureau of Immigration "the forces of American colonialism" in action.[46] They provided the Bureau of Immigration with Disneyfied depictions of Pueblo peoples which appeared authentic to the untrained masses.[47] The economics of tourism in New Mexico were shaped, at least in part, by some people's desire to witness what Nieto-Phillips has called the "last vestiges of a 'dying race' (Indians) and the sons of the conquistadores."[48] Tourism in New Mexico created a fetish with all things "Indian" and "Spanish." Like Bandelier and Cushing's efforts, the photography of William H. Brown and George Bennett also helped spread such depictions of New Mexico throughout the US.[49] The existing villages and Native traditions became a form of colonization in that both groups and their histories were frozen in time.[50] Sociologist Thomas Guthrie explains that tourist-oriented myths (i.e., fantasy heritage) place Indians and Spaniards in the past, stripping them of their respective cultures to allow Anglos to profit off tourists. These actions "inspir[ed] an industry based on cultural differences."[51] The omission of Anglos from the fantasy heritage gave them invisibility and converted them into "the standard or norm … against which others are measured"[52] and more importantly "leaving Anglo-Americans to claim 'modernity' and New Mexico's future for themselves."[53]

While Anglo interest in Santa Fe began a century ago, in 1981 *U.S. News and World Report* hailed it as the place to be. *Esquire* magazine shared similar views at the time. This framing and comparable media attention led to increased tourism and an influx of wealthy residents to Santa Fe during the 1980s and 1990s. Land prices soared as film stars, business leaders, and artists increasingly wanted to call Santa Fe home. By the 1990s, Anglos outnumbered *Hispano* or long-standing Latina/o-origin residents, according to Lovato, who also linked this change to a decline in the local middle class.[54]

120 *Inclusive tourism and public memory*

Tourism colonized Pueblo culture, leading to both its exploitation as a cultural commodity and raising questions about its authenticity. Pueblo life was simplified for tourists.[55] Then, Santa Fe faced an important need to balance its tourist friendly framing while avoiding the Disneyfied representations that could later hurt the economic bottom line of "tourist magnet areas."[56] Excessive tourism diminishes an area's charm as places become crowded, exploited, and lacking in appeal. Plus, labor in tourism areas typically consists of low-paying service jobs that support pricey restaurants, hotels, and tourist amusements but do not afford workers a high standard of living. Santa Fe was forced to raise its minimum wage to minimize this tendency.[57] It continues to struggle to meet the water supply needs of its skyrocketing population and heavy tourist traffic.[58] Today, *Hispano* Santa Feans feel underappreciated, underemployed, and underrepresented, as a new form of colonialism is imposed upon them under a fantasy heritage façade.[59] Their traditional culture, well documented by George I. Sánchez[60] and Robert Coles,[61] among others, has been replaced by a fine-tuned system of tourism activities and structures. The ease with which one finds Santa Fe brochures throughout the entire state of New Mexico and Canyon Road's more than 200 art galleries outside the Santa Fe plaza are but two examples of these elements. Many other locales have had to build themselves into a tourism mecca, as evidenced by the decades-long efforts that took place in Okinawa (See Case study 4.1).

Case study 4.1 Creating a tourism mecca in Okinawa

During World War II, the Battle of Okinawa off Japan's south coast stripped the area of all vegetation. Two notable landmarks, the Seiden Gateway and Shuri Castle, lay in ruins after the war. The castle was demolished and only subterranean outlines of a few walls remained. In the 1950s, locals wanted to return to the lives that they had lost to the war or to something similar. However, business leaders could not resist the allure of tourist dollars and their chance to rebuild the island. They worked hard to convert the city into part heritage tourism site, part tropical island paradise by planting palm trees and hibiscus flowers. These items were not indigenous to the island and had to be imported. Ironically, they became Okinawa's calling card and they were used on many tourism brochures.

When visitors noted their hosts' lack of hospitality and slow nature during the 1950s, the Okinawa Tourism Development Corporation (OTDC) trained tourism workers in customer service. In the 1960s, the OTDC used privately-owned bus lines for guided tours of Okinawa given by attractive young women who had been tutored in area history. To improve customer service and stronger local pride, competitions were held between each bus line and its tour guides. Each wanted to be rated better than the others. In the 1970s, a move was made to convert the island to a more convincingly tropical locale and its promotion continued into the 1980s. In the 1990s tourism officials launched a successful public relations campaign, with support from the Japanese Prime Minister's Office, that linked the reopening of Shurijo Park with the filming and eventual broadcast of a soap opera, *Ryukyu no Kaze* (*Winds of Ryukyu*). The title referenced the "original" rulers that resided in the Shuri Castle. The campaign included images of Japanese warriors and was featured in the magazine of All Nippon Airways. Yet, critics suggested that preserving was what left of the original Shuri Castle and Seiden would have had much more historical value than the reproductions that were being promoted as local history. Today, Okinawa is recognized as a tropical island, lined with palm trees and thriving with hibiscus flowers. Its tourism industry is recognized for its hospitality. The people of Okinawa no longer oppose the inaccuracies related to its tourism representations (at least not in great numbers).

Discussion questions

The following questions highlight the tensions between historical commemoration as a tourism strategy and as fantasy heritage:

1. Can a place be authentic if it imports its flora and rebuilds ruins as a tourism ploy?
2. Critics suggest that the new structures are reproductions. How might they react differently if the ruins had been preserved and a battle memorial had been erected there?
3. How many and what types of tourists do you think Okinawa would be able to attract if it had not rebuilt the Seiden gateway and Shuri Castle? Would tourism have still become so successful? Why do you think as you do?
   Source: Gerald Figal. "Between War and Tropics: Heritage Tourism in Postwar Okinawa." *Public Historian* 30, no.2 (2008), 83–107.

El Paso v. Santa Fe: from Spaniards in the North to Oñate in the Valley

El Paso community leaders' support for the Oñate fantasy is a longstanding tradition, as they have dreamed of drawing tourists to the broader area in numbers similar to Santa Fe (or even San Antonio). Many of these efforts were delegated to the EPMTA. However, that organization has been fraught with much internal tension and has been unable to generate community interest in the Spanish fantasy heritage, despite a thirty-year effort. EPMTA's energies have focused on the area "missions" (San Elizario has a chapel) and the First Thanksgiving fantasy myth. However, few locals identify as Spanish (we have met only one Native El Pasoan in the decade we have researched this phenomenon) and most do not see colonialism as a positive part of area history, based on the level of support from everyday El Pasoans and their regional neighbors. Even EPMTA President Suki Ramos has admitted that EPMTA efforts have not gone as planned. She stated that "the organization itself, hasn't met its goals of its mission statement to preserve, promote, and

122 *Inclusive tourism and public memory*

educate the public on the history of the mission trail."[62] This situation may be due to the group's "vision [being] about as brittle as its arrangement,"[63] according to Ramos. The group apparently has a difficult time working together.[64] Mary Davis, who held the EPTMA presidency after Ramos, and before Ramos subsequently regained it, noted: "It's difficult to get everyone thinking together on the same page. Each mission: Socorro, Ysleta, and San Elizario is pushing its own interests."[65] There has also been a backlash against the Oñate fantasy by some power brokers, for example, former Texas State Representative Norma Chavez: "I acknowledge the history of that era, but I don't celebrate or honor the statue of Oñate; I abhor the cruelty he inflicted on native and indigenous people."[66] As noted earlier, former San Elizario Historical Society President Al Borrego questioned the legitimacy of San Elizario's claim to the first Thanksgiving in the Americas.[67] In 2014, Texas Senator José Rodríguez organized a second heritage tourism conference in El Paso. Comments made by the senator surprised the audience when he reminded them of the area's indigenous history. In contrast, local county commissioner Vincent Pérez referred to the other panellists as history buffs and framed most of his comments by talking about history in Washington, DC; he repeatedly noted that policymakers need to help El Pasoans feel a connection with San Elizario's history. Although his district includes the Lower Valley, he admitted to the same panel that he did not know much about local history and had not studied it until assuming his elected position.[68] Yet, in 2015, Pérez and other officials unveiled three designs for 115 roadway signs to be installed throughout a forty-five mile stretch of El Paso county, declaring portions of local roadways the "Camino Real Auto Tour Route."[69] Delays have long plagued the XII Travelers and First Thanksgiving fantasy efforts, coupled with a lack of community support. Apparently, few El Pasoans have developed the connection the commissioner hoped for. Perhaps these signs will help or perhaps they are too little too late. Either way, the EPTMA has faced challenges in providing easy tourist access to the First Thanksgiving play and San Elizario plaza. It also has yet to promote more than fantasy heritage framing in its tourism events.

Although Destination El Paso, the local convention and visitors' bureau, recognizes the Mission Trail road course, the Lower Valley remains an underdeveloped portion of the metro area. Self-guided tours of the missions are required as no guided bus tours or information centers exist at any of the three mission sites. The omission of such elements, San Elizario's distance from downtown El Paso, and many negative local stereotypes of the Lower Valley likely preclude much tourism. A mobile phone app is currently available to help people as they visit the missions. We also recently saw a small bus covered in Mission Trail decals, but were unable to confirm that it served tourists wanting to visit the Lower Valley churches. In contrast to San Elizario and its missions, the plaza and tourist district in Old Mesilla, New Mexico, forty-five miles west of El Paso, receives a heavy stream of tourists, generating hundreds of millions of dollars annually from visitors.[70] The First

Inclusive tourism and public memory 123

Thanksgiving reenactment currently fails to draw anywhere near those figures, attracting only 150–200 people per year and almost all of them leave the plaza immediately after the reenactment. An event with broader appeal among locals and tourists would surely improve area profits. Perhaps this situation explains the shift in focus toward a revitalized downtown.

In recent years, the "Visit El Paso" website,[71] a key El Paso marketing brand has included the Lower Valley missions/chapel and some area tourism sites. Yet, the framing may mislead visitors who expect a highly developed tourism mecca, not poorly paved roads with a few road signs announcing the mission trail. Over all, El Paso's elite are now better coordinated and recognize the bigger value of a revitalized downtown, an area whose heritage tourism includes the El Paso Museum of History, a set of newly launched and refurbished classic street cars, and the *Museo Urbano*, a volunteer led community Mexican/American museum described in Chapter 5. Numerous downtown buildings are passable as local heritage but they are often run-down and either vacant or have only their first floors rented out to retailers that target low-income shoppers. Regentrification efforts are under way. For example, the Camino Real Hotel, an El Paso landmark, fell into a bad state of disrepair during the 2010s. It was purchased in 2017 by a pair of developer organizations, including the Meyers Group, "a Miami real estate development company with El Paso family ties."[72] The new owners entered into an eighteen-month renovation project with a cost of $70 million, partially offset by $34 million in city incentives.[73] The renovated Hotel Paso del Norte will be billed as a Marriott Autograph Collection Hotel.[74]

Another important downtown landmark is the *Plaza de los Lagartos* sculpture by world renowned sculptor, the late, Luis Jiménez, an El Paso native. Local developers gentrifying the area made efforts to have *Los Lagartos* removed from its San Jacinto Plaza home. Its Chicana/o aesthetic was argued to be unappealing to the tenants targeted for downtown living. It is, perhaps, overly empowering in its colorful defiance of El Paso's neocolonial reality. Community protests led the developers to back down. The city paid to refinish the sculpture and had it returned to the plaza.[75] *Los Lagartos* currently sits under a large glass canopy. While people still congregate in *la placita* as locals call it, many who grew up going to the original plaza may find the new one lacking in traditional (i.e., Chicano) El Paso flavor. Finally, the first Traveler, a fourteen-foot tall representation of Fray García de San Francisco, stands in Pioneer Plaza, a tiny plot of land outside the historic Plaza Theater. The most recent El Paso Museums and Cultural Affairs Department (MCAD) Arts District map lists Pioneer Park but not the monument.[76] Current efforts to redevelop the downtown have eclipsed the Oñate fantasy heritage but for how long? El Paso has invested in the Spanish colonial fantasy for decades and in 2017 the First Thanksgiving received support from a number of important local charities, for example, the Hunt Family Foundation, a private charity that funds "local heritage"[77] events and other projects in El Paso. This support suggests the First Thanksgiving may

124   *Inclusive tourism and public memory*

continue, even if it, or perhaps because it, like a vast majority of area tourism venues, omits the Mexican community and its local heritage.

El Paso typically limits Mexican history to *Cinco de Mayo* and *16 de Septiembre*, events easily promoted via alcohol sales. Yet, the Mexican Revolution played a major part in El Paso's history, as well as Mexico's.[78] Mexican revolutionaries laid battle plans in downtown buildings. One of the most important treatises on the revolution, *The Underdogs*, [79] was written in El Paso's *Segundo Barrio*. Little, if any, of this history is celebrated in any complex manner at any public event. Even the Salt War of 1877 has fallen victim to local historical amnesia. The conflict involved the struggle of San Elizario's community to overturn the appropriation of an open salt bed harvested by Mexicans for use in their homes to dry meat, season food, and other household uses. Despite generations of such use, Judge Charles Howard announced that hundreds of acres of salt beds were now his property and that he would charge a fee for salt. Louis Cardis had recently been elected to the state legislature and advocated for the Mexican people. San Elizario's population was especially supportive of him. His conflict with Howard went beyond words to include fisticuffs. On October 10, 1877, Howard, carrying a shotgun, found Cardis at a local El Paso store and fired both barrels into him.[80] Howard was tracked to San Elizario by a group of Mexicans from both sides of the river. He was killed by firing squad, along with two of his associates. Howard supporters had their homes ransacked; even a group of Texas Rangers were forced to surrender to the Mexicans. It took a posse of thirty volunteers from Silver City, New Mexico, to restore order. While this is part of El Paso history few of our students know about this and other important Mexican/ American or Chicano events, unless they have discovered such important information in university classes. Therefore, we strive to make the point to them about the importance of learning history. This example highlights the selective and dangerous tendencies in fantasy heritage. If this type of racial prejudice is erased from the historical records, current and future generations will fail to understand the machinations that influence how we understand our world. One city that engaged in a powerful and effective effort to maintain its history, while reclaiming its identity is Chemnitz, Germany, as can be seen in Case study 4.2.

Case study 4.2 Maintaining historical accuracy to create local identity: the case of Chemnitz, Germany

Chemnitz, Germany, traces its history to Slavic tribes who camped near the river after which the city is named. In 1143, a Benedictine monastery was established in the area and a city grew up around it. In the Middle Ages, Chemnitz became a textile center, earning the name, "the Manchester of Saxony" by the 1800s for its production of fabrics. During the early 1900s, Auto-Union was centered in Chemnitz for a time. This is one of the four companies that merged to create Audi, now the luxury automobiles division of Volkswagen. During World War II, a labor camp composed of 500 female prisoners operated in the city to produce military hardware. Perhaps the most interesting event to take place in Chemnitz's long history occurred after World War II. In 1953, when Chemnitz was controlled by the German Democratic Republic (DDR), the former East Germany, the DDR leadership renamed the city Karl-Marx-Stadt or Karl Marx City. The Socialists also installed a bust of Karl Marx, done in the Soviet realist tradition by Lev Kerbel, in the city center. The monument is approximately two and a half stories tall and sits in front of a former government building. Behind the monument, a large section of the building has the phrase "workers of the world unite" inscribed in multiple languages across an even taller concrete plaque that covers about one-third of the building. The sculpture is the largest bust in the world. After reunification, the people of Chemnitz needed to decide what to do about their city's name and about the socialist era statue in their city center. In the end, they voted to reinstitute the city's traditional name. They also voted to keep the sculpture as a reminder of their history. Many of Kerbel's other works were torn down and destroyed, an understandable reaction on the part of those who had, like their peers in Chemnitz, been victim to socialist politics and brutality. Fortunately, Chemnitzers saw their statue's historical value.

Today, the Karl Marx Monument retains its prominent place in the city center. Referred to as the Nischel or "head" by locals, in the local Saxsonian dialect, it is both a reminder of the past and a testament to the indelible desire of the community to never return to a socialist system of government. This form of political governance was imposed on them when the allies divided Germany amongst themselves after the World War II. Tourists who visit Chemnitz pass in front of the Nischel as they make their way to the city center from the main train station. Those staying at the Chemnitzer Hof, one of the city's finest hotels, walking to the local opera house, or art museum are also likely to encounter the monument. It has become a popular tourist attraction that reminds people of Chemnitz's past and its much more positive future after reunification in 1990. Tragically, in August 2018 German nationalists and far-right "soccer fans" protested against the death of a thirty-five year-old German man at the hands of an immigrant by meeting in front of the Nischel and inviting others via social media to protect Germany from immigrants, according to the *New York Times* (August 28, 2018). The racists began to attack people they thought were foreigners and the city had to close an event celebrating its 875th anniversary. The violence continued for a few days.

Discussion questions

1. What are the costs and benefits of leaving the Karl Marx Monument in place after reunification?
2. Do you think that Chemnitz's identity would be different if they had decided to tear down the Karl Marx Monument? Why or why not?

126 *Inclusive tourism and public memory*

3. What can Chemnitzers do to prevent or minimize similar events from happening?

Source: This case study is based on conversations author Frank G. Pérez had with people from the Chemnitz, Germany area over a series of five visits between 2001 and 2007. The information is consistent with multiple sources. However, it should not be cited for any public or academic purposes.

Another issue affecting El Paso tourism is the state's fiscally conservative nature, Texas politicians often campaign on limiting government support. For example, 2010 gubernatorial candidate Bill White ran on a promise to eliminate the state tourism office's advertising budget.[81]

The history of development in downtown El Paso provides an example of local power dynamics. Prior to White, in 2006, the Paso del Norte Group (PDNG), a conglomerate of local business owners, issued a plan to revitalize downtown, including a large section of the *Segundo Barrio*, an important Mexican/American cultural area and historical part of downtown. This community sits adjacent to the US-Mexico border and has traditionally been home to Mexican immigrants and working-class Mexican Americans. The PDNG hoped to acquire real estate in *Segundo Barrio* for development, likely because of its low cost and prime location. The PDNG failed to ask for any community input before announcing their plan which included using eminent domain. This omission generated a strong backlash that fostered much support for *Segundo Barrio*'s people. The PDNG wrongly assumed that the area's working-class Mexican Americans would capitulate to their plans; however, the *Segundo Barrio* community fought against the gentrification efforts. People from throughout the city have bonds to the area. Many people raised in *Segundo Barrio* typically retain strong ties to the community and quickly spoke out against the PDNG's efforts.[82] *Segundo Barrio* survived intact, at least for now, but developers cannot resist the lure of downtown real estate.

Current gentrification efforts focus on *Duranguito*, tied to efforts to build a concert and/or soccer arena. This controversy is ongoing and beyond the scope of the current project. Suffice it to say that legal battles, a concerted effort by owners to begin to tear down buildings (even after a court order instructed that no demolitions begin), and much community protest are in the midst of playing out as we write. Our work seeks to promote a more inclusive and culturally sensitive approach to tourism in El Paso (and other locales). We believe that empowering students by sharing this type of information with them can help to generate more culturally appropriate tourism efforts. Provided, of course, that our students take these examples to heart when they enter the area's professional class. The point here is that whether it is the business community or the city council—often it is both—many local elites believe they can do what they want to Mexican/Americans. Many of these individuals still believe stereotypes about passive Mexicans.

Figure 11 A mural in El Paso's *Segundo Barrio*. The legacy of Father Harold Rahm who served at the Sacred Heart Catholic Church from 1952 to 1964 is represented by the man on the bicycle.
Credit: Leonel Monroy

Tourism and Mexican/American exclusion

El Paso's tourism struggles have been ongoing for more than a century, beginning at least with Mayor Tom Lea's efforts to promote the region's past in the 1910s.[83] In 1985, Charles Ponzio[84] wrote an editorial asserting the problems with tourism resulted from city and county leaders' lack of vision. He argued that the local chamber of commerce's failure to upgrade and improve downtown led to its decline, including as a tourist draw. Citing El Paso developer Marcus Meyer, Ponzio notes "for El Paso to be successful, it must aggressively accept and promote the genuine friendliness of the Mexican American people."[85] He suggested that El Paso replicate an Austin, Texas, $11 million bond issue that created a Mexican American Cultural Center. While such a move passed in recent years, after community debate about its name, its future location remains an issue. The city announced it will be housed in an as yet unbuilt annex to the main library. It was supposed to be in a stand-alone building.

Local filmmaker and radio talk show host, Jackson Polk has promoted the idea of heritage tourism for the city. In an *El Paso Times* column he writes, "our region's rich and diverse history and heritage can help turn El Paso into a destination city that's world class."[86] While we certainly agree with Polk's views on the area's rich history, we noted that his column, as well as in an

128　*Inclusive tourism and public memory*

interview in *El Paso, Inc.* newspaper in 2014, fails to mention anything about Mexican Americans as part of local heritage. El Paso was the first major US city to elect a Mexican American mayor, Raymond Telles, who held the office for two terms (1957–1961). He was also the first Mexican American to be appointed as a US ambassador and held other important national-level posts. The most highly decorated World War I veteran from Texas, Marcelino Serna, was born in Mexico but lived in El Paso after the war. The zoot suiter style adopted by Chicanos during the 1940s is often attributed to El Paso's Mexican American youths. Among the most important Chicano civil rights meetings, organized by Rodolfo "Corky" González, were held at the El Paso County Coliseum in the early 1970s. El Pasoan John Daniel "Danny" Olivas, a UTEP graduate, served on two space shuttle missions to the international space station. The University of Texas at El Paso is the only emerging national research university recognized as a Research 1 institution under the Carnegie classification system with a majority Mexican/American student population. There are many other important Mexican/American contributions to El Paso's heritage. Regrettably, few local leaders seem to know about or promote them.

Rethinking tourism along the border

Juan de Oñate will continue to hold a key position in El Paso's tourism narrative for the foreseeable future. City elites must practice much greater cultural inclusion if they hope to see local heritage tourism succeed. Mexican Americans, the Tigua tribe, African Americans, and other minorities will contest their exclusion from the city's current economic goals. Yet, it appears that city leaders desire to maintain El Paso's neocolonial reality. Whites are less than twenty percent of the population but dominate the city's economic spheres and have a large influence on local politics. A handful of Mexican American politicians appear content to serve as bridges between their largely working-class brethren and the elites. Such politicians promote agendas that often benefit El Paso's white population—again, see the example of the renamed roadway and park. A small number of Mexican American politicians and business leaders advocate for Mexican/American issues.

The EPMTA was created in the hope of developing a tourist path along Socorro Road from the Ysleta neighborhood in El Paso, through Socorro, Texas, and into the heart of San Elizario. Since the late 1990s, the EPMTA has also supported the XII Travelers of the Southwest Memorial project that is under the control of an eponymously-named committee. Three statues have been completed and installed as public art at the time of this writing: Fray García de San Francisco, Juan de Oñate, and Susan Magoffin. There are plans for nine more but the project continues at a glacial pace. According to sculptor John Houser, the first statue, Fray García, was the tallest statue in bronze in Texas at the time of its installation.[87] It is also the only one in downtown and the XII Travelers project was initially designed to benefit tourism there. Yet, even this statue is small in comparison to the four-story tall Oñate/Equestrian statue. The statue is gigantic and finding a place to install it proved a challenge. At one time, the Oñate/Equestrian piece was to be installed in Cleveland Park, outside the main public library. Opponents convinced civic leaders that this locale would allow Oñate's shadow to literally and figuratively fall over the library, a symbol of El Paso's knowledge. There was also talk of installing the statue along the banks of the Río Grande. However, concern that the people of Ciudad Juárez might not want a large horse's ass facing their city led to a search for another locale. West El Paso City Representative Jan Sumerall suggested placing it on property owned by the El Paso International Airport (EPIA) and far from public view. Oñate sympathizers objected and threatened to sue the city if this action were taken. The statue was finally installed in a prime location outside EPIA, which minimizes possible defacement. To vandalize it here would result in federal criminal charges, which carry significant penalties. The airport manager held a press conference announcing that the airport is one of the few city entities that generates profit; as such, the EPIA offered to cover the Oñate/Equestrian's final funding shortfall. In recognition of this action, the city did then decide to install the statue at EPIA.

Concerns endure over who shall be represented in the XII Travelers' series and financing the remainder of the project. At this time, Susan Magoffin was selected as the first female Traveler, and a maquette was showcased for El Pasoans via a series of what the XII Travelers Committee frames as "community outreach programs."[88] The final statue has been installed at Keystone Heritage Park in El Paso's Upper Valley. The XII Travelers committee claims Magoffin represents the economic exchange that occurred between the Santa Fe/Chihuahua Trail during the 1800s. Known for her diary, Magoffin's gender limited her agency, due to the era's social mores. We question whether a wealthy Anglo woman born in Kentucky and with limited time in El Paso is really an apt representation of El Paso in the 1800s. Gender inclusion is now part of the XII Travelers' memorial but where are the women of color? Mexican/Americans? Native Americans? That community leaders promote a heritage monument without a single Mexican American, not even on the list of proposed Travelers, in a city that is eighty-two percent Mexican/American is blatantly racist.[89] Interestingly, the XII Travelers Committee found other Spaniards to deify, including Álvar Núñez Cabeza de Vaca who is referenced, along with Estebanico, as "Conquistadors of the Heart." The callousness and cluelessness of El Paso leaders knows no bounds. John Houser's passing suggests the key sculptor is now his son, Ethan, who is driving the project.[90] That two White sculptors can lead such a racially biased work highlights the disproportionate power of El Paso's White elite, often transplants from other cities or from El Paso's oldest Anglo families. Mexican/Americans battle against a hegemony that keeps their wealth and political power largely in check. They must also compete against economically elite families from

130 *Inclusive tourism and public memory*

Cuidad Juárez. It is this situation that necessitates a scholarly calling out of fantasy heritage and tourism in West Texas. El Paso is one of the twenty poorest cities in the nation, and we must come face-to-face with the Spaniards' legacy of viciousness, but these issues must not relegate Indians and Mexicans to invisible historical bystanders.

There are multiple strategies a city might use to develop its tourism market. Places across the globe promote heritage tourism events, memorials, and venues. Rather than promoting the same tired myths about Spanish nobles, we suggest the three local area communities—Ciudad Juárez, El Paso, and Las Cruces—develop a tri-city tourist network composed of ethnically diverse members. As we searched for possible answers for how to develop such a plan, we discovered a paper by Tomas J. Cuevas Contreras and Isabel Zizaldra Hernández, scholars based at the *Universidad Autonoma de Ciudad Juárez* (Autonomous University of Juárez City). They suggest that successful tourism requires the support and participation of multiple tourism stakeholders, particularly people from the local populations.[91] This means a working agreement of strategic alliances between public and private tourist activities across the various communities to develop a "cross-border network"[92] of tourism support.

Globally, tourism provides an estimated 194.6 million jobs, about one of every thirteen jobs on the planet. In 2005, tourism and related activities generated more than $6 trillion in sales, world-wide. Tourist development includes many different activities but in terms of sustainable tourism, the areas of historic preservation, natural resources, cultural activities, and heritage tourism are vital. The logistics of creating and sustaining such a network across state and international lines may be fraught with difficulties, including intercultural competition and conflict, but it remains a manner by which the three cities can benefit from tourism that is closely grounded in historical facts, presented in a complex and holistic manner. These suggestions offer potential insights for readers facing similar issues. We have also developed a series of suggestions based on our research and experiences looking at tourism in El Paso for over a decade.

A framework for inclusive heritage tourism: lessons from El Paso

The elections of Presidents Barrack Obama and Donald Trump, the murder of many Black men by law enforcement, the rise of the "alt right" (i.e., White supremacists), attacks on "elitist" university professors, rampant homophobia, and many other examples reveal the strong racial discord and social animosity that permeate contemporary US culture. Our study has been an attempt to explain the underlying racial aspects of the Juan de Oñate myth and its impact on local tourism via fantasy heritage. The bigger challenge will be to convince heritage tourism proponents and Oñate sympathizers that history is complex and should be sold as such to locals and tourists. Critics have suggested that progressive voices, like ours and countless others', need to move on or get past this issue. However, it is imperative in this day and age for all of us to talk about and acknowledge the contributions people of color have made to the Southwest (and the rest of the nation).

Here, we offer eight steps for any person or entity entering into heritage tourism to adopt to minimize fantasy heritage: (1) follow all relevant laws and work to reach minority groups beyond minimum requirements; (2) include appropriate experts on art, culture, city planning, and other areas throughout the entire project's development and implementation; (3) have project representatives conduct extensive community outreach, request and seriously consider feedback from these efforts; (4) work to generate community involvement, paying attention to individuals or groups that represent or are opinion leaders[93] to minority or marginalized populations; (5) move the project along at a moderate pace—do not let it linger for years or decades; (6) consider the environmental and long-term effects of the project, and what people will likely think years into the future; (7) conduct feasibility studies before, during, and after, each phase of the project to ensure it is economically prudent; and (8) above all else maintain and support transparency (see Table 1).

We invite readers to review the previous chapters to find ways El Paso's leadership failed to follow these steps at various points in the development of local fantasy heritage. Below, we offer a short assessment of how these guidelines relate to the fantasy heritage that has been imposed on a largely Mexican/American community.

Include the appropriate experts through the project's development and completion

The XII Travelers Memorial of the Southwest proposal brought before the El Paso city council in the late 1980s led to the establishment of the XII Travelers Committee. Its charge was to provide expertise and oversight relatively early on in the project. Yet, it failed to consider the views of a large portion of the local population. This requirement must move beyond forming an official organization of like-minded people. Our research suggests that few, if any, committee members were academics. The number of members with doctoral degrees appears to be nil, same for folks with advanced training, if any, in anthropology, Chicano studies, intercultural communication, or a related area. For example, noted El Paso historian Leon Metz was on the committee but we found not a single humanities or social science area professor from the local university or any other. The University of Texas at El Paso awards a PhD degree in Southwest history and master's level degrees in many relevant areas. Had the XII Travelers Committee sought out and considered the views of those community experts who know the area's working-class people and their lifeways, much of the controversy could have been avoided. Many Oñate supporters can legitimately claim to be native El Pasoans, some with multigenerational family ties. Few, however, can also claim strong ties to the Mexican/

Table 1 A framework for culturally inclusive heritage tourism and related projects

Recommendation	Description	Example or Rationale
Follow all legal requirements for Requests for Proposals (RFPs) and work to exceed those requirements.[94]	Post/distribute RFPs in legally mandated spaces and allow ample time for the development of competitive proposals.	Ensure members of minority groups receive the information. Allowing ample time gives people the opportunity to prepare compelling proposals, particularly those starting their careers, programs, or facing other constraints.
Include art, culture, city planning, legal, and related experts on relevant project committees and boards throughout the project. Heterogeneous groups face more initial conflict but typically produce more and more diverse results than homogenous groups.[95]	Each committee and board needs members who will understand the project and related issues from different points of view.	While there are comparatively few people of color with credentialed expertise (e.g., PhD, MFA, JD), many are available to work on heritage projects or may help identify others who may.
Conduct extensive outreach to engage a diverse group of possible RFP applicants and proposals.	Share RFPs with different minority social categories, to include ethnicity, gender, sexual orientation, and so on.	Minorities may rely on networks outside formal or mainstream sources. Announcing the RFPs in minority media or different languages may mitigate this tendency.
Take seriously and thoroughly consider the concerns of minorities and/ or minority leaders.	Invite and analyze community input to understand and reconcile differing points of view. Heritage is a contested field. It is also often publicly funded, at least partially.	Community feedback must be considered. When political actors or units receive a request for feedback and ignore it, they jeopardize community trust and support.
Move project at a moderate pace.[96]	Provide ample time for each project phase and solicit or accept public feedback where appropriate. Projects done too quickly may deny feedback. Projects that linger may lose community support. Controversial projects may unnecessarily prolong community discord.	Only three of twelve XII Travelers project statues have been completed in thirty-one years. The project has spawned community debate about classism and racism for three decades as a result of its glacial pace. It has also overshadowed most, if not all, other heritage tourism/ public art projects in the city for that time.

Inclusive tourism and public memory   133

Recommendation	Description	Example or Rationale
Consider environmental and long-term cultural effects.[97]	Identify, to the extent possible, how the project will affect the cultural and physical environment. How will the project's representation of culture and ethnicity affect the area?	Many tourism cites encounter challenges related to pollution, traffic congestion, sewage, and others. Thus, heritage tourism efforts must consider more than simply potential profits.
Conduct feasibility studies throughout the project to ensure it is likely to be a solid investment, yielding the desired results (e.g., tourism dollars).[98]	Periodically conduct feasibility studies from the RFPs until the project's completion to ensure the project is attainable and will provide the desired economic impact.	Periodic economic and public review of projects serve as barometers to guide project managers and relevant stakeholders and audiences.
Always maintain transparency.	Making information publicly available builds trust among all interested stakeholders and audiences.	Honesty is the best policy.

American communities south of I-10, the interstate that separates local middle-class or higher status folks from the rest of the people. Elites often shape public art and it is incumbent upon them to do so in a culturally sensitive manner.

Inclusion via extensive community outreach

It is logical to believe that community image is typically in the realm of area leaders and those with middle-class or higher incomes. Yet, in the current socio-cultural climate it is imperative that those involved in shaping a community's image inform the rest of the local/regional population. While no heritage project can conceivably win 100 percent community support, sharing information about the project builds community awareness. More importantly, it can also be used to gauge community views and then to modify the project to better reflect community mores. This does not necessarily mean scrapping a project or altering it completely but it may mean seriously reconsidering how the topic or message is presented. Art's function may be to act as a cultural barometer or to move society forward by pushing the envelope;[99] however, heritage art and events aimed at tourists tend to avoid controversy. The goal is to represent the community in a way that draws visitors, particularly in terms of contemporary norms.

In a conversation one of the authors had while presenting research in Germany, after talking about fantasy heritage in El Paso, a well-dressed, somewhat elderly business professor asked why El Paso's leaders were celebrating

134 *Inclusive tourism and public memory*

colonialism in the contemporary period. He noted that Germany had ended this practice decades ago if not longer. Had the XII Travelers Committee and other key players listened early on to critics who see Oñate as a reminder of the colonial past and the statue as veneration, they may have found a way to alter the memorial in a way that contextualized his importance to local history. We must point out that most scholars see Oñate as a historical footnote and we found no work other than our own commenting on the First Thanksgiving fantasy heritage.

The image of El Paso (or any municipality) affects everyone in the community, even if it is promulgated by a handful of people. The local population is affected by campaigns that in turn affect how tourists see a place, local heritage events, and other quality of life factors. The number of tourists visiting a locale also affect locals' quality of life. Thus, it is incumbent on community leaders to be ethical in the messages and images they use. Here is the problem in El Paso. Community leaders for the past thirty or more years have focused on Oñate, gunslingers, and little else. How can a community that is eighty-two percent of Mexican origin be so oblivious to its Mexican/American past, present, and future? We are reminded of Eduardo Bonilla Silva's notion of color blind racism. Many Whites throughout the Southwest are unaware of their racial biases. For example, many local Whites appear oblivious to the city's racist past. When confronted with inconvenient truths about racial segregation (e.g., El Paso had a "Black" school during the early 1900s), the marginalization of Mexican/Americans that made them second-class citizens, and the importance of El Paso to the Chicano Movement (1965–1978), many community leaders suggest that these phenomena are in the past or are exaggerated.

Failure to recognize the Mexican/American population is also tied to what we see as a flawed approach. In April 2015, the El Paso County Commissioners Court renamed Miguel Aguilera Highway, named after a retired Texas Department of Transportation engineer. When asked about the change, County Judge Veronica Escobar replied on behalf of the court: "We hope that it [the highway name change] will increase tourism [sic], we hope it will increase cross-border trade, and we hope it will have a positive impact on our economic development."[100] This decision was made despite protests from the Aguilera family. So long as community leaders, particularly those of Mexican American background, see no value in the contributions of their fellow ethnic El Pasoans, changing the name reinforces the dominant Anglo hegemony and neocolonial feel of the city. For the record, Escobar is a progressive and serves as a member of the US House of Representatives. She is one of El Paso's most popular politicians. She spoke for the entirety of the court and that body's decision. Yet, such political actions make it easy for fantasy heritage to thrive. Despite protests from the family, the county commissioners went ahead with the name change. We urge anyone involved in heritage tourism or any historical or branding efforts to inform the community of their plans and to take community concerns to heart. Their desires should be considered as a community moves forward to develop new tourist attractions.

Inclusive tourism and public memory   135

Pace the project moderately

Building on the previous item, we also advocate for planning and carrying out projects in a timely manner. After thirty years the XII Travelers project remains a divisive work-in-progress that pits local elites against a large segment of the metro area. Had the project been properly scheduled and funded from its inception it would have been completed in a timely manner. The XII Travelers' delays are analogous to community death by a thousand paper cuts or the notorious battle between the Hatfields and McCoys. No one benefits from thirty years of argument. A three-day symposium titled, *Memory and Monuments: Commemorating and Confronting History on the US-Mexico Border*, was held at our campus in February 2007, twenty years into the XII Travelers' efforts to edify the Oñate fantasy with a four-story monument. Even in this august setting, tempers flared and many of the same points advanced by those for and those against the local Spanish fantasy heritage were voiced publicly. The aforementioned 2013 and 2014 Heritage Tourism Summits allowed for similar scenes to play out. The key, positive difference is that Senator Rodríguez voiced the concerns of many progressives, advocating for the greater cultural inclusion of Native Americans and other marginalized groups in El Paso history. What these examples offer is support for the idea that heritage projects need to avoid fantasy heritage, must contextualize or "complicate" history, and move quickly to prevent years of community discord. Again, had the XII Travelers' project been sufficiently funded from its inception it could have been completed in a matter of years not decades. A prompt resolution would have allowed for other issues to be addressed. If nothing else, the XII Travelers could have served as a learning opportunity that would have allowed future projects to be more historically correct and ethnically inclusive.

Consider the environmental and long-term effects of the project

No one can foresee the future. What social norms will be in years, decades, or centuries is often beyond one's ability to predict. Still, one needs to consider the environmental and long-term effects of heritage tourism projects. In El Paso's case, the environmental toll of the statues, installed and proposed, was not an issue. However, celebrating the cultural impact of twelve dead Europeans and the colonialization of the area has a very real impact. Socially conscious and politically aware people, particularly Mexican/Americans, will be frequently reminded of their second-tier status.[101] This project and the area's promotion of fantasy heritage in other realms (e.g., First Thanksgiving, Oñate High School) potentially foments ethnic distrust or conflict. We can imagine progressive thinkers being cynical of community leaders who often side with Anglo desires to downplay the reality of local demographics in the present. Future generations of El Pasoans will likely be more sensitive to these issues. They will question why current leaders celebrated colonialism a

136 *Inclusive tourism and public memory*

century after such views fell out of favor. Heritage projects should unite communities, inform vistiors, generate tourism, and improve a locale's quality of life. To do this, planners must design programs that fit with contemporary mores and periodically update heritage programs/venues to ensure inclusion and community support.

Maintain transparency and share information with the community

El Paso's Spanish colonial heritage tourism efforts are primarily a mix of public and private monies. Whether such efforts are public or private we argue that they should have a large degree of transparency to inform the community of their message, progress, goals, and economic impact. To their credit the XII Travelers Committee and the EPMTA share some information with the public. One key omission on the part of the City of El Paso is that our research found nothing to indicate a feasibility study has been conducted to show how having the world's tallest equestrian statue may help tourism. One of the authors often asks his students if the fact that Cawker City, Kansas has the world's largest ball of twine makes them want to visit that city instead of Los Angeles or New York. The point is not to bash Kansas but to show them that communities need to empirically show their efforts to attract tourists will likely work. El Paso's leadership has devoted thirty years to the promotion of a Spanish colonial fantasy that lacks any apparent way to gauge its performance. Those working in public areas, and heritage tourism is one, are ethically bound to show their audiences the economic impact of their efforts. Had El Paso leaders requested such a study early on in the Spanish fantasy development they may have discovered its potential to actually lure tourists. It is likely that tourists are interested in many elements other than El Paso's sanitized account of its colonial past. No set of guidelines is exhaustive and heritage tourism interests must consider the uniqueness of their respective projects. We offer these suggestions to help minimize the same types of community-level disruptions that the imposition of the fantasy heritage has yielded in El Paso. We remind readers of Edward T. Hall's premise that intercultural exchange requires respect for and a sincere desire to learn about another culture.[102] For three decades many El Paso leaders have failed to follow these simple premises.

Conclusions

Our study has been an attempt to explain the theme of Juan de Oñate and fantasy heritage as it relates to El Paso area tourism. Though well ingrained into the community's collective psyche, fantasy heritage is a form of neocolonial racism that erases the area's Mexican/American and indigenous populations, privileges an incomplete and sanitized Eurocentric framing of the past, and supports the Anglo-dominant status quo. It is imperative that heritage framing be inclusive in the contemporary era. Heritage tourism efforts must acknowledge the contributions and represent the roles played by a locale's various groups. In El Paso Mexican/Americans, Native Americans, African Americans, and other social categories must be included. When heritage organizers are ignorant about the role minority categories have played in an area's history they must practice due diligence and reach out to various experts to ensure they develop a comprehensive, complex, and marketable tourism framework free from fantasy heritage.

We previously noted that Juan de Oñate was a man who reflected the realities of his era. No one can be completely good or all evil; yet, that is how he is often framed in the civic debates about Spanish conquest. Thus, the First Thanksgiving myth must correct its assumptions about Spanish colonialism. The El Paso area thanksgiving took place in 1598, but let us not worry about whose European celebration was first. The first thanksgiving in America was not celebrated by Juan de Oñate. It did not take place in St. Augustine, Florida, or in Santa Fe, New Mexico. Cabeza de Vaca's celebration in San Pedro Creek, Texas, was not first either. It must have been an indigenous celebration because Native Americans have been on the continent for centuries, if not millennia. It is astounding to think that only one key player in this debate, State Senator Rodríguez, has ever publicly acknowledged this point. The degree of cultural sensitivity and common sense that envelops the Spanish fantasy must increase.

Heritage tourism events should focus on the experiences of the entire community, but as the First Thanksgiving example illustrates that is not always the case. The El Paso area community should acknowledge its Mexican/American population, incorporating lessons on their history in public schools. The Texas Legislature recently approved the development of high school-level ethnic studies courses and the knowledge provided via such courses may help to begin to inform students and communities throughout Texas about the experiences of people of color.[103] Schools must adopt such curricula and parents must support them. Despite what has happened in Arizona, we are cautiously optimistic. Mexican American studies were cancelled in Arizona, bringing national attention to the topic. Texas also has a strongly conservative population in much of the state that may want to avoid the promotion of this knowledge. Tourists would benefit from conferences, dialogues, lectures, and reenactments that provide them with greater context and insight that transcends fantasy heritage representations. Mexican American studies in high school and Chicana/o Studies and similar areas of study at university would offer future heritage cultural workers a solid base from which to operate. Learning about Oñate is important in West Texas and New Mexico, even in other places where his impact was much smaller or indirect. Our concern is about how the symbols, behaviors, attitudes, and practices used to "teach" tourists about Spanish colonialism are framed and what those elements ignore. Ortíz-González, for example, refers to the border as a "hyper-real curio-shop" where:

138 *Inclusive tourism and public memory*

> Tourists, overtaken by the contrast – real and assumed – between the border and their hometown, experience the border in such stark ways that the exposure creates the simulacra of knowledge. Many such travelers become instant experts after a short visit. The intensity of the experience gives them an immediate expertise based on their circumscribed forays into the region.[104]

The problem with this experience is that the tourist finds expertise in "curio-shops, bars, and brothels, which cater to reaffirm the tourist's expectations and demands."[105] This is the hyperreal: the images or representations of drug trafficking, poverty, chaos, and violence. And this fantasy adds to the region's allure for some, leading the visitor to take fantasy representations as accurate. Such perceptions account for the fantastic or mythical view of the border as a supermarket of vices. The fantasy is consumed but never understood beyond its most stereotypic and largely erroneous level. The border becomes an Aztec calendar, a charro hat, and maracas with no understanding of the cultural context where these and myriad other signs exist. These trinkets are disposable, as are Mexican/Americans, to many tourists. Border residents who sell blankets or other items are viewed at times with hostility. For example, one of the authors overheard a tourist say in English to an indigenous woman who approached selling blankets: "You won't con me. You can't scam me, so don't try it." The indigenous woman looked confused and did not reply because she did not speak English. What she said to trigger such a reaction was simply the price of the blanket.

The danger for us is the possibility of inauthenticity, fostered by fantasy heritage elements since business entrepreneurs may conclude that if Mexican/ American culture can be sold to tourists, the community may become a focal point for development, according to Lawrence Herzog.[106] At the same time, some residents become aware that tourism might improve the economy of the community. These sorts of ventures have led scholars to argue that corporations or entrepreneurs look to homogenize products and how people interact with them. Such strategies are used in conjunction with easily recognized logos, tag lines, and other readily recognized elements that influence consumer behavior.[107] The homogenization of communities and cultures via fantasy heritage and related efforts destroy cultural spaces and the physical environments that surround them. These items are prostituted and have their authenticity stolen. Consumption trumps culture.

Successful heritage tourism relies on physical sites, supporting sociocultural elements (e.g., news media coverage), material items (e.g., tourism brochures, tee-shirts), and capital investments. These items can be met without fantasy heritage framing unto historical places.[108] The Lower Valley's missions provide the heritage sites and the city has worked hard to create the proper fantasy heritage for them. What is missing is infrastructure, cultural inclusion, and a complex retelling of the Spanish colonial era. Tourism may create enclaves where tourist activity is isolated from the community. Herzog looks to Barrio

Logan in San Diego and San Ysidro, California, twenty-five miles south on the border with Tijuana, Mexico. Ongoing debates in that region address similar tourism issues. Barrio Logan cannot compete with the San Diego Zoo or other big-ticket places but Herzog believes it is an ideal space for heritage tourism. But can such an endeavor work in unison with packaged tourism and tour buses? San Ysidro is the gateway to Mexico; El Paso makes the same claim. San Ysidro has also considered developing museums, media experiences, and perhaps mini-theme parks.[109] How such measures affect cultural identity there remains to be seen. In the end, we can see the role of fantasy heritage in shaping tourism. In West Texas and New Mexico the problem has been the resulting invisibility of Mexican/American, Indigenous, and African American communities from the El Paso tourism landscape. These omissions are disconcerting and must change. As we turn to the final chapter, our focus examines the question of identity, suggestions from El Paso residents for tourism, and suggestions for inclusiveness.

Notes

1 David E. Lorey *The U.S. – Mexico Border in the Twentieth Century* (Wilmington, DE: Scholarly Resources Books, 1992), 102.
2 Susan G. Davis. "Landscapes of Imagination: Tourism in Southern California." *Pacific Historical Review, vol. 68, No. 2* (May 1999), 175.
3 Tamar Diana Wilson. "Economic and Social Impacts of Tourism in Mexico." *Latin American Perspectives* 35, no. 3, (2008, May), 37–52.
4 See: I. Glenn Cohen. "Medical Tourism: The View from Ten Thousand Feet." *The Hastings Center Report* 40, no. 2, (March–April 2010), 11; and Matthew D. Dalstrom. "Winter Texans and the Re-creation of the American Medical Experience in Mexico." *Medical Anthropology* 31, no. 2 (March–April 2012).
5 Alicia Swords and Ronald L. Mize. "Beyond Tourist Gazes and Performances: U.S. Consumption of Land and Labor in Puerto Rican and Mexican Destinations." *Latin American Perspectives* 35, no. 3 (May 2008), 54.
6 The center's mail is sent to PO Box 399, San Antonio, New Mexico 87832, according to the Friends of the Camino Real Historic Trail website. See: http://www.elcaminoreal.org/html/museum.html. Downloaded August 1, 2017.
7 See: https://www.facebook.com/pg/EPMissionTrail/about/?ref=page_internal.
8 See: https://www.boston.com/news/national-news/2015/11/26/tbt-did-the-first-thanksgiving-really-take-place-in-plymouth-it-depends-who-you-ask.
9 Metz's previously published and undated column ran as part of journalist Trish Long's column, Tales from the Morgue, a space used to recount notable historical events from the area's past. At the time of this writing, to column was available at: http://www.elpasotimes.com/story/news/history/blogs/tales-from-the-morgue/2016/11/23/leon-metz-el-paso-take-pride-first-thanksgiving/94354642.
10 See: Valdez and Ibarra, *The Last Conquistador*, (2008, PBS Video), 53:04–53:18.
11 In 2006, a San Elizario business owner alleged that his store's lease was not renewed in the San Elizario plaza because he hung a Mexican flag inside. This person alleged he/she was harassed by local merchants who want to promote the Spanish fantasy for tourists. This person did not know why we were at the event. Rather he/she shared the story with an undergraduate research assistant who accompanied us and who knew the business owner.

140 *Inclusive tourism and public memory*

12 For an example of this point, see: Steve Mandal, Finola O'Carroll, and Denis Shine. "The Black Friary." *Archeology Ireland* (Spring 2015), pp. 34–38.
13 See: Christian M. Rogerson. "Tourism and Regional Development: The Case of South Africa's Distressed Areas." *Development in Southern Africa* 32, no. 3 (2015), 277–291.
14 David J. Weber, *The Spanish Frontier in North America.* (New Haven, CT: Yale University Press, 1992)..
15 Frank G. Pérez and Carlos F. Ortega. "Mediated Debate, Historical Framing, and Public Art: The Juan de Oñate Controversy in El Paso." *Aztlán: A Journal of Chicano Studies* 33, no. 2, 121–140; Pérez, Frank G. "Communicating for Social Justice: Juan de Oñate, and the Struggle for Chicano Cultural Representation in Public Art." *Noesis* 16 (2007): 98–121; Pérez, F.G., and T.E. Ruggiero. "Juan de Oñate as Public Art: A Case Study of Cultural Representation and Tourism," in *Communication for Development and Social Change Journal* 1, no. 3 (2007), 233–250.
16 Pérez and Ortega, "Mediated Debate."
17 Thomas H. Guthrie, *Recognizing Heritage: The Politics of Multiculturalism in New Mexico* (Lincoln, NB: University of Nebraska Press, 2013), 148
18 Ibid.
19 Ibid; Pérez and Ruggiero, "Juan de Oñate as Public Art."
20 Guthrie, *Recognizing Heritage*, 97–167.
21 See Charles Montgomery, "Becoming 'Spanish American': Race and Rhetoric in New Mexico Politics, 1880–1928." *Journal of American Ethnic History* 20, no. 4 (Summer 2001): 59–84.
22 Cited in Joanna Kempiak, Lindsey Hollywood, Peter Bolan, and Una McMachon-Beattie, "The Heritage Tourist: An Understanding of the Visitor Experience at Heritage Attractions." *International Journal of Heritage Studies* 23, no. 4 (January 2017): 376.
23 Cited in Daniel Cooper Alarcón, *The Aztec Palimpsest: Mexico in the Modern Imagination* (Tucson, AZ: University of Arizona Press, 1997): 152.
24 Alarcón's point builds on Dean MacConnell's question in *The Tourist: A New Theory of the Leisure Class.* (New York: Random House, 1976): "What do you call an expeditionary force without guns? Tourists." See Alarcón, *The Aztec Palimpsest*, 153.
25 Alarcón, citing Denison Nash, "Tourism as a Form of Imperialism." In *Hosts and Guests: The Anthropology of Tourism*, Ed. Valene L. Smith (Philadelphia, PA: University of Pennsylvania Press, 1989), 37–52.
26 Debbie Nathan, "The Best Laid Plan." *Texas Monthly* 41, no. 2, (February 2013), 90, 174–175.
27 Elida, S. Perez. "Mayoral Candidates discuss Downtown Arena at Forum." *El Paso Times* (April 13, 2007):
    http://www.elpasotimes.com/story/news/politics/2017/04/13/mayoral-candidates-discuss-downtown-arena-forum/100406090.
28 While Margo received the most votes, it was in an election that, according to KVIA-TV, saw the lowest voter turnout in sixteen years. Only 30,000 people voted for a mayoral candidate, an additional 1,100 others voted in the election but cast no vote for mayor. Perhaps El Paso's elites may have finally succeeded in discouraging even more people from voting and allowing them to further consolidate their power.
29 Daniel Borunda, "No Sports, No Basketball, No Ice-rink in Downtown El Paso Arena, Judge Says." *El Paso Times*, 4 October, 2017. See: http://www.elpasotimes.com/story/news/local/el-paso/2017/10/04/no-sports-no-basketball-no-ice-rink-downtown-el-paso-arena-judge-says/733169001. Retrieved October 23, 2017.
30 Ibid.

Inclusive tourism and public memory   141

31 Andrew Leo Lovato, *Santa Fe Hispanic Culture: Preserving Identity in a Tourist Town* (Albuquerque, NM: University of New Mexico Press, 2006).
32 Richard L. Nostrand. *The Hispano Homeland.* (Norman, OK: University of Oklahoma Press, 1992) 31–32.
33 Weber, *The Spanish Frontier.*
34 Nostrand, *The Hispano Homeland*, 31–32.
35 Lovato, *Santa Fe Hispanic Culture*, 9–10.
36 John M. Nieto-Phillips, *The Language of Blood: The Making of Spanish American Identity in New Mexico, 1880s–1930s* (Albuquerque, NM: University of New Mexico Press, 2004), 107.
37 Ibid., 107–108.
38 Ibid., 107.
39 Ibid., 107–108.
40 Linda C. Noel. "'I am an American': Anglos, Mexicans, Nativos, and the National Debate over Arizona and New Mexico statehood," *Pacific Historical Review* 80, no. 3 (August 2011), 430–467.
41 Gabriel Melendez, "Nuevo Mexico by any Other Name." In *Contested Homeland: A Chicano History of New Mexico*, Ed. Erlinda González-Berry and David R. Maciel (Albuquerque, NM: University of New Mexico Press, 2000) 14.
42 Noel. "'I am an American'."
43 Chris Wilson, *The Myth of Santa Fe*: Creating a Modern Regional Tradition (Albuquerque, NM: University of New Mexico Press, 1997).
44 James F. Zimmermann, "The Coronado Cuarto Centennial." *The Hispanic American Historical Review* 20, no. 1(nd..), 158–162.
45 Lovato, *Santa Fe Hispanic Culture,* 108.
46 Nieto-Phillips, *Language of Blood,* 125
47 Ibid., 125
48 Ibid., 108
49 Wilson, *The Myth of Santa Fe*, 82–83.
50 Guthrie, *Recognizing Heritage*; Nieto-Phillips, *The Language of Blood.*
51 Nieto-Phillips, *The Language of Blood,* 49.
52 Guthrie, *Recognizing Heritage*, 12
53 Ibid., 12.
54 Lovato, *Santa Fe Hispanic Culture*, 26–28.
55 Guthrie, *Recognizing Heritage.*
56 Lovato, *Santa Fe Hispanic Culture*, 98–99.
57 Ibid., 101.
58 Lovato, *Santa Fe Hispanic Culture.*
59 Ibid., 109–112. See A. Gabriel Melendez's discussion of the film, "This Town is Not for Sale," in *Hidden Chicano Cinema: Film Dramas in the Borderlands* (New Brunswick, NJ: Rutgers University Press, 2013), 234–235. The film is a documentary that recounts some of the political struggles of lower- and middle-class *Hispanos* via Debbie Jaramillo's 1994 campaign for the mayorship of Santa Fe.
60 George I. Sánchez. *Forgotten People: A Study of Mexicans.* (Albuquerque, NM: University of New Mexico Press, 1940/1996.).
61 Robert Coles. *The Old Ones of New Mexico.* Photographs by Alex Harris. Revised ed. (Albuquerque, NM: University of New Mexico Press, 1973/1989).
62 Maribel Santoyo, "Older than Plymouth Rock, but Still behind," *newspapertree. com*, posted June 26, 2006. Retrieved June 20, 2007.
63 Ibid.
64 Ibid.
65 Ibid.
66 Ibid.

142 *Inclusive tourism and public memory*

67 See Aileen B. Flores. "San Eli's Claim is Labeled Campaign: Historical Society's Chief Calls It a Creation to Attract Tourists." *El Paso Times* (January 12, 2014), A1, A7.

68 The points made by Senator Rodríguez and Commissioner Pérez were taken from notes compiled by Frank G. Pérez during the aforementioned Texas Heritage Tourism Summit organized by the Senator's office. The panel is available online: https://www.youtube.com/watch?v=S0j39KGyvPI&list=PL7G8Zp1nSwkWYKIOy 9p0vZEQVHRf-w4zg&index=11. Retrieved July 28, 2019.

69 See: http://www.elpasotimes.com/story/news/local/el-paso/2015/11/24/project-in crease-awareness-el-camino-real/76325010.

70 The City of Mesilla identifies itself as the "the best known and most visited historical community in Southern New Mexico" (http://www.mesillanm.gov). Information retrieved on July 2, 2017. Citing a report by *Tourism Economics*, the *Las Cruces Sun Times* newspaper reported in October 2016, that Doña Ana county, home to Mesilla, that visitors had spent more than $360 million dollars in 2015. See: http://www.lcsun-news.com/story/money/business/2016/10/23/new-m exico-las-cruces-see-record-tourism-numbers/92396830.

71 See https://visitelpaso.com. Information referenced here downloaded on October 2, 2017.

72 The other ownership group is not mentioned in the *El Paso Times'* story: http://www.elpasotimes.com/story/money/business/2017/08/16/el-paso-downtown-ho tel-renovation/570616001. Retrieved October 2, 2017.

73 See Vic Kolenc's story at: http://www.kvia.com/news/top-stories/camino-rea l-hotel-sign-to-be-taken-down-wednesday/207680000 and Sara Sanchez's at: http://www.elpasotimes.com/story/news/2016/12/14/historic-makeover-camino-rea l-sign-comes-down/95436776. Retrieved August 22, 2017.

74 Kolenc, "'Camino Real Hotel' sign to be taken down Wednesday."

75 El Paso activist Miguel Juárez provides his version of events in *Fusion Magazine*: http://thefusionmag.com/keeping-los-lagartos-at-san-jacinto-plaza. Student journalist Dave Acosta covered the controversy for borderzine.com: borderzine.com/ 2011/07/saving-luis-jimenez'-gators-—-el-pasoans-won't-let-go-of-a-beloved-city-centerpiece. Both articles were retrieved on October 2, 2017.

76 See: https://mcad.elpasotexas.gov/arts-district. Retrieved June 2, 2017.

77 The term local heritage appears on http://www.huntfamilyfoundation.com/a bout-us. Retrieved July 2, 2017. The 2017 First Thanksgiving website listed the Hunt Foundation as sponsors.

78 David Romo. Ringside Seat to a Revolution: An Underground Cultural History of El Paso and Juárez, 1893–1923. (El Paso, TX: Cinco Puntos Press, 2006).

79 Mariano Azuela, *The Underdogs* (New York: Penguin Classics, 2008).

80 W.H. Timmons, *El Paso: A Borderlands History* (El Paso, TX: Texas Western Press, 1990), 165.

81 Bill Blazick, "Dumping State Tourism Budget Would Hurt El Paso," *El Paso Times*, September 26, 2010.

82 Nathan, "The Best Laid Plan. See also Miguel Juárez, "Demolish Convention Center Complex for Arena," *El Paso Times*, December 11, 2016.

83 See Shawn Lay, *War, Revolution, and the Ku Klux Klan: A Study of Intolerance in a Border City.* (El Paso, TX: Texas Western Press, 1985).

84 Charles Ponzio, "Absence of Vision," *El Paso Times*, June 11, 2000.

85 Ibid.

86 Jackson Polk, "El Paso Can Benefit from Heritage Tourism," *El Paso Times,* December 11, 2006.

87 Houser makes this statement in John J. Valadez and Christine Ibarra's documentary *The Last Conquistador* (2007; PBS Video).

88 See: http://xiitravelers.org/susan.html. Retrieved October 2, 2017.

Inclusive tourism and public memory 143

89 At the time of this writing, the XII Travelers' website (http://xiitravelers.org) lists four statues that are completed or underway: Fray García de San Francisco, Juan de Oñate, Susan Magoffin, and Benito Juárez. The proposed remaining statues include: Alvar Nuñez Cabeza de Vaca, Estebanico The Black [sic], Governor Juan Moro, Bartolo Pique, Juan Bautista de Anza, Juan María Ponce de León, Lozen, Lt. Henry O. Flipper, and John Wesley Hardin.

90 We visited the XII Travelers website and found that both John and Ethan Houser are listed as authors. However, we did not find anything officially listing Ethan Houser as the head sculptor now that his father has passed. See: https://www.xiitravelers.org/artist.html. Retrieved March 13, 2019.

91 Tomas J. Cuevas Contreras and Isabel Zizalda Hernández, "Cross-border Tourism Networks, Cuidad Juárez, Chihuahua, México, and El Paso, Texas, United States," unpublished manuscript, 2011.

92 Ibid.

93 The concept of opinion leadership was pioneered by Paul Felix Lazarsfeld and is a central construct in Everett M. Roger's diffusion of innovations theory. See: Everett M. Rogers, *Diffusion of Innovations*. 5th ed. (New York: Free Press, 2003), 303–305. For more on Lazarsfeld's contributions to communication research see: Everett M. Rogers, *A History of Communication Study: A Biographical Approach*. (New York: Free Press, 1994), 244–315.

94 Various public oriented disciplines have adopted this process in recent years. For example, community-based participatory research (CBPR) and positive deviance approaches work with medical and/or academic institutions, government, and the public to generate solutions to problems being faced, often, by marginalized or minority populations. For CBPR examples see: Christine Makosky Daley, Aimee S. James, Ezekiel Ulrey, Stephanie Joseph, Angelia Talawyma, Won S. Choi, K. Allen Greiner, and M. Kathryn Coe, "Using Focus Groups in Community-Based Participatory Research: Challenges and Resolutions," *Qualitative Health Research* 20, no. 5 (May 2010), 697–706; also Nina B. Wallerstein and Bonnie Duran, "Using Community-Based Participatory Research to Address Health Disparities," *Health Promotion Practice* 7, no. 3 (July 2006), 312–323. For an positive deviance see: Michael J. Papa, Arvind Singhal, and Wendy H. Papa, *Organizing for Social Change: A Dialectical Journey of Theory and Praxis.* (Thousand Oaks, CA: Sage), 2006.

95 See Stella Ting-Toomey and John G. Oetzel, *Managing Intercultural Communication Conflict.* 2nd ed. (Thousand Oaks, CA: Sage), 2001.

96 Hammad Al Nassieri and Radhlianh Aulin, "Enablers and Barriers to Project Planning and Scheduling Based on Construction Projects in Oman," *Journal of Construction in Developing Countries* 21, no. 2 (2016), 1–20.

97 See Xing Huibin, Azizan Marzuki, and Arman Abdul Razak, "Conceptualizing a Sustainable Development Model for Cultural Heritage Tourism in Asia." *Theoretical and Empirical Researches in Urban Management* 8, no. 1 (February 2013), 51–66.

98 See Bruce Prideaux, "Creating Rural Heritage Visitor Attractions: The Queensland Heritage Trail Project," *International Journal of Tourism Research, 4* (2002), 313–323. Prideaux notes that "rural heritage attractions face many challenges as they balance the need for authenticity with the need for community support, marketing, and generating ongoing funding" (p. 316). One way to build this support is to freely provide information, fiscal and otherwise, to interested community members and stakeholders to build trust between the project and relevant audiences.

99 Nestor Garcia Canclini. Art Beyond Itself: Anthropology for a Society Without a Storyline. Durham, NC: Duke University Press, 2014.

144 *Inclusive tourism and public memory*

100 KDBC-TV. County Leaders Vote to Rename Miguel Teran Park, Manuel Aguilera Highway. For Escobar's quote see: http://cbs4local.com/news/local/county-leaders-vote-to-rename-miguel-teran-park-manuel-aguilera-highway. Retrieved July 27, 2017. See also: http://www.kvia.com/news/highway-renaming-plan-draws-emotional-protest-from-namesake-family/56195559. Retrieved July 27, 2017.

101 Here we are influenced by Rodney Hero's work on social divisions in contemporary US society. Rodney Hero, *Latinos and the U.S. Political System: Two-tiered Pluralism.* (Philadelphia, PA: Temple University Press, 2010).

102 Edward T. Hall. *The Silent Language.* (New York: Anchor Books, 1959).

103 See: http://www.legis.state.tx.us/tlodocs/85R/billtext/html/SB00695I.htm and https://www.dallasnews.com/opinion/commentary/2017/02/11/students-might-get-kick-proposed-new-ethnic-studies-course-texas-schools. Both retrieved on October 2, 2017.

104 Victor M. Ortíz-González, *El Paso: Local Frontiers at the Global Crossroads.* (Minneapolis, MN: University of Minnesota Press, 2004), 17. We have seen a similar phenomenon in the scholarly realm where scholars of color are often asked if they are doing scholarship or advancing an ethnic agenda. Both authors have directly experienced this phenomenon and many scholars of color have shared similar stories with us. One example involves author Pérez who presented a history of the Chicano Movement at a symposium at the University of New Mexico. As part of a four-person panel he was astounded when a woman in the audience asked a fellow panelist, "Can I believe anything he [Pérez] said? Because I have often heard that Chicanos have their own agendas."

105 Ortíz-González, *El Paso*, 17

106 Lawrence Herzog. "Globalization of the Barrio: Transformation of the Latino Cultural Landscapes of San Diego, California," in *Hispanic Spaces, Latino Places: Community and Cultural Diversity in Contemporary America.* Ed. Daniel Arreola. (Austin, TX: University of Texas Press, 2004), 116.

107 Ibid.

108 Greg Dickinson, Carole Blair, and Brian L. Ott, *Places of Public Memory: The Rhetoric of Museums and Memorials* (Tuscaloosa, AL: University of Alabama Press, 2010).

109 Herzog, "Globalization of the Barrio," 116.

5 On public memory and ethnic conflict in the current era

Our account of the Spanish fantasy heritage phenomena in West Texas and New Mexico focused on events that begin in 1988 as anticipation mounted for the 1998 quadricentennial of Oñate's arrival. We specifically began with an account from 1998 when individuals sawed off the right foot of a Juan de Oñate monument in Alcalde, New Mexico.[1] At the time, a year-long series of Spanish- and Oñate-related activities had been scheduled throughout the state. A note to the *Albuquerque Journal* indicated the amputation of the right foot was in support of the Acoma people, who endured this same form of violence under Oñate's orders in the 16th Century.[2] Alcalde is one mile from the Ohkay Owingeh Pueblo where Oñate established his base of operations in 1598. The Oñate Monument and Visitors Cultural Center's proximity is a constant reminder to the Pueblo people of their colonial existence.

In 2015, author Carlos Ortega stopped in Alcalde to view the statue and visitor center. To his dismay, the center was closed. Weeds surrounded the Oñate statue and no one was there to answer questions. To understand what happened we must go back to the early 1990s when then-New Mexico state senator Emilio Naranjo introduced a bill proposing the statue and center to the state legislature, claiming it would *attract tourism* and *help the economy* [our emphasis]. The legislature approved the bill, Rio Arriba County donated land, and funding came through tax bonds, grants, the Small Business Administration, and the Rio Arriba County Commission in the amount of $2 million dollars.[3] A 2016 KRQE news story suggested that the center was a financial disappointment. Dr. Robert McGeash, retired history professor and the center's first director, remarked that the center "never functioned according to the original purpose:" to bolster tourism. While the center opened in 1994, a business plan to draw in visitors was never prepared. Naranjo was then Rio Arriba County manager but was removed from his position and the county appears to have lost interest in the project. The center closed in 1998 due to this lack of planning and the state senators who supported it moved on to other projects.[4] Over the years, the county leased the site for a Montessori School, a charter school, a flea market, a part-time yoga studio and now, as home for the Northern Rio Grande National Heritage Area offices.[5] We wonder if people see the irony that the center's development and demise were due more to political gamesmanship than the needs of the state. People driving down Highway 68 can easily Alcalde's Oñate statue, but few apparently stop. Author Carlos Ortega noted during his stop that the "scar" where the replacement foot was soldered on is quite visible. The center's closure possibly conveys a loss of interest in the Spanish fantasy in Alcalde. The Alcalde action set off a series of controversies that soon reached El Paso, Texas. In fact, El Paso's own XII Travelers project has been questioned for its lack of a feasibility study.[6] Will tourism increase merely from an as yet unfinished collection of statues and an annual event with few visitors, even after three decades of effort?

In October 2017, the *New York Times* featured a front-page story about Oñate's missing foot. Here, Simon Romero recounts a recent meeting with a man who now has the statue's amputated foot and who claims to have stolen it, along with a New Mexican friend. The thief identifies as Iroquois, a tribe whose homeland, and allegedly the thief's, is situated in the Northeast. Romero's piece highlights the history of conflict between Hispanics and Indians. However, we find it problematic that his story, like so much of the fantasy heritage, omits the Anglo power brokers and residents who continue to develop and promote these erroneous myths. Still, Romero's analysis is spot on when he notes the longstanding distrust and interconnections between the Hispanics and Indians in New Mexico. As other places move to alter the fantasies of earlier generations, El Paso's colonial mentality remains as intact and culturally insensitive as ever. On October 21, 2017, the city held its first annual Running of the Bulls 5km fun run, organized by the [El Paso] Downtown Management District. The run was funded by corporate and non-profit sponsors, including Amstel Bier.[7] So much for stereotypes of sophisticated Europeans (Amstel began as a Dutch brewery and is now owned by Heineken). European philosopher John Locke advocated for parents to teach their children "an abhorrence of killing or tormenting any living creature"[8] more than 400 years ago. Yet, Amstel/Heineken supported this brutal neocolonial theme, an appalling idea to many in the current era. Sadly, a large enough group of people remain supportive of or indifferent to animal suffering. Perhaps El Pasoans are oblivious to the death by bullfight that awaits these animals.

The city's heritage tourism efforts with the 5km run, like much of the Juan de Oñate fantasy, highlight El Paso's reliance on fantasies that ignore the violence Spaniards brought to the region. Oñate's image, the First Thanksgiving, the Equestrian statue, school curricula, and other related elements promote and sustain the local Eurocentric hegemony that benefits area powerbrokers, a disproportionately White population. Issues arising from this narrative have held sway over local culture for generations throughout the Southwest.[9] While fantasy heritage is only one perspective, locals and tourists alike do not typically encounter alternative narratives in mainstream media and venues. This "cultured" perspective is safe, as one colleague told us, "One cannot get ahead in El Paso, unless one is a safe Mexican," meaning a

Mexican/American who upholds, or minimally ignores, the dominant fantasy heritage. What rubs many Mexican/Americans in the community the wrong way, leading them to resist the fantasy heritage, is that it validates only history told from an Anglo point of view. For a time, Oñate coloring books and Bea Bragg's sympathetic telling of Oñate's exploits were assigned to elementary students by local area school districts. The experiences of many in the Mexican/American community are apparently of little consequence, although they constitute eighty-two percent of the local population. In fact, El Paso has always been largely Mexican/American. The absence of specific Mexican/American namesakes throughout much of the city is obvious by omission. Not a single regular high school is named in honor of a Mexican American.[10] One high school uses the conquistador as its mascot, another uses the Ranger. The Spanish conquistadors' violent legacy is addressed throughout the book. The Texas Rangers are an equally curious mascot choice, as the law enforcement agency terrorized Mexican/Americans, particularly in South Texas.[11] In fact, on March 3, 2018, as the book was in final preparation, the *New York Times* featured a story about this topic. It included an interview with an El Paso woman whose great grandfather was murdered by the Rangers in Presidio, Texas. It is hard to believe that a Mexican American neighborhood would choose the Ranger mascot unless there were few to no other choices.

Omission and misrepresentation have also given way to cultural erasure via fantasy heritage. Such efforts have included efforts to tear down the building where Mariano Azuela drafted his account of the Mexican Revolution (1910–1920), *Los de abajo* (*The Underdogs*), to gentrify *Segundo Barrio* (the Second Ward), and more recent attempts to eradicate the entire *Duranguito* Mexican/American neighborhood show the existing community-level ignorance of or hostility against local about Mexican/American history. Heritage tourism bus or walking tours of these areas would possibly lure tourists to the areas and possibly lead some travelers to see Mexican/Americans as more than the sum of a series of negative stereotypes. These actions also speak to local elites' machinations at economic exploitation and historical amnesia, much of it advanced under the guise of heritage tourism. Local mainstream media and politicians suggest that the only history is the official or safe one offered in schools or the one narrated by those designated as experts by the powers that be. Apparently, few, if any, of these "experts" have terminal university degrees in the liberal arts (e.g., communication, history). For many years, the local media relied on a local popular writer of history as the de facto area expert, ignoring the university's faculty. Such local tendencies help to explain why El Paso's heritage tourism is mired in fantasies and is bent on making a fast buck via historical accounts of "food, fun, and fiesta."

The unseen Mexican community

In the mid-1960s, the Chicano Movement emerged as a full blown call to action for Mexican American civil rights in the US.[12] At the time, and in

148 *Public memory and ethnic conflict*

many ways today, writers and intellectuals viewed Mexican Americans as foreigners in their native land.[13] This prejudice served to justify the marginalization of the Mexican American community that had been reduced to second-class status from at least the 1820s, despite their citizenship status.[14] They had fought and died for the US in two world wars, participated in politics, raised families, paid taxes, educated their children (often in segregated schools), and worked in urban and rural settings. Yet, they were and remain under attack. Shamefully, the government deported as many as two million Mexican/Americans, many of them native-born US citizens, in the 1930s via repatriation efforts.[15] In the 1940s, the harassment of Chicano youths by police and media led to escalated conflicts between pachucos and US servicemen.[16] The landmark case of *Mendez v. Westminster* (1946) led to the desegregation of schools in California and laid the legal foundation for the *Brown v. Board of Education* (1954) Supreme Court case.[17] Repatriation sentiments arose again in the 1950s via *Operation Wetback.* [18] As recently as November 2015, then-presidential hopeful Donald Trump spoke favorably of *Operation Wetback*, telling viewers of a presidential debate:

> [President] Eisenhower moved immigrants just beyond the border; they came back. Moved them again beyond the border; they came back. Didn't like it. Moved them way south; they never came back. Dwight Eisenhower. You don't get nicer, you don't get friendlier.[19]

Trump's racist comment and subsequent voter support is hardly surprising given the racist, anti-minority sentiments many Whites espoused in reaction to President Barack Obama and his administration. Yet, as Paula Ioanide notes, Whites' "widespread social panics over the perceived threats of criminality, terrorism, welfare dependence, and undocumented immigration in the post-civil rights era are … dismissive of facts and evidence" contrary to the dominant hegemony.[20] Such fears are part of a centuries old mentality that predates the founding of the original thirteen colonies. As labor union members, Mexican Americans helped advance worker rights for much of the previous century, for example, Emma Tenayuca's work in San Antonio, Texas[21] and the more widely known legacies of César Chávez[22] and Dolores Huerta.[23] These brave individuals faced great personal danger and risked imprisonment for their actions. Mexican American journalist and Chicano martyr, Ruben Salazar was born in Ciudad Juárez, graduated from Texas Western College, now the University of Texas at El Paso, and began his career at the now defunct *El Paso Herald-Post*. The first national La Raza Unida convention was held here. Sadly, this history is not part of El Paso's heritage efforts, despite its relevance to area history. Mexican/American or not, people in the region need to learn about the racism that has and continues to relegate many of the city's people to second class status. These elements and those earlier in the chapter suggest ample opportunities for heritage events in El Paso of potential interest to locals and tourists, particularly in the current era.

During the first half of the 20th Century, assimilation was a common theme that permeated society and academe. Mexican Americans were taught in school that they needed to shed their ethnic identity to become "American,"[24] part of the dominant national culture, while being systematically denied the opportunity. The Chicano Movement and pioneering scholars in Chicano Studies of the same era demonstrated that the experience of working class and poor Mexican Americans was different from that of earlier European immigrants. Sociologist Alfredo Mirandé addresses these differences via a transmigration model.[25] He notes how shifts in contemporary social theory finally acknowledge the limitations of the assimilationist model and the ways social marginalization have affected Mexican immigrants.[26]

How are the aforementioned items related to fantasy heritage and tourism? When we discuss fantasy heritage, we refer to a style of historical and cultural memory that romanticizes the Spanish (i.e., European), vilifies the Mexican American (i.e., mestizo), and that builds on myths that engage in the denial of historical realities. This romanticism takes many forms: naming a Las Cruces, New Mexico school after Oñate, El Paso business leaders dressing as Spanish explorers at press conferences, and rationalizing the colonization of Mexico and the Southwest. Such fantasies cling to the notion that northern New Mexico is more Spanish than southern New Mexico or West Texas. Many local heritage events seek to impose that rubric unto area culture and commerce. These efforts, in and of themselves, do not contribute to the invisibility of the Mexican/American community, issues such as social class, race, gender and economics do. How each has been interpreted historically and by whom also impacts the community. These issues have been a major part of the Mexican/American working-class experience. As our key theme, fantasy heritage helps explain why Juan de Oñate was rationalized as important for tourist activity. Why the monument built in his name was thirty-six feet tall rather than twelve. And why his memory is represented to El Pasoans and tourists through the First Thanksgiving reenactment, El Paso area school curricula, and public art, creating a fantasy heritage that never existed.

If, as his sympathizers argue, Oñate is our history, a bringer of civilization and culture, what does it say for the Mexican/American and indigenous communities of New Mexico and Texas? Have they not contributed? This is one reason so many criticisms of heritage tourism sites and festivals, public art, and the school curriculum exist. Children in Southwest schools, Anglo and Mexican American alike, learn next to nothing about the history, culture and heritage of Mexico and Mexican/Americans. It is not surprising that students would be confused or conflicted about who they are. Assimilation succeeds when basic knowledge of the native culture is lost. Art historian Trinidad Rico observes that little "attention has been dedicated in the growing critical heritage corpus of literature to the circumstances under which attempts to heritagize certain objects, places, or practices has been unsuccessful."[27] This treatise seeks to help address this scholarly omission by considering both the latent and manifest ways Mexican/Americans are marginalized, omitted, or vilified in West Texas tourism. We offer this work and the framework in Chapter 4 to help remedy these tendencies by

150 Public memory and ethnic conflict

calling out and providing methods for replacing fantasy heritage in any number of venues throughout the US and beyond.

In relation to El Paso, we also suggest the community broaden its support for and interactions with *Museo Urbano* (Urban Museum) and other community-oriented entities, such as our university's Center for Community Engagement (CCE), formerly Center for Civic Engagement. The CCE links undergraduate students with local non-profits. Students engage in collaborative and mutually beneficial partnerships with organizations where they apply their academic knowledge and ideas that benefit community organizations that are typically short on funding and personnel resources. Meanwhile, these organizations serve as co-teachers to students seeking to broaden their community awareness and knowledge. Having these and similar organizations tie into and work on local heritage tourism would allow for greater input from everyday El Pasoans, particularly Mexican/Americans and other marginalized social categories. Together with the local chamber of commerce, county, and municipal government, these groups could help develop tourism festivals and identify sites that would interest both the local community and tourists. More importantly, such efforts could abandon fantasy heritage framing in favor of more culturally inclusive approaches to teach visitors about the city and region.

Possibilities: culture and space

With respect to El Paso, one can posit that the Oñate/Equestrian statue fiasco may have taught leaders a lesson, even if it is one with limited prosocial impact. Municipal development is largely funded by bonds on which locals vote. Once approved, however, bond projects tend to pit local White and assimilated Hispanics against much of the community. A 2012 quality of life bond impacted what downtown El Paso has become, site to a minor league baseball park and home to many new eateries and bars. Yet, conflict continues over the potential razing of the *Duranguito* neighborhood, El Paso's

Figure 12 Skyline of El Paso
Credit: Leonel Monroy, Jr.

oldest and populated by working-class Mexican/Americans, to build a sports arena. Despite much talk of funds being used for a Mexican American cultural center and children's museum, at this time the cultural center has been reduced to an annex to the main library. The children's museum appears to be on hold. One observer, Rev. Rafael García, suggests that a solution to the impasse would be for local leaders to acknowledge and support a cultural identity that reflects the area's rich Mexican and Tigua history.[28] Another possibility is to hold an annual conference on area culture that allows for a frank academic discussion where competing perspectives are encouraged and openly discussed. Such an idea would both dispel many fantasy heritage myths as well as help promote academic tourists.

At the time of this writing, the XII Travelers list contains no Mexican Americans. This omission is consistent with the project's longstanding bias against mestizos, again in a city that is eighty-two percent Mexican American. The problem is further complicated when younger generations of Hispanic El Pasoans buy into the fantasy heritage and promote it. For example, El Paso educator Joe Estala appeared on the *Texas Standard* radio program in November 2017 to promote the *First Thanksgiving*. His framing of the event was apologetic and consistent with the Oñate fantasy. He refers to the Spanish colonial entry to the region as "two cultures from different parts of the world coming together to help each other."[29] We fail to see how the murder, rape, and forced religious conversion that went hand-in-hand with colonization helped the Indians. Yet, such interpretations dominate El Paso's public memory.

To counter the fantasy heritage, we suggest El Paso recognize the contributions of its Mexican American people. The XII Travelers should include one or more of the following people: Chicano artist Luis Jiménez (1940–2006), a native El Pasoan and one of the most important artists of the modern era; Victor Leaton Ochoa (1850–1945), inventor, newspaper editor, spy, science fiction writer and politician; Marcelino Serna (1896–1992), most highly decorated World War I Texas veteran; Father Harold Rahm, Jesuit Priest at Sacred Heart Church and housing activist; Teresa Urrea (1873–1906), folk healer and Mexican revolution era religious icon; and writer José Antonio Burciaga (1940–1996), a highly recognized writer and El Paso native.

Public art is for the entire community, at least in theory. A statue of Susan Shelby Magoffin was completed in 2012, and is to be followed by one of Benito Juárez sometime in 2019 or 2020. While the second Traveler statue, Juan de Oñate (Fray García de San Francisco is the first), is viewed by some as reflecting the history and culture of an entire community, it simply is not. Dionne Mack writes that whether we love or hate a piece of public art, the goal should be to initiate "conversations about who we are and who we want to be."[30] But getting people to sit and discuss these questions becomes a problem, particularly in one of the poorest cities in the US. Perhaps this is where museums and heritage tourism festivals can play a key role. Besides being sources of learning about culture, history, and art, museums and

152   *Public memory and ethnic conflict*

festivals can do more. They should strive to capture the local culture as seen in the diverse populations, whether in El Paso or anywhere in the Southwest. One might say it is all about tolerance, and yes, this word comes up a great deal in discussions of our multicultural world. However, there must be a better alternative than to merely tolerate.[31] We believe the goal should be acceptance, not easy to achieve but certainly a worthwhile goal. In other words, like writing a film script, the author must prepare a narrative where the journey becomes an arc. In such a situation, the inciting incident—such as the Oñate statue—leads to a journey where conflict is resolved: from tolerance to acceptance.

School curricula must be used to help correct and then banish fantasy heritage accounts from public memory. In April 2018, the Texas State Legislature "approved creating statewide academic standards for Mexican-American studies in high school."[32] Regrettably, state republicans insisted the course be labeled ethnic studies.[33] While these courses will be electives, they also open the door to alternative forms of information, and not just for students of representative ethnic communities. These courses will be open to all students and White students will then be exposed to information that would enhance their own understanding of difference, expand their critical thinking skills, as well as open their minds to alternative perspectives.

The last thing we would want to see is a conflict where individuals are cut off from their "symbolic moorings ... where they are rendered vulnerable to forms of anomie,"[34] something against which John Mandalios cautions. Examining the conflicts caused by globalization, he drives home the following point:

> The risk potential for those human communities which are not merely politically and socially disenfranchised but also culturally marginalized is greater than the unrelenting forces of modernization, mass consumerism, and tourism, where globalism may simply be another pseudonym for California, Tokyo, or Brussels.[35]

In the Third World, there are cases where indigenous people have been removed from their homes and land. This is especially true of beachfront property. Cases where people were removed for the building of hotels or for creating tourist beaches occurred in Gambia, Togo, and Djerba (an island off the coast of Tunisia), to name only a few. The creation of the tourist playground serves to make the indigenous invisible to tourists, unless the native is working at the tourist site.[36]

It is this type of invisibility our study has sought to confront. Elites in El Paso have worked to create a fantasy heritage that omits the area's largest ethnic group. El Paso hegemony makes it easy to ignore the Mexican/American community and the Tigua tribe until there is a celebration of culture that is presented as a fantasy packaged for tourists.

The presence of the Mexican/American community can be enhanced through existing activities. One example is the Annual Chicano Heritage Festival which takes place in the Segundo Barrio. Sponsored by La Fe Culture and Technology Center, the weekend event celebrates El Paso's Mexican/ American community. More importantly, the event also reaches out to the city's Mexican/American youth. *Museo Urbano* was developed by the faculty and students of the history department at the University of Texas at El Paso, most notably under the direction of Professors Yolanda Chávez Leyva and David D. Romo, then a doctoral candidate. The museum is underfunded, in comparison to other local museums, and is largely staffed by volunteers. It provides a service whereby diverse items, whether art, material or cultural items, and photography are collected to display a look at the city's Mexican/ American community. These items are displayed with a large degree of cultural authenticity. *Museo Urbano* offers visitors a more organic experience than more traditional museums. It offers street exhibits and works with other area museums to curate exhibits, for example, *La Frontera*, which told the history of the last century on the US-Mexico border and *Viva La Causa*, an exhibit on the Chicano Movement at the University of Texas at El Paso. Leyva also directs the Institute of Oral History on campus, which gathers fronterizo histories to share and preserve for future generations. Some have compared El Paso to the Ellis Island of the Southwest. If properly promoted, these types of efforts can potentially lure tourists to a cultural space that will enlighten their understanding of Mexican/American and border culture.

El Paso's importance to, and proximity, with Ciudad Juárez also make it an ideal locale for international field research experiences. Many faculty members conduct research on issues directly related to this type of intercultural experience, as do students and classes from other universities that visit the region, often during the summer. Their findings may also provide insights useful to tourism that move beyond the same tired Spanish fantasies. "Community-based field experiences involve interdisciplinarity, cultural exchange, and intellectual reflection. They also enable students to develop deep understandings of the ways people connect with the past."[37] What better way to engage students in shaping the stories the El Paso community tells about its people? Such efforts can also extend to the notion of El Paso as a gateway city to international tourism, specifically to Ciudad Juárez or Chihuahua, Mexico, or to Latin America via the Ciudad Juárez airport.

Alternately, instead of focusing on cities, community leaders could utilize the idea of gateway heritage.[38] The area's history extends back to a time before the United States existed and well before the time that Mexico or New Spain were on a map. Historian Oscar J. Martínez suggested that one way to acknowledge this heritage is with identical arches, connected at the top with flags and banners. His idea is to celebrate history and the future. It is a way of bringing the region together through public education rather than to divide it. On the other hand, the Greater El Paso Chamber of Commerce (GEPCC) provides an example of fantasy heritage dangers. Their messages are naturally directed at the business community and often include a focus on Oñate and

154 *Public memory and ethnic conflict*

colonization as a buy-in to future business, especially tourism. To them the message is presumably "authentic" but it is misguided, at best. It becomes a process where Mexican/Americans and the Tigua are excluded as if they have nothing economically important to offer in tourism efforts.

Case study 5.1 Gastronomy as a tool for culturally sensitive tourists

Food is often associated with a specific ethnic group or region and food tourism can add to a region's "economic, social and environmental sustainability" (p. 15). Combined with geography and regional identity, food often helps to attract visitors. When a region focuses on its culinary traditions it may gain visitors who enjoy fine dining and other gastronomic delights. In some locales, this strategy allows a community to expand its tourism appeal, say beyond the summer months. Yet, reliance on dining forces people to engage in a balancing act between "authentic" dishes that are indigenous to the area and experimenting with new ways of cooking. If the region remains overly focused on the same way of doing things people may grow tired and retreat from the area. The locale has grown stale. If the region's chefs stray too far in the other direction people may abandon the locale because it has lost its way. They may believe that the region has commercialized itself to a point where it is no longer authentic.

Cornwall, England, has balanced this tension well, allowing the city, faced with a stagnating economy in other sectors, to thrive as a tourist site. The impetus for this transformation is tied to the rise of bovine spongiform encephalopathy (BSE, or mad cow disease) and outbreaks of aphtae epizooticae (hoof and mouth disease) during the late 1990s. In 2001, the British government launched programs to help with the outbreak's negative economic impact. England's South West was seen as a region with a unique degree of patriotism and a beautiful geography. Cornwall reinvented itself as a regional food tourism venue to counter the demise of its fishing and farming businesses. Food tourism provided an avenue for growth but some locals feared that appealing to tourists would jeopardize or water-down Cornwall's culture. Would "Cornishness" remain a viable cultural marker? Yet, the possibility of appealing to people with high disposable incomes and who would visit to try new or revisit favorite restaurants was an option too tempting to avoid. While the plan was an economic success for Cornwall, critics blamed tourists for the related environmental costs and their perceived break down the area's traditional social ties. Supporters saw food tourism as something positive for the entire community. Interviews with Cornish people suggested that many dying professions have been revived because of tourist demand for authentic artifacts. Tourists' interests have also allowed some locals to open companies devoted to local produce. Existing small farms have remained in business by selling to the invigorated local markets rather than competing with large

Public memory and ethnic conflict 155

industrial growers. Fishing has also seen some growth as locals source area marine life for seafood.

Cornwall has managed to see its area culture grow into a prosperous tourist industry. Part of this success is due to the concern for local culture being open to its evolution vis-à-vis new ways of doing as well as affluent, year-round visitors. Locals report that food tourists are of higher income levels than the traditional summer tourists. Appealing to such people via an extended tourism season that transcends the summer months has had a strong and positive economic impact for Cornwall. It has also revived some local traditions.

Discussion questions

1. Everett and Aitchison's work suggests tourism is working well in Cornwall. Their research suggests that when food (and/or cultural) tourism is managed with a concern for the old and an accommodation of the new, locals maintain their culture and tourists find places to visit. Yet, most such endeavors are driven by business and political leaders. How might that reality affect these findings? Businesses benefit from increased sales and politicians can site growth in jobs and taxes when they seek reelection. What are benefits you imagine the average person gains from Cornish tourism? Relate your answers to your own experiences if possible.
2. Is it possible to promote local or regional culture in a manner that does not Disneyfy it but that allows it to thrive as a source of tourism, while remaining "authentic?" What does it mean for a culture to be authentic, considering that culture is fluid and constantly changing?
3. Marketing via "local culture" campaigns may lead people to visit a region or city. Do you think communities engaged in such endeavors can remain "authentic?" Why or why not?

   Source: Sally Everett and Cara Aitchison. "The Role of Food Tourism in Sustaining Regional Identity: A Case Study of Cornwall, South West England." *Journal of Sustainable Tourism* 16, no. 2 (2008): 150–167.

The first step in ending fantasy heritage accounts is to recognize cultural diversity and to use this concept to develop a message for locals and tourists alike. The local audience is comprised of students (at all levels), academics, workers, retirees, politicians, historical experts, established businesses, government employees, and the area's general population. The tourist audience includes potential businesses, entertainment companies, talent, politicians, artists, and technology organizations from outside El Paso, as well as those who at this point do not care. Considering the breadth of such audiences requires that an organization like the local Chamber offer heterogeneous messages instead of homogeneous ones. We believe that by developing a complex and multicultural message framework, the Chamber can capture the link that has eluded government, non-profits, and stakeholders in the area tourist industry.[39] A campaign that celebrates El Paso's various ethnic categories would unite a far greater number of people behind the tourism effort. One idea is for El Paso to do a better job of promoting its Mexican food tradition. Many here are familiar with San Antonio's claims to being the Mexican food capital of the world. Yet, San Antonio is perhaps the Tex-Mex food capital. El Paso is arguably the Mexican food capital because its proximity to Mexico keeps its gastronomy closer to Mexican than Tex-Mex or Santa Fe's fame for New Mexican food, a unique take on traditional Mexican food characterized by different seasonings and presentation. For example, one local Mexican café has been recognized for its award-winning menu and sits across from Concordia Cemetery in Central El Paso. Concordia is the final resting place of outlaw John Wesley Hardin. This café also has a colorful past from the Prohibition era. Another Mexican restaurant has been recognized as one of the top fifty in the US. Finally, an area steakhouse has been ranked among the best in Texas and operates out of a working ranch. Yet, some restaurants along the "Mission Trail" (Socorro Road) have waited in vain for years for tourism to increase. A food crawl that perhaps focused on different parts of the city by day would perhaps help tourism efforts. It would be culturally sensitive, as these are local venues with many years of tradition. Additionally, bringing people together over food and drink, while perhaps offering heritage talks, short plays, or musical performances would open people to learning more about the region's Indian, Mexican/American, Spanish, or Anglo past. More needs to be done but perhaps this suggestion could serve as a first step to move beyond El Paso's fantasy-driven neocolonial reality.

Figure 13 Los Lagartos fountain at San Jacinto Plaza, a symbol of El Paso's Mexican American cultural reality and a denial of its fantasy heritage.
Credit: Leonel Monroy, Jr.

As El Paso moves its tourism agenda forward it will face many challenges in competing against well-established West/Southwest tourism destinations (e. g. Santa Fe, NM; Reno, NV, etc.) and we advocate for abandoning fantasy heritage in the development of new tourism strategies. Although El Paso is one of the twenty largest cities in the US by population, it lags behind most other large metroplexes across many socioeconomic and quality of life measures. A large population is not the sole criterion for becoming a tourism mecca. One view on this topic, the central place model, suggests that places such as El Paso, termed secondary or regional cities, act as satellites that are influenced by larger cities' economic and political climates.[40] Another explanation, the network model, posits that secondary cities are part of associative networks with other cities that, again, are established through the influence of larger metropolitan areas. From this perspective, secondary cities do not have the ability to form more economically beneficial associative networks. How have other cities handled this challenge? We offer the following case study to highlight some of the frustrations other communities have faced.

Case study 5.2 Tourism efforts in a second-tier city

Oil-related industries and military installations triggered growth for Corpus Christi from the 1920s through the 1970s. Yet, starting in the 1960s concerns about the sustainability of this growth and its economic benefit led the local leaders to explore how to deal with the inevitable drop in growth that would take place. During the 1960s out-migration of the area's "best and brightest" young people took a strong hold. Approximately 12.7 percent of the 1960 population, 28,000 people moved out of the city. As a result, for the last forty years local leaders have sought to enhance the city's image. A regional university and the additional resources for the local community college helped. Then, in the 1980s, the petrochemical industry seemed a less reliable source of taxes and jobs. Petrochemical corporations became increasingly merged and promoted ever increased efficiencies. Fewer people were required to do certain jobs and others were sent to other locales. The city adapted as best it could and maintained economic growth through the early 2000s. Yet, the 2005 closure of Ingleside Naval Station found city leaders waylaid. They lobbied to keep it open but failed to plan for the shutdown that occurred.

Fortunately, Corpus Christi is home to one of the largest US sea ports, with an ideal geographic proximity to the oil-producing nations of Mexico, Venezuela, and Nigeria, as well as to the Middle East. Civic leaders then focused on establishing the port as the premier locale for the import of oil and other goods from Veracruz and from throughout Mexico. Yet, the city again found itself as "roughly what it was in 1960: a port and regional service center dependent on petrochemicals, the military, and tourism" (pp. 118–119). The city then pursued an anchor strategy that included building and housing three replicas of Columbus' Spanish fleet at the Corpus Christi

158 *Public memory and ethnic conflict*

Museum (fantasy heritage). The Texas State Aquarium, opened in 1990, became a key tourism ploy, and the USS Lexington, a decommissioned aircraft carrier, was established as a floating museum that links Corpus Christi with WWII history. Yet, such projects drew opposition from those against higher taxes. In 2003, tensions exploded when Houston-based company Landry's sought to lease a downtown marina for a restaurant. The deal failed and the city remained divided between those who want economic growth, leading it to eventually become closer to a top-tier city, and those who are fine with the city remaining as it is. These tensions reflect a secondary city that has reached maturity and is struggling to (re)define itself. The book's authors believe that recent geopolitical challenges, for example, in Venezuela, have complicated these efforts.

Discussion questions

1. Lessoff suggests that Corpus Christi's three major economic areas are "petrochemicals, the military, and tourism" (pp.118–119). Does it appear from the information above that Corpus Christi has had much success with tourism? Often communities must invest a great deal of money and resources to create tourism venues, hoping that visitors will follow. Does it seem from this article that Corpus Christi has done a sufficient job in this area? What could the city have done differently? What can they add or do to entice more people to visit? Or, do you think they have done all that is reasonably possible? If so, why?
2. The use of tourism as a local economic engine often reveals social rifts between the business and political classes and many locals who oppose the costs of such efforts (e.g., questions of cultural representation, increased traffic, pollution, costs of living). How might the opposition unite to promote cultural sensitivity in representation and to minimize the direct impact of increased taxes and more people living in the community? What concessions might business and political leaders make to gain more community support?
3. Corpus Christi invested in a fantasy heritage tourism site via the acquisition of reproductions of Christopher Columbus' Spanish ships. Do you associate Columbus with Corpus Christi? How do you think people will factor in these replicas in determining whether or not to visit the city? Alternately, once there, how likely do you think it is that people visiting Corpus Christi will go and see the ships? Given the information in this book, what type of heritage retellings do you think people will encounter when they visit?

> **Source:** Lessoff, Alan. (2008). "Corpus Christi, 1965–2005:
> A Secondary City's Search for a New Direction."
> *Journal of Urban History* 35, no. 1 (2008).

Conclusion: public memory in the era of Donald Trump

Despite the specificity of our analysis, themes of neocolonialism and tourism occur throughout the world. In the US, one need merely think about the speech used by Donald J. Trump to launch his bid for the US presidency on June 16, 2015. Trump suggested that: "When Mexico sends its people, they're not sending their best … They're sending people that have lots of problems … They're bringing drugs. They're bringing crime. They're rapists. And some, I assume, are good people."[41] Initially dismissed, Trump built a coalition of presumably upset "Americans" who believe their world is changing to the detriment of their way of life. His racist bravado includes the desire to build a wall between the US and Mexico. Trump claimed that Mexico would pay for the wall, no less. This idea and its popularity among his base, if not within even his own party, highlight the contempt many Americans have against people of color. This sentiment is exemplified by those who hide behind the cowardly "alt right" label, the term "white supremacist" being less politically expedient in mainstream venues. Tensions between alt right racists and progressives broke out in Charlottesville, Virginia, in October 2017.[42] White nationalists held a "Unite the Right" rally to protest the removal of a Robert E. Lee statue from a local park. Counter protesters met them with calls for greater social inclusion. In the end, nineteen people were injured, and a thirty-two-year-old female was murdered when a car was purposely driven into a group of counter protesters.[43] Similar controversies and protests have plagued the US since Trump took office, particularly in the South. Fox News even maintains a "running list" of confederate statue removals.[44] While the South has received much media attention on this topic, statue controversies exist elsewhere. Yet, even in the Deep South one can find tourism venues that promote a multicultural perspective, such as the Martin Luther King, Jr. National Historical Park (Atlanta, Georgia) and the National Civil Rights Museum (Memphis, Tennessee).

Statues and other public art are also tied to area identity creation and management. For example, as recently as October 7, 2017, the *New York Times* featured two stories about the case of the removal of a foot from the Juan de Oñate statue in Alcalde, New Mexico that introduces this book. Twenty years after this action, the celebration of Oñate remains a controversial issue in far West Texas and New Mexico. Yet, tourists continue to encounter statues of conquistadors (e.g., El Paso International Airport, Old Town Albuquerque) and myriad other neocolonial elements (e.g., restaurants and high schools named after Spaniards, cowboy heroes, or gunslingers). Public art and heritage ignite people's passions. We hope this book will serve as a guide to those who advocate for greater respect and more culturally sensitive representations in public works. Regrettably, El Paso's Eurocentric, neocolonial attitudes remain ingrained in many locals, even among the younger generation, as evidenced by the comments made by a local educator to *The Texas Standard* radio news show.[45]

160 *Public memory and ethnic conflict*

Perhaps the best way to end this story is to draw on the words of Ruth Mojica-Hammer who in 2005 served as Executive Director of the El Paso Council for International Visitors. In an editorial in the *El Paso Times*, she noted the words of a delegate member from Morocco who had toured the US: "El Paso is perhaps the only American city in which the dynamics of bi-nationalism, immigration and acculturation are tangibly felt on the very faces of its inhabitants, in the accent and in the city's conflicting architectural designs."[46] The delegate continued: "[El Paso] reinforces the idea that the U.S. is in actual fact too large to be described as one country not only by virtue of its size but also because of the complexity of its history." This visitor highlighted El Paso's heterogeneous composition, noting how it allowed for many ways to understand the social and historical nature of the city and its peoples. The gathering of El Paso's diverse communities will only feel included when the city and its organizations, such as the local city council and area non-profit heritage entities, work to be more inclusive. Yes, Oñate will always be part of the narrative but unless a more expressive and captivating theme is utilized to reach tourists and residents, acceptance of diversity will continue to fall short.

Notes

1 Simon Romero, "Missing Foot Surfaces: A Symbol of New Mexico's Racial Divisions", *New York Times,* October 1, 2017, A1 and A24. A slightly different and shorter version is available online: https://www.nytimes.com/2017/10/02/insider/new-mexico-statue-conquistador-foot-thief.html. Retrieved February 22, 2019.
2 David J. Weber, *The Spanish Frontier in North America.* (New Haven, CT: Yale University Press, 1992), 86.
3 Larry Barker, KRQE News 13 Investigation, February 8, 2016.
4 Larry Barker, KRQE News; Also see, Michael L. Trujillo, "Oñate's Foot: Remembering and Dismembering in Northern New Mexico," *Aztlán: A Journal of Chicano Studies* 33, no. 2, (2008): 91–119.
5 Thomas M. Guthrie, *Recognizing Heritage: The Politics of Multiculturalism in New Mexico* (Lincoln, NB: University of Nebraska Press, 2013). See also: Simon Romero, "Missing Foot Surfaces: A Symbol of New Mexico's Racial Divisions," *New York Times,* October 1, 2017, A1 and A24.
6 Moises Bujanda, "Larger-Than-Life-Statues and Larger-Than-Life Price Tag," *El Paso Herald-Post,* March 22, 1991: B3.
7 At the time of this writing, the link to the race webpage is still available online: http://downtownelpaso.com/running-of-the-bulls-5k-in-downtown-el-paso. Retrieved October 30, 2017.
8 John Locke (1693/1989), cited in Elenora Gullone, "Historical and Current Conceptualizations of Animal Cruelty," *Animal Cruelty, Antisocial Behavior, and Aggression: More than a Link* (New York: Palgrave MacMillan, 2012), 5.
9 See, for example: Arnoldo De León, *They Called Them Greasers: Anglo Attitudes toward Mexicans in Texas, 1821–1900* (Austin, TX: University of Texas Press, 1983); Mario García, *Desert Immigrants: The Mexicans of El Paso, 1880–1920* (New Haven, CT: Yale University Press, 1981); Linda Gordon, *The Great Arizona Orphan Abduction* (Cambridge, MA: Harvard University Press, 1999); Shawn Lay, *War, Revolution, and the Ku Klux Klan: A Study of Intolerance in a Border City,*

Public memory and ethnic conflict   161

(El Paso, TX: Texas Western Press, 1985); David Montejano, *Anglos and Mexicans in the Making of Texas: 1836–1986* (Austin, TX: University of Texas Press, 1987).

10 The César Chávez Academy, a high school for at-risk students, and Silva Magnet School, with a medical focus, exist. However, neither has a large student body, traditional athletic and/or academic programs that could bring recognition to the general public that El Paso recognizes its Mexican/American role models.

11 Rolofo F. Acuña, *Occupied America: A History of Chicanos.* 4th Ed. (New York: Longman, 2000), 69–71; David Montejano, *Anglos and Mexicans,* 116; David J. Weber, *Foreigners in Their Native Land: Historical Roots of the Mexican Americans.* Rev. ed. (Albuquerque, NM: University of New Mexico Press), 153–154.

12 Juan Gómez-Quiñonez, *Chicano Politics: Reality and Promise, 1940–1990* (Albuquerque, NM: University of New Mexico Press, 1990).

13 Weber, *Foreigners in Their Native Land.*

14 García, *Desert Immigrants*; Gordon, *Great Arizona Orphan Abduction*; Monica Perales, *Smeltertown: Making and Remembering a Southwest Border Community* (Chapel Hill, NC: University of North Carolina Press, 2010).

15 Francisco E. Balderrama and Raymond Rodríguez, *Decade of Betrayal: Mexican Repatriation in the 1930s.* Rev. Ed. (Albuquerque, NM: University of New Mexico Press, 2006).

16 Luis Alvarado, *The Power of the Zoot: Youth Culture and Resistance during World War II* (Berkley, CA: University of California Press, 2008); Mauricio Mazón, *The Zoot-Suit Riots: The Psychology of Symbolic Annihiliation* (Austin, TX: University of Texas Press, 1984); Eduardo Obregón Pagán, *Murder at the Sleepy Lagoon: Zoot Suits, Race, and Riot in Wartime L.A.* (Chapel Hill, NC: University of North Carolina Press, 2003); Mark A. Weitz, *The Sleepy Lagoon Murder Case: Race Discrimination and Mexican-American Rights* (Lawrence, KS: University Press of Kansas, 2010).

17 Philippa Strum, *Mendez v. Westminster: School Desegregation and Mexican American Rights* (Lawrence, KS: University Press of Kansas, 2010), 2.

18 Juan R. García, *Operation Wetback: The Mass Deportation of Mexican American Undocumented Workers in 1954* (New York: Praeger, 1980).

19 See: http://www.npr.org/sections/thetwo-way/2015/11/11/455613993/it-came-up-in-the -debate-here-are-3-things-to-know-about-operation-wetback. Retrieved November 3, 2017.

20 Paula Ioanide, *The Emotional Politics of Racism: How Feelings Trump Facts in an Era of Colorblindness* (Stanford, CA: Stanford University Press, 2015), 34.

21 Michelle A. Holling, "A Dispensational Rhetoric in the 'The Mexican Question in the Southwest'," in *Border Rhetorics: Citizenship and Identity on the U.S.-Mexico Border,* ed. D. Robert DeChaine (Tuscaloosa, AL: University of Alabama Press, 2012), 65–85.

22 John C. Hammerback and Richard J. Jensen, *The Rhetorical Career of César Chávez* (College Station, TX: Texas A&M Press, 1998); John C. Hammerback and Richard J. Jensen, *The Words of César Chávez* (College Station, TX: Texas A&M University, 2002); Peter Matthiessen, *Sal Si Puede (Escape If You Can!): César Chávez and the New American Revolution* (Berkley, CA: University of California Press, 1969/2000).

23 Stacey K. Sowards, "Rhetorical Functions of Letter Writing: Dialogic Collaboration, Affirmation, and Catharsis in Dolores Huerta's Letters," *Communication Quarterly* 60, no. 2 (2012): 295–315. Sowards examines the letters between Huerta and César Chávez in the 1960s and 1970s to contextualize Huerta's many contributions to Chicana/o civil rights and the United Farm Workers. See also: Stacey K. Sowards, *Si, Ella Puede* (Austin, TX: University of Texas Press, 2019); Erin F. Doss and Robin E. Jensen, "Balancing Mystery and Identification: Dolores Huerta's Shifting Transcendent Persona, *Quarterly Journal of Speech* 99, no. 4 (2013):

162 *Public memory and ethnic conflict*

481–506. These scholars address the lack of scholarly interest in Huerta until relatively recently, and her work with Chávez.

24 Alfredo Mirandé, *Jalos, USA: Transnational Community and Identity* (Notre Dame, IN: University Notre Dame Press, 2014).

25 Mirande, *Jalos USA*.

26 Ibid. See also: D. Robert DeChaine, *Border Rhetorics*.

27 Trinidad Rico, "Thoughts on the Preservation of Old Doha, Qatar," *Public Historian* 41 no. 1 (2019): 111–120.

28 Rafael García, "Build on EP's Real Identity," *El Paso Times,* December 17, 2016. Available at: https://www.elpasotimes.com/story/opinion/columnists/2016/12/17/garcia-build-eps-real-identity/95569988. Retrieved April 1, 2018.

29 Estala appeared on the November 23, 2017 edition of the program. Available at: http://www.texasstandard.org/stories/in-el-paso-some-celebrate-thanksgiving-in-april. Retrieved November 27, 2017.

30 Dionne Mack, "El Paso's Public Art Serves Key Function, Even in Controversy," *El Paso Times,* October 19, 2014.

31 Maribel Villalva, "At Holocaust Museum, It's All about Tolerance," *El Paso Times*, February 9, 2011.

32 US News and World Report, "Texas OKs Mexican-American Studies Course-Without the Name, (April 13, 2018), https://www.usnews.com/news/best-states/texas/articles/2018-04-13/texas-oks-mexican-american-studies-course-without-the-name. Retrieved February 28, 2019.

33 Ibid.

34 John Mandalios, "Historical Sociology," in *The Blackwell Companion to Social Theory*, 2nd edition, ed. Brian S. Turner (Oxford: Blackwell Publishers, 2000), 389–415.

35 Ibid.

36 Armand Mattelart, *Transnationals and the Third World* (South Hadley, MA: Bergin and Garvey Publishers, 1983), 104–106.

37 Alicia Ebbitt McGill, "Examining the Pedagogy of Community-based Heritage Work through an International Public History Field Experience," *Public Historian* 30, no. 1 (2018): 54–83. McGill cites the extant literature on the topic of fieldwork and heritage studies (p. 55).

38 Oscar J. Martínez, "El Paso/Juárez Should Develop 'Gateway' Heritage," *El Paso Times*, June 27, 1999, 13A.

39 Miguel Torres, "The Missing Link of the El Paso Message," Term Project, College of Business, University of Texas at El Paso, nd.

40 Alan Lessoff, "Corpus Christi, 1965–2005: A Secondary City's Search for a New Direction," *Journal of Urban History* 35, no. 1 (2008). DOI: 10.1177/0096144208322462. Retrieved March 15, 2019.

41 Michelle Ye Hee Lee, "Fact Checker/Analysis: Donald Trump's False Comments Connecting Mexican Immigrants and Crime," *Washington Post*. https://www.washingtonpost.com/news/fact-checker/wp/2015/07/08/donald-trumps-false-comments-connecting-mexican-immigrants-and-crime/?utm_term=.5fe3655a57bd, Retrieved November 27, 2017.

42 Hawes Spencer, and Sheryl Gay Stolberg, "White Nationalists March on University of Virginia," *The New York Times*, August 11, 2017, https://www.nytimes.com/2017/08/11/us/white-nationalists-rally-charlottesville-virginia.html?_r=0. Retrieved: July 22, 2019.

43 Devon M Sayers, "Virginia Governor to White Nationalists: 'Go Home … Shame on You'." *CNN*. August 13, 2017, http://www.cnn.com/2017/08/12/us/charlottesville-white-nationalists-rally/index.html. Retrieved July 22, 2019.

44 We readily acknowledge the many valid criticisms levied against Fox News. However, an internet search entering the term "confederate statues" led us to the Fox News story from 2017: http://www.foxnews.com/us/2017/10/18/which-confedera

te-statues-were-removed-running-list.html. We searched again and found the following link for the same information. Its publication date appears as August 21, no year, presumably 2018: https://www.foxnews.com/us/which-confederate-statues-were-removed-a-running-list. Retrieved February 28, 2019.
45 Rhonda Fanning and Michael Marks, "In El Paso, Some Celebrate Thanksgiving in April," *Texas Standard,* November 23, 2017. The comments referencing El Paso high school teacher and El Paso Mission Trail Association Artistic Director Joe Estala can be accessed here: http://www.texasstandard.org/stories/in-el-paso-som e-celebrate-thanksgiving-in-april. Retrieved November 29, 2017.
46 Ruth Mojica-Hammer, "A Different View of El Paso," *El Paso Times,* April 3, 2005, 11B.

References

Acosta, David. "Saving Luis Jimenez's Gators: El Pasoans Won't Let Go of a Beloved Centerpiece." *Borderzine.* July 14, 2011. http://borderzine.com/2011/07/saving-luis-jimenez%E2%80%99-gators-%E2%80%94-el-pasoans-won%E2%80%99t-let-go-of-a-beloved-city-centerpiece.

Acuña, Rodolfo F. *Anything but Mexican: Chicanos in Contemporary Los Angeles.* New York: Verso, 1996.

Acuña, Rodolfo F. *Occupied America: A History of Chicanos.* 6th edition. New York: Pearson, 2007.

Acuña, Rodolfo F. *Occupied America: A History of Chicanos.* 4th edition. New York: Longman, 2000.

Acuña, Rodolfo F. *Sometimes There is No Other Side: Chicanos and the Myth of Equality.* Notre Dame, IN: University of Notre Dame Press, 1998.

Adams, David Wallace. *Education for Extinction: American Indians and the Boarding School Experience, 1875–1928.* Lawrence, KS: University of Kansas Press, 1995.

Agnew, Vanessa. "Introduction: What is Reenactment?" *Criticism* 46, no. 3 (Summer 2004 2004): 327–339.

Aitchison, Cara, Nicola E. Macleod, and Stephen J. Shaw. *Leisure and Tourism Landscapes: Social and Cultural Geographies.* New York: Routledge, 2000/2002.

Alarcón, David Cooper. *The Aztec Palimpsest: Mexico in the Modern Imagination.* Tucson, AZ: University of Arizona Press, 1997.

Alivizatou, Marilena. *Intangible Heritage and the Museum: New Perspectives on Cultural Preservation.* Walnut Creek, CA: Left Coast Press, 2012.

Almaguer, Tomas. *Racial Fault Lines: The Historical Origins of White Supremacy in California.* Berkeley, CA: University of California Press, 2008.

Alvarez, Luis. *The Power of the Zoot: Youth Culture and Resistance During World War II.* Berkeley, CA: University of California Press, 2008.

Armada, Bernard J. "Memory's Execution: (Dis)placing the Dissident's Body." In *Places of Public Memory: The Rhetoric of Museums and Memorials,* edited by Greg Dickenson, Carole Blair, and Brian L. Ott, 216–237. Tuscaloosa, AL: University of Alabama Press, 2010.

Ashworth, G.J. and J.E. Tunbridge. *The Tourist-Historic City: Retrospect and Prospect of Managing the Heritage City.* New York: Oxford University Press, 2000.

Assies, Willem. "Land Tenure and Tenure Regimes in Mexico: An Overview." *Journal of Agrarian Change* 8, no. 1 (January 2008): 33–66. DOI: doi:10.1111/j.1471-0366.2007.00162.x.

References 165

Auslander, Mark. "Touching the Past: Materializing Time in Traumatic 'Living History' Reenactments." *Signs and Society* 1, no. 1 (Spring 2013 2013): 161–183.

Azuela, Mariano. *The Underdogs.* Trans. New York: Penguin Classics, 2008.

Badner, John E. *Remaking America: Public Memory, Commemoration, and Patriotism in the Twentieth Century.* Princeton, NJ: Princeton University Press, 1992.

Balderrama, Francisco E. and Raymond Rodríguez. *Decade of Betrayal: Mexican Repatriation in the 1930s.* Revised edition. Albuquerque, NM: University of New Mexico Press, 2006.

Balderrama, Francisco E. and Raymond Rodríguez. "The Emergence of Unconstitutional Deportation and Repatriation of Mexicans and Mexican Americans as a Public Issue." *Radical History Review* 93 (2005): 107–110.

Barnes, J. "The Struggle to Control the Past: Commemoration, Memory, and the Bear River Massacre of 1863." *The Public Historian* 30, no. 1 (February 2008): 81–104. DOI: doi:10/1525/tph.2008.30.1.81.

Bates, Christopher. "Oh, I'm a Good Rebel: Reenactment, Racism, and the Lost Cause." In *The Civil War in Popular Culture: Memory and Meaning*, edited by Lawrence A. Kreiser and Randell Allred, 191–221. Lexington, KY: University of Kentucky Press, 2014.

Bedford, David and W. Thomas Workman. "Whiteness and the Great Law of Peace." In *Working Through Whiteness: International Perspectives*, edited by Cynthia Levine-Rasky, 25–41. Albany, NY: State University of New York Press, 2002.

Berger, Arthur Asa. "Semiotics and Society." *Society* 51, no. 1 (February 2014): 22–26. DOI: doi:10.1007/s12115–013–9731–4.

Berliner, David, "Multiple Nostalgias: The Fabric of Heritage in Luang Prabang." *Journal of the Royal Anthropological Institute* 18, no. 4 (December 2012): 769–786.

Blade, Melinda K. "Spanish Colonization of New Spain: Benevolent? Malevolent? Indifferent?" *OAH Magazine of History* 14, no. 4 (Summer 2000 2000): 54–58.

Blady, Rebecca. *Towards a Theory of Self-Critical Nationalism: Constructing a Moral National Identity in the Aftermath of the Dark Past.* Undergraduate Honors Thesis, Brandeis University, Waltham, Massachusetts, 2012.

Blair, Carol, Greg Dickinson and Brian L. Ott. (Eds.) "Introduction." In *Places of Public Memory: The Rhetoric of Museums and Memorials*, 1–54. Tuscaloosa, AL: University of Alabama Press, 2010.

Blanton, Carlos Kevin. *The Strange Case of Bilingual Education in Texas 1836–1981.* College Station, TX: Texas A&M University Press, 2004.

Blaut, J.M. *The Colonizer's Model of the World: Geographic Diffusionism and Eurocentric History.* New York: Guilford Press, 1993.

Boime, Albert. "Patriarchy Fixed in Stone: Gutzon Borglum's Mount Rushmore." *American Art* 5, nos. 1–2 (Winter–Spring, 1991): 143–167.

Bokovoy, Matthew F. *The San Diego World's Fairs and Southwestern Memory, 1880–1940.* Albuquerque, NM: University of New Mexico Press, 2005.

Bonilla-Silva, Eduardo. *Racism Without Racists: Color-Blind Racism and the Persistence of Racial Inequality in the United States* 4th edition. New York: Rowman and Littlefield, 2014.

Bonnett, Alastair. "A White World? Whiteness and the Meaning of Modernity in Latin America and Japan." In *Working Through Whiteness: International Perspectives*, edited by Cynthia Levine-Rasky, 69–106. Albany, NY: State University of New York Press, 2002.

166 *References*

Bragg, Bea. *The Very First Thanksgiving: Pioneers on the Rio Grande.* Niwot, CO: Robert Rhinehart Publishers, 1997. Printed in cooperation with the El Paso Mission Trail Association.

Bruner, Edward M. "Abraham Lincoln as Authentic Reproduction: A Critique of Postmodernism." In *The Political Nature of Cultural Heritage and Tourism: Critical Essays,* edited by Timothy J. Dallen, Vol. 3, 19–37. Burlington, VT: Ashgate Publishers, 2007.

Bryant, Jennings and Mary Beth Oliver (Eds.). *Media Effects: Advances in Theory and Research.* 3rd edition. New York: Routledge, 2009.

Bunten, Alexis Celeste. "Sharing Culture or Selling Out? Developing the Commodified Persona in the Heritage Industry." *American Ethnologist* 35, no. 3 (2008): 380–395.

Burke, Timothy. "Onate or the Equestrian." History News Network. Colombian College of Arts and Sciences, George Washington University, Washington, DC (January 12, 2004). Retrieved from https://historynewsnetwork.org/blog/3013.

de Buys, William. *Enchantment and Exploitation: The Life and Hard Times of a New Mexico Mountain Range.* Albuquerque, NM: University of New Mexico Press, 1985.

Canclini, Nestor Garcia. *Art Beyond Itself: Anthropology for a Society Without a Storyline.* Durham, NC: Duke University Press, 2014.

Carpignano, Paolo, Robin Andersen, Stanley Aronowitz, and William DiFazio. "Chatter in the Age of Electronic Reproduction: Talk Television and the 'Public Mind'." In *The Phantom Public Sphere,* edited by B. Robbins, 93–120. Minneapolis, MN: University of Minneapolis Press, 1993.

Castaneda, Antonia I. "Sexual Violence in the Politics and Policies of conquest: Amerindian women and the Spanish conquest of Alta California." In *Between Conquests: The Early Chicano Historical Experience,* edited by Michael Ornelas. 4th edition. Dubuque, IA: Kendall-Hunt, 2004.

Chambers, Erve. *Native Tours: The Anthropology of Travel and Tourism.* 2nd edition. Long Grove, IL: Waveland Press, 2000.

Cohen, I. Glenn. "Medical Tourism: The View from Ten Thousand Feet." *The Hastings Center Report* 40, no. 2 (March–April 2010): 11–12.

Coles, Robert. *The Old Ones of New Mexico.* Photographs by Alex Harris. Revised edition. Albuquerque, NM: University of New Mexico Press, 1973/1989.

Cordess, Christopher and Maja Turcan. "Art Vandalism." *British Journal of Criminology* 33, no. 1 (1993): 95–102.

Córdova, Teresa. "Power and Knowledge: Colonialism in the Academy." In *Living Chicana Theory,* edited by Carla Trujillo, 17–45. Berkeley, CA: Third Woman Press, 1998.

Craik, Jennifer. "The Culture of Tourism." In *Touring Cultures: Transformations of Travel and Theory,* edited by Chris Rojek and John Urry, 113–136. London: Routledge, 2007.

Crane, D., N. Kawashima, and K. Kawasaki. (Eds.). *Global Culture: Media, Arts, Policy, and Globalization.* New York: Routledge, 2003.

Crawford, Stanley. *Mayordomo: Chronicle of an Acequia in Northern New Mexico.* New York: Anchor Books, 1988.

Crawley, Catherine E. "Localized Debates of Agricultural Biotechnology in Community Newspapers: A Quantitative Analysis of Media Frames and Sources." *Science Communication* 28, no. 3 (2007): 314–346.

Crehan, Kate. *Gramsci, Culture and Anthropology.* Berkeley, CA: University of California Press, 2002.

References 167

Cuevas Contreras, Tomas J. and Isabel Zizalde Hernández. "Cross-border Tourism Networks, Ciudad Juarez, Chihuahua, Mexico and El Paso, Texas, United States." Unpublished Manuscript, 2011: 2–15.

Culler, Jonathan. *Framing the Sign: Criticisms and Its Institutions.* Norman, OK: University of Oklahoma Press, 1988.

Daley, Christine Makosky, Aimee S. James, Ezekiel Ulrey, Stephanie Joseph, Angelia Talawyma, Won S. Choi, K. Allen Greiner, and M. Kathryn Coe, "Using Focus Groups in Community-Based Participatory Research: Challenges and Resolutions." *Qualitative Health Research* 20, no. 5 (May 2010), 697–706.

Dalstrom, Matthew D. "Winter Texans and the Recreation of the American Medical Experience in Mexico." *Medical Anthropology* 31, no. 2 (March–April, 2012): 167–177.

D'Ambra, John, and Concepcion S. Wilson. "Use of the World Wide Web for International Travel: Integrating the Construct of Uncertainty Information Seeking and the Task-technology Fit (TTF) Model." *Journal of the American Society for Information Science and Technology* 55, no. 8 (2004): 731–742.

Davis, Susan G. "Landscapes of Imagination: Tourism in Southern California." *Pacific Historical Review* 68, no. 2 (May 1999): 173–191.

Deagan, Kathleen. "Colonial Origins and Colonial Transformations in Spanish America." *Historical Archeology* 37, no. 4 (2003): 3–13.

DeChaine, D. Robert (Ed.). *Border Rhetorics: Charting Enactments of Citizenship and Identity on the U.S. – Mexico Border.* Tuscaloosa, AL: University of Alabama Press, 2012.

DeGuzmán, María. *Spain's Long Shadow: The Black Legend, Off-Whiteness, and Anglo-American Empire.* Minneapolis, MN: University of Minnesota Press, 2005.

de Herrera, María Luisa, Kathleen Garcia, and Gail Goldman. "Public Art as a Planning Tool." Paper presented at Contrasts and Transitions: National Planning Conference of the American Planning Association, San Diego, CA. April 5–9, 1997, http://data.quaytest.net/apaproceedings/PRCDS97/herrera.html.

De León, Arnoldo. *They Called Them Greasers: Anglo Attitudes Toward Mexicans in Texas, 1821–1900.* Austin, TX: University of Texas Press, 1983.

de Toro, Fernando. *Theater Semiotics: Text and Staging in Modern Theater.* Toronto: University of Toronto Press, 1995.

Deverrell, William. *Whitewashed Adobe: The Rise of Los Angeles and the Removing of its Mexican Past.* Berkeley, CA: University of California Press, 2004.

de Villagrá, Gaspar Pérez. *Historia de la Nueva Mexico, 1610.* Translated by Miguel Encinias and Alfred Rodriguez. Albuquerque, NM: University of New Mexico Press, 1610/2004.

de Villagrá, Gaspar Pérez. *History of New Mexico.* Translated by Gilberto Espinosa. New York: Arno Press, 1967.

de Vries, Tity. "Ambiguity in an Alaskan Theme Park: Presenting 'History as Commodity' and 'History as Heritage." *The Public Historian* 29, no. 2 (Spring 2007 2007): 55–79.

Dickinson, Greg, Brian L. Ott and Eric Aoki. "Memory and Myth at the Buffalo Bill Museum." *Western Journal of Communication* 69, no. 2 (April 2005): 85–108. DOI: doi:10.1080/10570310500076684.

DiGiano, Maria, Edward Eliss and Eric Keys. "Changing Landscapes for Forest Commons: Linking Land Tenure with Forest Cover Change Following Mexico's

168   *References*

1992 Agrarian Counter-reforms." *Human Ecology: An Interdisciplinary Journal* 41, no. 5 (2013): 707–723. DOI: doi:10.1007/s10745–10013–9581–0.

Dixon, Travis L. (2008). "Who is the Victim Here? The Psychological Effects of Over-representing White Victims and Black Perpetrators on Television News." *Journalism* 9, no. 5 (2008): 582–605.

Dolezal, Claudia. "Community-based Tourism in Thailand: (Dis-)Illusions of Authenticity and the Necessity for Dynamic Concepts of Culture and Power." *Austrian Journal of South-East Asian Studies* 4, no. 2, (2011): 129–138.

Doss, Erin F. and Robin E. Jensen. "Balancing Mystery and Identification: Dolores Huerta's Shifting Transcendent Persona." *Quarterly Journal of Speech* 99, no. 4 (September 2013): 481–506.

Drinnon, Richard. *Facing West: The Metaphysics of Indian-Hating and Empire-Building*New York: New American Library, 1980.

Dunbar-Ortiz, Roxanne. *An Indigenous People's History of the United States.* Boston, MA: Beacon Press, 2014.

Dunbar-Ortiz, Roxanne. *Roots of Resistance: Land Tenure in New Mexico, 1680–1980.* Los Angeles, CA: Chicano Studies Research Center/American Indian Studies Center/University of California, 1980.

Dyer, Richard. *White.* New York: Routledge, 1997.

Elam, Keir. *The Semiotics of Theater and Drama.* New York: Psychology Press, 2002.

Escobedo, Elizabeth R. *From Coveralls to Zoot Suits: The Lives of Mexican American Women of the World War II Home Front.* Chapel Hill, NC: University of North Carolina Press, 2013.

Everett, Sally, and Cara Aitchison. "The Role of Food Tourism in Sustaining Regional Identity: A Case Study of Cornwall, South West England." *Journal of Sustainable Tourism* 16, no. 2 (2008): 150–167.

Fairclough, Norman. "The Discourse of New Labour: Critical Discourse Analysis." In *Discourse as Data: A Guide for Analysis,* edited by Margaret Wetherell, Stephanie Taylor, and Simeon Yates, 229–266. Thousand Oaks, CA: Sage, 2001.

Fanning, Rhonda and Michael Marks. "In El Paso, Some Celebrate Thanksgiving in April." *Texas Standard,* November 23, 2017.

Figal, Gerald. (2008). "Between War and Tropics: Heritage Tourism in Postwar Okinawa." *Public Historian* 30, no. 2 (2008): 83–107.

Filene, Benjamin. "'Outsider' History-makers and What They Teach Us." *Public Historian* 34, no.1 (Winter 2012 2012): 11–33.

Fiorini, Daniela and Paula Socolovsky. "Argentinian Myths: Semiotics and Cultural Identity." *Society* 51, no. 1 (February 2014): 27–30.

Fleming, Ronald Lee and Melissa Tapper Goldma. "Public Art for the Public." *The Public Interest* 159 (Spring 2005 2005): 55–76.

Florescano, Enrique. *Memory, Myth, and Time in Mexico: From the Aztecs to Independence.* Translated by Albert G. Bork. Austin, TX: University of Texas Press, 1994.

Foucault, Michel. *The Archeology of Knowledge & The Discourse on Language.* Translated by A. M. Sheridan Smith. London: Tavistock, 1972.

Fregoso, Rosa-Linda. *MeXicana Encounters: The Making of Social Identities on the Borderlands.* Berkeley, CA: University of California Press, 2003.

García, Ignacio Manuel. *Chicanismo: The Forging of a Militant Ethos Among Mexican Americans.* Tucson, AZ: University of Arizona Press, 1997.

García, Juan R. *Operation Wetback: The Mass Deportation of Mexican American Undocumented Workers in 1954.* New York: Praeger, 1980.

References 169

García, Mario T. *Desert Immigrants: The Mexicans of El Paso, 1880–1920*. New Haven, CT: Yale University Press, 1981.

Gaspar de Alba, Alicia. *Chicano Art Inside/Outside the Master's House: Cultural Politics and the CARA Exhibition*. Austin, TX: University of Texas Press, 1998.

Gerbner, George, and Larry Gross. "Living with Television: The Violence Profile." *Journal of Communication* 26, no. 2 (1976): 172–199.

Gerbner, George, Larry Gross, Michael Morgan, Nancy Signorielli, and James Shanahan. "Growing Up with Television: Cultivation Processes." In *Media Effects: Advances in Theory and Research*, edited by Jennings Bryant and Dolf Zillmann, 2nd edition. 43–67. Mahwah, NJ: Lawrence Erlbaum Associates, 2002.

Ghartey-Tagoe Kootin, Amma Y. "Lessons in Blackbody Minstrelsy: Old Plantation and the Manufacture of Black Authenticity." *TDR/The Drama Review* 57, no. 2 (Summer2013): 102–122.

Giles, Howard, Daniel Linz, Doug Bonilla, and Michelle LeahGomez. "Police Stops of and Interactions with Latino and White (non-Latino) Drivers: Extensive Policing and Communication Accommodation." *Communication Monographs* 79, no. 4 (September 2012): 407–427.

Glazer, Nathan. "Monuments in an Age without Hero's." *The Public Interest* 123 (Spring 1996 1996): 22–39.

Glover, N. "Co-produced Histories: Mapping the Uses and Narratives of History in the Tourist Age." *The Public Historian* 30, no. 1 (2008): 105–124.

Gómez, Laura E. *Manifest Destinies: The Making of the Mexican American Race*. New York: New York University Press, 2007.

Gómez-Quiñones, Juan. *Chicano Politics: Reality and Promise, 1940–1990*. Albuquerque, NM: University of New Mexico Press, 1990.

González, Deena J. *Refusing the Favor: The Spanish-Mexican Women of Santa Fe, 1820–1880*. Albuquerque, NM: University of New Mexico Press, 1999.

González, Gilbert G. *Culture of Empire: American Writers, Mexico & Mexican Immigrants, 1880–1930*. Austin, TX: University of Texas Press, 2004.

Gonzalez, Manuel G. and Cynthia M. Gonzalez. *En Aquel Entonces [In Years Gone By]: Readings in Mexican American History*. Bloomington, IN: Indiana University Press, 2000.

Gordon, Linda. *The Great Arizona Orphan Abduction*. Cambridge, MA: Harvard University Press, 1999.

Graham, Brian, G.J. Ashworth, and J.E. Tunbridge. *A Geography of Heritage: Power, Culture, and Economy*. New York: Oxford University Press, 2000/2002.

Griffin, Larry J. and Peggy G. Hargis. "Surveying Memory: The Past in Black and White." *Southern Literary Journal* XL, no. 2 (2008): 42–69.

Grimes, Ronald L. *Symbol and Conquest: Public Ritual and Drama in Santa Fe*. Albuquerque, NM: University of New Mexico Press, 1976/1992.

Grundlingh, Albert. "Revisiting the 'Old' South Africa: Excursions into South Africa's Tourist History Under Apartheid, 1948–1990." *South African Historical Journal* 56, no. 1 (March 2009): 103–122. DOI: doi:10.1080/02582470609464967.

Gutiérrez, José Ángel. "The Chicano Movement: Paths to Power." *The Social Studies* 102 (2011): 25–32.

Griswold del Castillo, Richard. *The Treaty of Guadalupe Hidalgo: A Legacy of Conflict*. Norman, OK: University of Oklahoma Press, 1990.

Griswold del Castillo, Richard. *World War II and Mexican Americans*. Austin, TX: University of Texas Press, 2008.

170 *References*

Gullone, Elenora. "Historical and Current conceptualizations of Animal Cruelty." In *Animal Cruelty, Antisocial Behavior, and Aggression: More Than a Link*, edited by Phil Arkow and Elenora Gullone. New York: Palgrave MacMillan, 2012.

Guthrie, Thomas H. *Recognizing Heritage: Multiculturalism in New Mexico*. Lincoln, NB: University of Nebraska Press, 2013.

Gutiérrez, Ramón. *When Jesus Came, the Corn Mothers Went Away: Marriage, Sexuality, and Power in New Mexico, 1500–1846*. Stanford, CA: Stanford University Press, 1991.

Hall, Edward T. *The Silent Language*. New York: Anchor Books, 1959.

Hammer, Andrea. "Memory Lines: The Plotting of New York's Military Tract." In *Rhetoric, Remembrance, and Visual Form: Sighting Memory*, edited by Anne Teresa Demo and Bradford Vivian, 15–32. New York: Routledge, 2012.

Hammerback, John C. and Richard J. Jensen (Eds.). *The Words of César Chávez*. College Station, TX: Texas A&M Press, 2002.

Hammerback, John C. and Richard J. Jensen. *The Rhetorical Career of César Chávez*. College Station, TX: Texas A&M Press, 1998.

Hammett, Daniel. "British media representations of South Africa and the 2010 FIFA World Cup." *South African Geographical Journal* 93, no. 1 (2011): 63–74.

Hammond, George P. and Agapito Rey. *Don Juan de Oñate: Colonizer of New Mexico, 1595–1628 Vols V & VI*. Albuquerque, NM: University of New Mexico Press, 1953.

Hero, Rodney. *Latinos and the U.S. Political System: Two-tiered Pluralism*. Philadelphia, PA: Temple University Press, 2010.

Herzog, Lawrence. "Globalization of the Barrio: Transformation of the Latino Cultural Landscapes of San Diego, California." In *Hispanic Spaces, Latino Places: Community and Cultural Diversity in Contemporary America*, edited by Daniel Arreola, 103–124. Austin, TX: University of Texas Press, 2004.

Hogan, Maureen P., and Timothy Pursell. "The 'Real Alaskan': Nostalgia and rural masculinity in the 'last frontier'." *Men and Masculinities* 11, no. 1 (October 2008): 1–23. DOI: doi:10.1177/1097184X06291892.

Hoig, Stan. *Came Men on Horses: The Conquistador Expeditions of Francisco Vasquez de Coronado and Don Juan de Oñate*. Boulder, CO: University of Colorado Press, 2012.

Holling, Michelle A. "A Dispensational Rhetoric in 'The Mexican Question in the Southwest'." In *Border Rhetorics: Charting Enactments of Citizenship and Identity on the U.S.-Mexico Border*, edited by D. Robert DeChaine, 65–85. Tuscaloosa, AL: University of Alabama Press, 2012.

Horowitz, Tony. *A Voyage Long and Strange: Rediscovering the New World*. New York: Henry Holt and Company, 2008.

Horton, Sarah. "New Mexico's Cuarto Centario and Spanish Nationalism: Collapsing Past Conquests and Present Dispossession." *Journal of the Southwest* 44, no. 1 (Spring 2002 2002): 49–60.

Hou, Jeffrey, and Michael Ríos. "Community-Driven Place Making: The Social Practice and Participatory Design in the Making of Union Point Park." *Journal of Architectural Education* 57, no. 1 (2003): 19–27.

Hunner, Jon. "Preserving Hispanic Ways in New Mexico." *Public Historian* 23, no. 4 (Fall 2001): 29–40.

Huggard, Christopher J. and Terrence M. Humble. *Santa Rita del Cobre: A Copper Mining Community in New Mexico*. Boulder, CO: University Press of Colorado, 2012.

Imada, Adria L. "The Army Learns to Luau: Imperial Hospitality and Military Photography in Hawai'i." *Contemporary Pacific* 20, no. 2 (2008): 329–361.

References   171

Ioanide, Paula. *The Emotional Politics of Racism: How Feeling Trump Facts in an Era of Colorblindness*. Stanford, CA: Stanford University Press, 2015.

Jacoby, Eric. *Man and Land*. London: Andre Deutch, 1971.

Jamal, Tazim and Mike Robinson. "Introduction: the Evolution and Contemporary Positioning of Tourism as a Focus of Study." In *The Sage Handbook of Tourism Studies*, edited by Tazim Jamal and Mike Robinson, 1–16. Thousand Oaks, CA: Sage, 2009.

Johnson, Julia R. "Bordering on Social Practice." In *Border Rhetorics: Charting Enactments of Citizenship and Identity on the U.S.-Mexico Frontier*, edited D. Robert DeChaine, 33–47. Tuscaloosa, AL: University of Alabama Press, 2012.

Juárez, Miguel. "Keeping Los Lagartos at San Jacinto Plaza." *Fusion Magazine.* http://thefusionmag.com/keeping-los-lagartos-at-san-jacinto-plaza. Retrieved October 2, 2017.

Keen, Benjamin. "The Black Legend Revisited: Assumptions and Realities." *The Hispanic American Historical Review* 49, no. 4, (November 1969): 703–719.

Kempiak, Joanna, Lindsey Hollywood, Peter Bolan and Una McMachon-Beattie. "The Heritage Tourist: An Understanding of the Visitor Experience at Heritage Attractions." *International Journal of Heritage Studies* 23, no. 4 (January 2017): 375–392.

Kessell, John. *Kiva, Cross, and Crown: The Pecos Indians and New Mexico, 1540–1840*. Washington, DC: Government Printing Office for the National Park Service, US Department of the Interior, 1979.

Kessell, John. *Spain in the Southwest: A Narrative History of Colonial New Mexico, Arizona, Texas, and California*. Norman, OK: University of Oklahoma Press, 2002.

Kessell, John L. *Pueblos, Spaniards, and the Kingdom of New Mexico*. Norman, OK: University of Oklahoma Press, 2008.

Avraham, Eli, and Eran Ketter. "Marketing Destinations with Prolonged Negative Images: Towards a Theoretical Model." *Tourism Geographies* 15, no. 1 (March 2012): 145–164.

Kirk, Camille M. "Authenticity and Place: An Interpretation of Resident Response to Tourism in Santa Fe, New Mexico." Master's Thesis, University of California, Los Angeles, 1994.

Klapp, Orrin E. "The Creation of Popular Hero's." *American Journal of Sociology* 54, no. 2 (September 1948): 135–141.

Knauer, Lisa Maya and Daniel J. Walkowitz. "Introduction: Memory, Race, and the Nation in Public Spaces." In *Contested Histories in Public Space: Memory, Race, and Nation*, edited by Daniel Walkowitz and Lisa Maya Knauer, 1–27. Durham, NC: Duke University Press, 2009.

Knox, Dan. "The Sacralised Landscapes of Glencoe: From Massacre to Mass Tourism, and Back Again." *International Journal of Tourism Research* 8, no. 3 (August 2006): 185–197.

Kozol, Jonathan. *The Night is Dark and I am Far from Home*. New York: Bantam Books, 1977.

Kuan-HsingChen and David Morely (Eds.). *Stuart Hall: Critical Dialogues in Cultural Studies*. New York: Routledge, 1996.

Lamadrid, Enrique. "Ig/Noble Savages of New Mexico's Silent Cinema, 1912–1914." Special Issue: Border Crossings: Mexican and Chicano Cinema. Chon A. Noriega, Guest Editor. *Spectator*, USC School of Cinema (1992): 12–23.

172 *References*

Lay, Shawn. "Imperial Outpost on the Border: El Paso's Frontier Klan 100." In *The Invisible Empire in the West: Toward a New Historical Appraisal of the Ku Klux Klan in the 1920s*, edited by Shawn Lay, 67–96. Urbana, IL: University of Illinois Press, 2004.

Lay, Shawn. *War, Revolution, and the Ku Klux Klan: A Study of Intolerance in a Border City*. El Paso, TX: Texas Western Press, 1985.

Lessoff, Alan. "Corpus Christi, 1965–2005: A Secondary City's Search for a New Direction." *Journal of Urban History* 35, no. 1 (2008). Online: DOI: doi:10.1177/0096144208322462.

Lewis, Jeff. *Cultural Studies: The Basics*. London: Sage, 2002.

Leyva, Yolanda Chavez. "Monuments of Conformity: Commemorating and Protesting Onate on the Border." *New Mexico Historical Review* 82, no. 3 (2007): 343–367.

Light, Duncan. "Dracula Tourism in Romania: Cultural Identity and the State." *Annuals of Tourism Research* 34, no. 3 (2008):746–765. DOI: doi:10.1016/j.annals.2007.03.004.

Lippmann, Walter. *Public Opinion*. New York: Free Press, 1922/1997.

Lorey, David E. *The U.S.-Mexico Border in the Twentieth Century*. Wilmington, DE: Scholarly Resources Books, 1992.

Lovato, Andrew Leo *Santa Fe Hispanic Culture: Preserving Identity in a Tourist Town*. Albuquerque, NM: University of New Mexico Press, 2006.

Luibhéid, Eithne. *Entry Denied: Controlling Sexuality at the Border*. Minneapolis, MN: University of Minnesota Press, 2002.

MacConnell, Dean. *The Tourist: A New Theory of the Leisure Class*. New York: Random House, 1976.

Maharaj, Brij, Reshma Sucheran and Vino Pally. "Durban – A Tourism Mecca? Challenges of the Post-Apartheid Era." *Urban Forum* 17, no. 3 (July 2006): 262–281.

Mandal, Steve, Finola O'Carroll and Denis Shine. "The Black Friary." *Archeology Ireland* (Spring 2015 2015): 34–38.

Mandalios, John. "Historical Sociology." In *The Blackwell Companion to Social Theory*, edited by Brian S. Turner, 2nd edition, 389–415. Oxford: Blackwell Publishers, 2000.

Marques, Rigoberto. "What's in the 'X' of Latinx?" Center for Comparative Studies in Race and Ethnicity, Stanford University, July 9, 2018.

Martorella, Rosanne. "Cultural Policy as Marketing Strategy: The Economic Consequences of Cultural Tourism in New York City." In *Global Culture: Media, Arts, Policy, and Globalization*, edited by Diana Crane, Nobuko Kawashima, and Ken'ichi Kawasaki, 118–131. New York: Routledge: 2002.

Martínez, Oscar J. *The First Peoples: A History of Native Americans at the Pass of the North*. El Paso, TX: El Paso Community Foundation, 2000.

Mattelart, Armand. *Transnationals and the Third World*. South Hadley, MA: Bergin and Garvey Publishers, 1983.

Matthiessen, Peter. *Sal Si Puedes (Escape if You Can): César Chávez and the New American Revolution*. Berkeley, CA: University of California Press, 1969/2000.

Mazón, Mauricio. *The Zoot-Suit Riots: The Psychology of Symbolic Annihilation*. Austin, TX: University of Texas Press, 1984.

McCombs, Maxwell and Donald Shaw. "The Agenda-setting Function of Mass Media." *Public Opinion Quarterly* 36, no. 2 (1972): 176–187.

McDougall, Kathleen L. "Just Living: Genealogic, Honesty, and the Politics of Apartheid." *Anthropology Southern Africa* 37, no. 1 and 2 (2014): 19–29.

References 173

McGeagh, Robert. *Juan de Oñate's Colony in the Wilderness: An Early American History of the Southwest*. Santa Fe, NM: Sunstone Press, 1990.

McGill, Alicia Ebbitt. "Examining the Pedagogy of Community-based Heritage Work Through an International Public History Field Experience." *Public Historian* 30, no. 1 (2018): 54–83.

McKay, R. Reynolds. "The Impact of the Great Depression on Immigrant Mexican Labor: Repatriation of the Bridgeport, Texas Coalminers." *Social Science Quarterly* 62, no. 2 (1984): 354–363.

McKercher, Bob, Karin Weber, and Hilary Du Cros. "Rationalizing Inappropriate Behavior at Contested Sights." *Journal of Sustainable Tourism* 16, no. 4 (December 2008): 369–385.

McWilliams, Carey. *North from Mexico: The Spanish-speaking People of the United States*. Revised edition. Alma M. García. New York: Praeger, 1948/2016.

Medina, Lara. "Los Espíritus Siguen Hablando: Chicana Spiritualities." In *Living Chicana Theory*, edited by Carla Trujillo, 189–213. Berkeley, CA: Third Woman Press, 1998.

Melendez, A. Gabriel. *Hidden Chicano Cinema: Film Dramas in the Borderland*. New Brunswick, NJ: Rutgers University Press, 2013.

Melendez, Gabriel. "Nuevo Mexico by any Other Name." In *Contested Homeland: A Chicano History of New Mexico*, edited by Erlinda González-Berry and David Maciel, 143–168. Albuquerque, NM: University of New Mexico Press, 2000.

Meltzer, Milton. *Columbus and the World Around Him*. New York: Franklin Watts, 1990.

Memmi, Albert. *The Colonizer and the Colonized*. Boston, MA: Beacon Press, 1957/1991.

Menchaca, Martha. *Recovering History, Constructing Race: The Indian, Black, and White Roots of Mexican Americans*. Austin, TX: University of Texas Press, 2001.

van der Merwe, Clinton David, "The Limits of Urban Heritage Tourism in South Africa: The Case of Constitution Hill, Johannesburg." *Public Forum* 24, no. 4, (December 2013): 573–588. DOI: doi:10.1007/s12132–013–9197-x.

Mesa-Bains, Amalia. "Chicano Bodily Aesthetics." In *Body/Culture: Chicano Figuration*, edited by Richard Kubiak, Elizabeth Partch, Amalia Mesa-Bains, and V.A. Sorell, 6–13. Sonoma, CA: University Art Gallery/Sonoma State University, 1990.

Mirandé, Alfredo. *Jalos, USA: Transnational Community and Identity*. Notre Dame, IN: University of Notre Dame Press, 2014.

Mirandé, Alfredo. *Hombres y machos: Masculinity in Latino Culture*. Boulder, CO: Westview Press, 2007.

Mirandé, Alfredo. *The Chicano Experience: An Alternative Perspective*. Notre Dame, IN: University of Notre Dame Press, 1985.

Mirandé, Alfredo, and Evangélina Enríquez. *La Chicana: The Mexican American-Woman*. Chicago, IL: University of Chicago Press, 1979.

Monroy, Douglas. *Thrown Among Strangers: The Making of Mexican Culture in Frontier California*. Berkeley, CA: University of California Press, 1990.

Montejano, David. *Anglos and Mexicans in the making of Texas, 1836–1986*. Austin, TX: University of Texas Press, 1987.

Montgomery, Charles. "Becoming 'Spanish-American': Race and Rhetoric in New Mexico Politics, 1880–1928." *Journal of American Ethnic History* 20, no. 4 (2001): 59–84.

Montgomery, Charles. *The Spanish Redemption: Heritage, Power, and Loss on New Mexico's Upper Rio Grande*. Berkeley, CA: University of California Press, 2002.

Morales, Ed. *Latinx: The New Force in American Politics and Culture*. New York: Verso Press, 2018.

174   *References*

Morin, Raul. *Among the Valiant: Mexican Americans in World War II and Korea.* Los Angeles, CA: Borden Publishing, 1963.

Murray, Gregory. "'Tears of the Indians' or Superficial Conversion? José Acosta, the Black Legend, and the Spanish Evangelization in the New World." *Catholic Historical Review* 99, no. 1 (January 2013): 29–51.

Nash, Denison. "Tourism as a Form of Imperialism." In *Hosts and Guests: The Anthropology of Tourism.* Edited by Valene L. Smith, 37–52. Philadelphia, PA: University of Pennsylvania Press, 1989.

Al Nassieri, Hammad, and Radhlianh Aulin. "Enablers and Barriers to Project Planning and Scheduling Based on Construction Projects in Oman." *Journal of Construction in Developing Countries* 21, no. 2 (2016), 1–20.

Nathan, Debbie. "The Best Laid Plan." *Texas Monthly* 41, no 2 (February 2013): 90, 174–175.

Nericcio, William Anthony. *Tex(t)-Mex: Seductive Hallucinations of the Mexican in America.* Austin, TX: University of Texas Press, 2007.

Nieto-Phillips, John M. *The Language of Blood: The Making of Spanish American Identity in New Mexico, 1880s–1930s.* Albuquerque, NM: University of New Mexico Press, 2004.

Noel, Linda C. "'I am an American': Anglos, Mexicans, Nativos, and the National Debate Over Arizona and New Mexico Statehood." *Pacific Historical Review* 80, no. 3 (August 2011): 430–467.

Noriega, Chon. "Editor's Commentary: Preservation Matters." *Aztlán: A Journal of Chicano Studies* 30, no. 1 (Spring 2005 2005): 1–20.

Nostrand, Richard L. *The Hispano Homeland.* Norman, OK: University of Oklahoma Press, 1992.

Ortíz-González, Victor M. *El Paso: Local Frontiers at the Global Crossroads.* Minneapolis, MN: University of Minnesota Press, 2004.

Pagán, Eduardo Obregón. *Murder at the Sleepy Lagoon: Zoot Suits, Race and Riots in Wartime L.A.* Chapel Hill, NC: University of North Carolina Press, 2003.

Papa, Michael J., Arvind Singhal, and Wendy H. Papa, *Organizing for Social Change: A Dialectical Journey of Theory and Praxis.* Thousand Oaks, CA: Sage, 2006.

Paredes, Américo. *"With His Pistol in His Hand": A Border Ballad and Its Hero.* 11th edition Austin, TX: University of Texas Press, 1970.

Parish, Timothy C. "Class Structure and Social Reproduction in New Spain/New Mexico." *Dialectical Anthropology* 7, no. 2 (September 1982): 137–153.

Paulsen, Krista E. "Strategy and Sentiment: Mobilizing Heritage in Defense of Place." *Qualitative Sociology* 30 (March 2007): 1–19.

Peck, Douglas T. "Revival of the Spanish 'Black Legend': the American Repudiation of Their Spanish Heritage." *Revista de la Historia de America* 128 (January–June 2001): 25–39.

Pegler-Gordon, Anna. *In Sight of America: Photography and the Development of U.S. Immigration Policy.* Los Angeles, CA: University of California Press, 2009.

Perales, Monica. *Smeltertown: Making and Remembering a Southwest Border Community.* Chapel Hill, NC: University of North Carolina Press, 2010.

Pérez, Frank G. "Communicating for Social Justice: Juan de Oñate, and the Struggle for Chicano Cultural Representation in Public Art." *Noesis* 16 (2007): 98–121.

Pérez, Frank G. "Effectively Targeting Hispanics in the Southwest: Views from Public Relations Professionals in a Border City." *Public Relations Quarterly* 47, no. 1 (2002): 18–21.

Pérez, Frank G., and Carlos F. Ortega. "Hegemony and Civic Discourse in Public Art: The Debate on Juan de Oñate." *Aztlán: A Journal of Chicano Studies* 33, no. 2, (Fall 2008): 121–140.

Pérez, Frank G., and Carlos F. Ortega. "Mediated Debate, Historical Framing, and Public Art: The Juan de Oñate Controversy in El Paso," *Aztlán: A Journal of Chicano Studies* 33, no. 2 (2008): 121–140.

Pérez, Frank G., and T.E. Ruggiero. "Juan de Oñate as Public Art: A Case Study of Cultural Representation and Tourism." *Communication for Development and Social Change Journal* 1, no. 3 (2007): 233–250.

Pérez-Torres, Rafael. *Mestizaje: Critical Uses of Race in Chicano Culture.* Minneapolis, MN: University of Minnesota Press, 2006.

Petrakos, Christopher Ross. "We Would Live Like Brothers: A Reexamination of Diego de Vargas' Reconquest of New Mexico and the Pueblo Indian Revolt, 1692–1696." *Delaware Review of Latin American Studies* 15, no. 1 (2014).

Pope, Melody K., April K. Sievert, and Sheree L. Sievert. "From Pioneers to Tourist: Public Archeology at Spring Mill State Park." *International Journal of Historical Archeology* 15, no. 2 (June 2011): 206–221.

Prideaux, Bruce. "Creating Rural Heritage Visitor Attractions: The Queensland Heritage Trail Project." *International Journal of Tourism Research* 4 (2002): 313–323.

Pycior, Julie Leininger. *LBJ & Mexican Americans: The Paradox of Power.* Austin, TX: University of Texas Press, 1997.

Quintana, Benito. "Damas Indias: America's Iconic Body and the Wars of Conquest in the Spanish Comedia." *Bulletin of the Comediantes* 62, no. 1 (2010): 103–122.

Rabasa, José. *Writing Violence on the Northern Frontier: The Historiography of New Mexico and Florida and the Legacy of Conquest.* Durham, NC: Duke University Press, 2000.

Ramírez, Catherine S. "Deus ex Machina: Tradition, Technology, and the Chicanafuturist Art of Marion C. Martinez [sic]." *Aztlán: A Journal of Chicano Studies Researc* 29, no. 2 (Fall 2004): 55–92.

Ramírez, Catherine S. *The Woman in the Suit Zoot: Gender, Nationalism, and Cultural Politics of Memory.* Durham, NC: Duke University Press, 2009.

Ramírez, Manuel R. "El Pasoans: Life and Society in Mexican El Paso, 1920 1945." PhD diss., Department of History, University of Mississippi, 2000.

Rickly-Boyd, Jillian M. "Commentary – Existential Authenticity: Place Matters." *Tourism Geographies* 15, no. 4 (2013): 680–686.

Rico, Trinidad. "Thoughts on the Preservation of Old Doha, Qatar." *Public Historian* 41, no. 1 (2019): 111–120.

Rinderle, Susana. "The Mexican Diaspora: A Critical Examination of Signifiers." *Journal of Communication Inquiry* 29, no. 4 (2005): 294–316.

Ricard, Robert. *Spiritual Conquest of Mexico: An Essay on the Apostolate and the Evangelizing Methods of the Mendicant Orders in New Spain, 1523–1572.* Library Reprint. Translated by Lesley Byrd Simpson. Berkeley, CA: University of California Press, 1974.

Rivas-Rodriguez, Maggie. *Beyond the Latino World War II Hero: The Social and Political Legacy of a Generation.* Austin, TX: University of Texas Press, 2010.

Rivas-Rodriguez, Maggie. *A Legacy Greater Than Words: Stories of U.S. Latinos and Latinas of the World War II Generation.* Austin, TX: US Latino and Latina World War II Oral History Project/University of Texas Press, 2006.

176 *References*

Rivas-Rodriguez, Maggie. *Mexican Americans and World War II*. Austin, TX: University of Texas Press, 2005.

Robinson, Mike and Smith, Melanie. "Politics, Power and Play: The Shifting Contexts of Cultural Tourism." In *Cultural Tourism in a Changing World: Politics, Participation, and (re)Presentation*, edited by Mike Robinson and Melanie Smith, 1–17. Clevedon: Channel View Publications, 2005.

Rogerson, Christian M. "Tourism and Regional Development: The Case of South Africa's Distressed Areas." *Development in South Africa* 32, no. 3 (2015): 277–291.

Romero, Mary. "El Paso Salt War: Mob Action or Political Struggle?" *Aztlán: A Journal of Chicano Studies* 16, no. 1 and 2, (1985): 119–143.

Romi, Schlomo and Michal Lev, "Experiential Learning of History Through Youth Journeys to Poland." *Research in Education* 78 (November 2007): 88–102.

Rogers, Everett M. *Diffusion of Innovation*. 5th edition. New York: Free Press, 2003.

Rogers, Everett M. *A History of Communication Study: A Biographical Approach*. New York: Free Press, 1994.

Romo, David. *Ringside Seat to a Revolution: An Underground Cultural History of El Paso and Juárez, 1893–1923*. El Paso, TX: Cinco Puntos Press, 2006.

Said, Edward W. *Orientalism*. New York: Vintage Books, 1978.

Sánchez, George J. *Becoming Mexican American: Ethnicity, Culture and Identity in Chicano Los Angeles, 1900–1945*. New York: Oxford University Press, 1993.

Sánchez, George I. *Forgotten People: A Study of Mexicans*. Albuquerque, NM: University of New Mexico Press, 1940/1996.

Sánchez, Joseph P. "Introduction: Juan de Oñate and the Founding of New Mexico, 1598–1609." *Colonial Latin American Historical Review* 7, no. 2 (1998): 89–107.

San Miguel, Guadalupe. *"Let Them All Take Heed": Mexican Americans and the Campaign for Educational Equality in Texas. 1910–1981*. College Station, TX: Texas A&M Press, 2000.

Sargent, Hillary. "#TBT: Did the First Thanksgiving Really take Place in Plymouth? It Depends on Who you Ask." *Boston*, November 26, 2015. http://www.boston.com/news/national-news/2015/11/26/tbt-did-the-first-thanksgiving-really-take-place-in-plymouth-it-depends-who-you-ask.

Scheurer, Timothy E. *Music and Mythmaking in Film*. Jefferson, NC: McFarland & Company, 2008.

Shaff, Howard and Audrey Karl Shaff. *Six Wars at a Time: The Life and Times of Gutzon Borglum, Sculptor of Mount Rushmore*. Sioux Falls, SD: Augustana College, Center for Western Studies, 1985.

Sharp, Joanne, Venda Pollack, and Ronan Paddison. "Just Art for a Just City: Public Art and Social Inclusion in Urban Regeneration." *Urban Studies* 42, no. 5 and 6 (May 2005): 1001–1023.

Shohat, Ella and Robert Stam. *Unthinking Eurocentrism: Multiculturalism and the Media*. New York: Routledge, 1994/2004.

Simmons, Marc. *The Last Conquistador: Juan de Oñate and the Settling of the Far Southwest*. Norman, OK: University of Oklahoma Press, 1993.

Singer, Allan J. *Social Studies for Secondary Schools*. New York: Lawrence Erlbaum and Associates, 2008.

Slack, Jennifer Daryl. "The Theory and Method of Articulation." In *Stuart Hall: Critical Dialogues in Cultural Studies*, edited by David Morley and Kuan-Hsing Chen, 112–127. New York: Routledge, 1996.

References 177

Smith, Cynthia Duquette and Teresa Bergman. "You Were on Indian Land: Alcatraz Island as Recalcitrant Memory Space." In *Places of Public Memory: The Rhetoric of Museums and Memorials*, edited by Greg Dickinson, Carole Blair and Brian L. Ott, 160–188. Tuscaloosa, AL: University of Alabama Press, 2010.

Smith, Linda Tuhiwai. "Colonizing Knowledges." In *Education, Globalization, and Social Change*, edited by Hugh Lauderet. al, 557–569. New York: Oxford University Press, 2006

Smith, Linda Tuhiwai. *Decolononizing Methodologies: Research and Indigenous Peoples*, 7th edition. London: Zed Books, 1999.

Smith, Margaret. "The Many Functions of Historical Memory." Paper presented at the Annual Meeting of the International Studies Association, May 17, 2001, Montreal, Quebec, Canada.

Sowards, Stacey K. *Si, Ella Puede*. Austin, TX: University of Texas Press, 2019.

Sowards, Stacey K. "Rhetorical Functions of Letter Writing: Dialogic Collaboration, Affirmation, and Catharsis in Dolores Huerta's Letters." *Communication Quarterly* 60, no. 2 (May 2012): 295–315.

Sperling-Cockcroft, Eva, and Holly Barnet-Sanchez. "Introduction." In *Signs from the Heart*. Venice, CA: Social and Public Art Resource Center, 1990.

Spicer, Edward H. *Cycles of Conquest: The Impact of Spain, Mexico and the United States on the Indians of the Southwest, 1533–1960*. Tucson, AZ: University of Arizona Press, 1962.

Stacks, Don W. and Michael B. Salwen. "Integrating Theory and Research: Starting with Questions." In *An Integrated Approach to Communication Theory and Research*, edited by Don W. Stacks and Michael B. Salwen, 3–14. 2nd edition. New York: Routledge, 1996/2009.

Stannard, David E. *American Holocaust: The Conquest of the New World*. New York: Oxford University Press, 1993.

Strum, Phillipa. *Mendez v. Westminster: School Desegregation and Mexican American Rights*. Lawrence, KS: University Press of Kansas, 2010.

Swords, Alicia and Ronald L. Mize. "Beyond Tourist Gazes and Performances: U.S. Consumption of Land and Labor in Puerto Rican and Mexican Destinations." *Latin American Perspectives* 35, no. 3 (May 2008): 53–69.

Timmons, W.H. *El Paso: A Borderlands History*. El Paso, TX: Texas Western Press, 1990.

Ting-Toomey, Stella, and John G. Oetzel, *Managing Intercultural Communication Conflict*. 2nd edition. Thousand Oaks, CA: Sage, 2001.

Torres, Miguel. "The Missing Link of the El Paso Message." Term Project in Corporate Communications, College of Business, University of Texas, El Paso, (nd): 1–6.

Treviño, Robert T. "Facing Jim Crow: Catholic Sisters and the 'Mexican Problem' in Texas." *Western Historical Quarterly* 34, no. 2 (Summer 2003 2003): 139–164.

Trujillo, Carla. "La Virgen de Guadalupe and Her Reconstruction in Chicano Lesbian Desire." In *Living Chicana Theory*, edited by Carla Trujillo, 214–231. Berkeley, CA: Third Women Press, 1998.

Trujillo, Michael. "Oñate's Foot: Remembering and Dismembering in Northern New Mexico." *Aztlán: A Journal of Chicano Studies* 33, no. 2 (Spring 2008 2008): 91–119.

Tucker, Hazel and John Akama. "Tourism as Postcolonialism." In *The Sage Handbook of Tourism Studies*, edited by Tazim Jamal and Mike Robinson, 504–520. Thousand Oaks, CA: Sage, 2009.

Tucker, Josiah. "Instructions for Travellers, 1757." In Erwe Chambers (Ed.). *Native Tours: The Anthropology of Travel and Tourism*. 2nd edition. Long Grove, IL: Waveland Press, 2010.

178 References

Turner, Fredrick Jackson. "The Significance of the Frontier in American History." Presentation at the American Historical Association, Chicago, IL, 1893.

Urrea, Jr., Luis. "Identity Production in Figured Worlds: How Some Mexican Americans Become Chicana/o Activist Educators." *Urban Review* 39, no. 2 (2007): 117–144.

U.S. News and World Report. "Texas Oks Mexican-American Studies Course Without the Name." (April 13, 2018). https://www.usnews.com/news/best-states/texas/articles/2018-04-13/texas-oks-mexican-american-studies-course-without-the-name. Retrieved February 28, 2019.

Vargas, George. "Border Artists in the Contemporary El Paso Mural Movement: Painting the Frontier." In *Chicano Studies: Survey and Analysis*, edited by Dennis Bixler-Marquez, Carlos F. Ortega, Rosalia Solorzano Torres, and Lorenzo G. LaFarelle, 3rd edition, 367–384. Debuque, IA: Kendall- Hunt Publishing, 2007.

Vasconcelos, José. *The Cosmic Race/La Raza Cosmica*. Translated by Didier T. Jaen, with afterword by José Gabilondo. Baltimore, MD: John Hopkins Press, 1979/1997.

Vigil, James Diego. *From Indians to Chicanos: The Dynamics of Mexican-American Culture*. 3rd edition. Long Grove, IL: Waveland Press, 2012.

Vila, Pablo. *Border Identifications: Narratives of Religion, Gender, and Class on the U.S.-Mexico Border*. Austin, TX: University of Texas Press, 2005.

Vila, Pablo. "The Competing Meanings of the Label 'Chicano' in El Paso." In *The U.S.-Mexico Border: Transcending Division, Contesting Identities*, edited by Kathleen Staudt and David Spencer, 185–211. Boulder, CO: Lynne Rienner Publishers, 1998.

Vila, Pablo. *Crossing borders, Reinforcing Borders: Social Categories, Metaphors, and Narrative Identities on the U.S.-Mexico Frontier*. Austin, TX: University of Texas Press, 2000.

Villa, Raúl Homero. *Barrio Logos: Space and Place in Urban Chicano Literature and Culture*. Austin, TX: University of Texas Press, 2000.

Visser, Gustav, "Social Justice, Integrated Development Planning and Post-Apartheid Urban Reconstruction." *Urban Studies* 38, no. 10 (Fall 2001): 1673–1699.

Voss, Barbara L. "Gender, Race, and Labor in Archeology of the Spanish Colonial Era." *Current Anthropology* 49, no. 5 (October 2006): 861–893. DOI: doi:10.1086/591275.

Wallerstein, Nina B. and Bonnie Duran. "Using Community-Based Participatory Research to Address Health Disparities." *Health Promotion Practice* 7, no. 3 (July 2006): 312–323.

Weber, David J. *Foreigners in their Native Land: Historical Roots of the Mexican Americans*. Revised edition. Albuquerque, NM: University of New Mexico Press, 1973/2004.

Weber, David J. *The Spanish Frontier in North America*. New Haven, CT: Yale University Press, 1992.

Weber, David J. *Myth and History of the Spanish Southwest*. Albuquerque, NM: University of New Mexico Press, 1990.

Weisiger, Marsha, "No More Hero's: Western History in Public Places." *Western Historical Quarterly* 42, no. 3 (Autumn 2011 2011): 289–296.

Weitz, Mark A. *The Sleepy Lagoon Murder Case: Race Discrimination and Mexican American Rights*. Lawrence, KS: University Press of Kansas, 2010.

West, Cornell. "Horace Pippin's Challenge to Art Criticism." In *The Cornell West Reader*, edited by Cornell West, 447–455. New York: Basic Civitas Books, 1999a.

West, Cornell. "The Indispensability Yet Insufficiency of Marxist Theory." In *The Cornel West Reader*, Cornell West Ed., 213–230. New York: Basic Civitas Books, 1999b.

References 179

West, Cornell. "The New Cultural Politics of Difference." *The Humanities as Social Technology* 53 (Summer 1990 1990): 93–109.

White, Jr., George. "I am Teaching Some of the Boys: Chaplain Robert Boston Dokes and Army Testing of Black Soldiers in World War II." *Journal of Negro Education* 81, no. 3 (Summer 2012 2012): 200–217.

Wilson, Chris. *The Myth of Santa Fe: Creating a Modern Regional Tradition.* Albuquerque, NM: University of New Mexico Press, 1997.

Wilson, Tamar Diana. "Economic and Social Impacts of Tourism in Mexico." *Latin American Perspectives* 35, no. 3 (May 2008): 37–52.

Wise, Tim. *Dear White America: Letter to a New Minority.* San Francisco, CA: City Lights Publishers, 2012.

Wise, Tim. *White Like Me* Berkeley, CA: Softskull Press, 2011.

Wright, Ronald. *Stolen Continents: The Americas through Indian Eyes Since 1492.* Boston, MA: Houghton-Mifflin, 1992.

Wynn, J. "Guiding Practices: Storytelling Tricks for Reproducing the Urban Landscape." *Sociology* 28, no. 4 (Winter 2005 2005): 399–417.

XingHuibin, Azizan Marzuki, and Arman Abdul Razak. "Conceptualizing a Sustainable Development Model for Cultural Heritage Tourism in Asia." *Theoretical and Empirical Researches in Urban Management* 8, no. 1 (February 2013): 51–66.

XuZi-lin, ShenJu-qin, LiuBo, and TanLiang. "Study of TOPSIS-based Evaluation of Urban Competitiveness." *Journal of Chemical and Pharmaceutical Research* 6, no. 7 (2014): 1843–1846.

Ying, Fan. "Space, Landscape, and Memory: Chengdu's Shaocheng Park and the Historical Memory of the Railway Protection Monument." *Chinese Studies in History* 47, no. 1 (2013): 6–28. DOI: doi:10.2753/CSH0009–4633470101.

Zanetell, Myrna. "Chicano Exhibit Advances Status of Newest American School of Art." Gallery Talk. *El Paso Scene.* (June 2003): 40–41.

Zimmerman, James F. "The Coronado-Cuatro Centennial." *The Hispanic American Historical Review* 20, no. 1 (nd.): 158–162.

Zinn, Howard. *A People's History of the United States: 1492 to the Present.* New York: Harper Collins, 1980/2003.

Newsletters and Pamphlets

Lincoln Park Conservation Committee. *The Murals of Lincoln Park: A Chicano Art Experience.* (n.d.).

El Camino Real Historic Trail. http://www.elcaminoreal.org/html/museum.html. Retrieved August 1, 2017.

John Jay College of Criminal Justice. *Latin American & Latina/o Studies Department Newsletter,* City University of New York (2016): 1–4.

League of El Paso, Junior. *An Art of Conscious: A Guide to Selected El Paso Murals.* (1996).

League of El Paso, Junior. *Los Murales: Guide and Maps to the Murals of El Paso.* 1992.

XII Travelers. *XII Travelers Memorial of the Southwest* (newsletter), November 27, 1995.

XII Travelers. *XII Travelers Memorial of the Southwest* (newsletter), April, 1990.

180 *References*

Newspapers

Albuquerque Journal – 1998
efniks.com – 2018
El Paso Herald-Post – 1989–1995
El Paso Scene – 1995
El Paso Times – 1989–2017
New York Times – 2006–2017
Newspaper Tree.com – 2007

Film/TV/Social Media

Ibarra, Christine. *Las Marthas.* DVD Produced by ITVS/Latino Public Broadcasting. (Alexandria, VA: PBS, 2014).

Picker, Miguel and Cyung Sun. *Latinos Beyond Reel.* DVD Produced by Miguel Picker, Edwin Pagan, and Lorena Manriquez, (Alexandria, VA: PBS, 2013).

Valdez, John J. and Christine Ibarra. *The Last Conquistador.* DVD Produced by John Valdez and Christine Ibarra (Alexandria, VA: PBS, 2008).

Valdez, John J. and Christine Ibarra. "Statement on Juan de Oñate." Produced by ITVS and Latino Public Broadcasting. (Warwick, NY: The Kitchen Sync Group, Inc./Valdez Media, n.d. Distributed by PBS.)

Index

Note: Locators in **bold** refer to case studies.

Acoma pueblo 1–2; adjudication 27, 88, 145; art vandalism 1, 10n22; atrocities 99; battle 27; resistance 27
Acuna, Rodolfo 29, 82
adelantados 2, 92
Akama, John 14
Alba, Alicia Gaspar de, 91
Albuquerque Journal 99, 145
Albuquerque Old Town District 29
Annual Chicano Heritage Festival 153
articulation perspective 31
assimilation 32, 41–42, 72, 77, 88, 149
Azar, Mayor Suzanne 92
Azuela, Mariano 147

Bandlier, Alfred 119
Bennett, George 119
Berliner, David 7
biracial tropes 118
Black Legend, The, 28, 30, 49n112, 50n113, 77, 115; *see* La Leyenda Negra
Blair, Carol 15,
Bokovoy, Matthew 32, 42
Boorstin, Daniel 17
Borglum, Gordon 57, 92
Borrego, Al 2, 122
Bragg, Bea 60, 146
Brown, William H. 119
Bujanda, Moises 102
Bureau of Immigration 119

Castaneda, Antonia 73
cedula 24–25
central place model, the 157
Cesar Chavez Border Highway 3, 92
Chavez, Norma 122

Chicanos 33; cultural erasure 38–39; murals, 90; public space 90–91, 105; struggles 34, 47 n59, 61, 94
Chicano Art: Resistance and Affirmation (CARA) 90
Chicano Movement 35, 42, 61, 134,147, 149; murals, 90
Chicano Visions 91
Chino, Darva 38
Ciudad Juarez, Chihuahua, MX 6, 28, 77, 90, 93; fantasy heritage 109; tri-city tourism 130
Coles, Robert 120
Colonialism, Spanish 7
Comprehensive Orders for New Discovery (1573) 25–26
confusion of the colonized 29, 59, 101
Cordoba, Teresa 29, 101
Coronado, Francisco Vasquez de 22
Creating a Tourist Mecca in Okinawa **120–21**
criollo 22
critical dialogue 6
Cuarto Centenario (the Fourth Centenary) 1
Cuevas-Contreras, Tomas 130
Culler, Jonathan 17
cultural diversity 155
cultural erasure 38–39
Cushing, Frank 119

Davis, Mary 122
Deagin, Kathleen 76
Deverall, William 37
dilenation perspective 31
Dickinson, Greg 15
Don Juan de Onate Trail 3, 92

182 *Index*

Dunbar-Ortiz, Roxanne 40
Duranguito, El Paso, TX 115, 117, 126, 150

El Paso Independent School District (EPISD) 59, 72
El Paso Mission Trail Association (EPMTA) 59, 62, 79, 115, 121–22, completed statues 128
El Paso Museum of Art 90
El Paso Museum of History 123
El Paso, TX 58, 61, 89–90, 130; critique, 101; downtown 92, 112, 116, 123; good for tourism, 101, 111, 121; International Airport 94, 112, 128; Mexican community 147; public memory 3, 9, 34, 43, 109, 118, 151; see, Equestrian/Juan de Onate critique 101
El Paso Salt War (1877) 90, 124
El Paso schools 137
El Paso Quadricentennial 97
Equestrian, The/Juan de Onate statue, 8, 78, 81, 94, 112, 114, 129; critics and supporters,102; installation 101; renaming, 94
Espanola, NM 115
Estala, Joe 62, 111, 157
Eurocentric fantasies 113, 146, 159

fantasies 17
fantasy heritage, 4, 6, 31–32, 42–43, 82, 149; fiestas, 7, 36, 38–39, 40, 42; identity15, 33, 37, 62, 70, 72; in practice 32–33, 55, 81; marketing, 34; oppressed groups 14; public memory 35; public space 34; Spanish 14, 31, 113, 145; tourism 37
fiestas, Day of the Dons 34; Fiesta Santa Fe 18, 36–37, 43; Mission Days 34, 43; Old Spanish Days 7, 11, 16
Filene, Benjamin 19; outside history-makers, 19
First Thanksgiving 1, 3, 71, 80; colonialism 57, 137; Eurocentrism 59, 67, 73; historical guide 68, 70, 114; play 58, 62–65 (2006), 65–67 (2016); reenactment 56, 122; Spanish conquest 72
functional perspective 31

Gastronomy as a Tool for the Culturally Sensitive Tourist **154–55**
Gonzalez, Deena J. 42

Gramsci, Antonio 100–01
Grimes, Ronald L. 18–19
Guthrie, Thomas 115, 119
Gutierrez, Ramon 36

Hall, Edward T. 80, 136
Hall, Sheldon 1, 8, 58–59, 61, 110
Hammond, George 3
hegemony 4, 67, 81–82, 88, 100, 102, 104
heritage tourism 14,137–38; cultural enterprise 14; El Paso 146; inclusivity in 131–37; Mexican Americans 14, 19
Herzog, Lawrence 138–39
Hispanic 5, 20, 29, 33–35, 42, 60, 71, 77, 117
Historia de Nuevo Mexico 29
historical reenactment 4, 15, 56, 72
Hoig, Stan 24–25
Horton Sarah 36
Houser, Ethan 129
Houser, John 2, 57, 92, 110, 115
How men become "real Alaskans" **74–75**

Ibarra, Christine 78, 84
identity 5–6, 33; labels, 12n25, 31,77; Spanish 79, 81
indigenous 71–72, 76–77, 91, 94, 137, 149
Ioanide, Paula 148

Kessell, John 76
Kozol, Jonathan 5
Ku Klux Klan 57, 83N8, 85N44, 100

Lamar, Howard 40
land tenure 39–40
La Farge, Oliver 119
La Leyenda Negra (The Black Legend) 28, 31, 41, 77, 115
La Raza Cosmica 72, 85, N46
Last Conquistador: Juan de Onate and the Settling of the Southwest, The 2, 21, 78
la toma (the taking) 4, 26, 64, 92
Lea, Tom 57–58, 92
Lea, Thomas Calloway 57, 92
Lewis, Mike 111
Leyva, Yolanda Chavez 153
Lombroso, Cesare 30
Los de Abajo (The Underdogs) 124, 147
Lovato, Andrew Leo 31, 119
Lower Valley 42, changed to Mission Valley 43, 70, 122

Mack, Dionne 151
Magoffin, Susan 105, 128–29

Index 183

Maintaining Historical Accuracy to Create Local Identity: The Case of Chemnitz, Germany **124–26**

Mandalios, John 152

Manso Indians 26

Marin, Cheech 91

Marketing Unpopular Tourism Destinations **102–104**

Marti-Flux, Ricardo 61

Martinez, Oscar 98–100, 153

Mattelart, Armand 162n36

McWilliams, Carey 4, 7, 15, 43

Media shaping attitudes 5, 19, 39, 42, 46n42, 88, 97, 100–01

Medina, Larry 2

Memmi, Albert 28

Mendez vs. Westminster (1946) 148

Mestizaje 30–31, 72, 76–79

Metz, Leon 98–100, 110

Mexican/Americans 9, 14, 19, 31, 40, 77, 146–48

Mexican Americans 5, 33, 60, 71–72, 104–05, 128; civil rights 148; contributions to El Paso 128, 148–49, 151; heritage tourism 14, 20, 112, 147; living in El Paso 149; marginalized 20, 134, 148–49, 152, 159; terminology 9–10

Mexican American Cultural Center (El Paso, TX) 90, 117, 151

Mexican origin community 35, 82, 90, 151; as Hispanic 5, 34; identity 12n26; unseen 147–50

Mexican problem 39–42, 53n183

Mills, David 7, 61

Mirande, Alfredo 149

Mission Revival (architecture) 34, 115

Mission Valley *see* Lower Valley

Mojica-Hammer, Ruth 160

Monroy, Douglas 35

Montejano, David 90

Montwood High School 62,65; *see* First Thanksgiving

monuments 18, 20, 29, 34, 49n97, 78, 88, 135

Museo Urbano 123, 150, 153

Narrihando, Cristobal Perez de 22; *see also* Juan de Onate

network model, the 157

New Mexico 37–38, 105; Pueblos 119; tourism 119

Nieto-Phillips, John 33, 123

North from Mexico (1948) 7

Northern Rio Grande National Heritage Area, Alcalde, NM 145

Ohkay Owingeh Pueblo 118; *see also* San Juan, NM

Old Spanish Days (Santa Barbara, CA), *see* Fiestas

Olvera St., Los Angeles, CA 37, 43

Onate, Cristobal de 22–24

Onate, Juan de birth 7, 24; bloodless conquest 3, 11n15; conquest of New Mexico 47n58; life 67–68; San Elizario, TX 5,10,15,26, 56–62, 79, 84n22, 86–87n76; sawing off right foot 1, 146; status 8, 28, 78, 81; tourist references to 8, 78, 81, 114; visitor center, Alcalde, NM 1, 145–46; *see* Equestrian/Juan de Onate statue

Onate, Juan Perez de 22

Onate, Manuel Gullon y de 2, 61

Onate Monument and Visitors Cultural Center, Alcalde, NM, *see* Northern Rio Grande National Heritage Area

Operation Wetback (1957) and Donald Trump 148

Orientalism 41

Ortiz-Gonzalez, Victor 137–38

Ott, Brian L. 15

Paso del Norte Group (PDNG) 126

Perez, Vince 122

Plaza de los Lagartos, (El Paso, TX) 123

Polk, Jackson 127

Ponzio, Charles 127

Pope, Melody K. 15

public art 88, 91, 94, 151

public memory 29, fantasy heritage 4, 7, 15, 36, 42–43, 152; premise, 14; reshaping 34, 159; Spanish 19

Pueblo culture 40, 120

Ramona 34

Ramos, Suki 67, 121

reenactments 56, 61, 72

repatriation 36, 148

requerimiento 27

Rey, Agapito 3

Richardson, Bill 29

Rico, Trinidad 149

Rodriguez, Jose 9, 28, 82, 135

Romero, Simon 99, 145

Romo, David D. 4, 153

184 *Index*

Said, Edward 41
San Elizario Chapel 66–67
San Elizario, TX 3, 7, 62, 79, 112, 122
Sanchez, Ben 2
Sanchez, George I. 40, 120
Santa Fe, NM 118–121; plaza 7
Santa Fe Fiesta 36–37; changes 119–20; founded 118; tourism 120; *see* Fiestas
Santa Fe Hispanic Culture: Preserving Identity in a Tourist Town 31
School curriculum 115, 152
Segundo Barrio 1, 4, 124, 126
Serrano, Hector 7, 61
Sievert, April K. 15
Sievert, Sheree L. 15
Simmons, Marc 21, 24, 92–100
Skin tone 77
Smith, Linda Tuhiwa 5
Socorro, NM 33, 37
Socorro, TX 58, 92, 122, 128
South Africa: The 2010 World Cup and Media Representations **96–97**
Spain: colonialism, 20, 34, 77, 115, 137
Spaniards 3, 8, 20, 26, 31–32, 35, 43, 45n21,57, 59, 75, 77, 80, 119; Acoma 89; heritage tourism 111; stereotype of, 28, 30, 49n112
Suarez, Jose Luis 58–60

The Very First Thanksgiving (1997) 60
Tigua Indians 114, 128, 151–52
Tolosa Cortes Moctezuma, Isabel de 24
Tourism 109; as colonial instrument 100; global strategies 130

Tourism Efforts in a Second-Tier City **157–58**
Tourists 79–80, 105,115; characteristics 17; material comforts 18; *see* visitors
Tucker, Hazel 14
Tucker, Josiah, 17, 46n33
Turner, Frederick Jackson, 29
XII Travelers project 56–58, 92–97, 100, 129, 135; possible Chicano/Mexican statues 106

Valadez, John J. 78
Vasconcelos, Jose 72
Vila, Pablo 42, 77
Villa, Raul Romero 35
Villagra, Gaspar Perez de 27, 29
Visit El Paso (website), 123
Visitors, 14, 20, 34, 56, 79, 84n26; characteristics 17; *see also* tourists

Weber, David J. 32, 75
Weisiger, Marsha 5
White, Jeff 70
Wilson, Chris 106
Wise, Tim 30
world's fair, Long Beach Pacific Southwest Exposition; Panama-California Exposition; San Diego Exposition 36

Zaldivar, Juan de 25, 27
Zaldivar, Vicente de 25
Zizaldra-Hernandez, Isabel 130